Granville Sharp's Uncovered Letter
and the *Zong* Massacre

Michelle Faubert

Granville Sharp's Uncovered Letter and the *Zong* Massacre

palgrave
macmillan

Michelle Faubert
University of Manitoba
Winnipeg, MB, Canada

ISBN 978-3-319-92785-5   ISBN 978-3-319-92786-2   (eBook)
https://doi.org/10.1007/978-3-319-92786-2

Library of Congress Control Number: 2018942883

This Palgrave Pivot imprint is published by the registered company Springer Nature
Switzerland AG
The registered company address is: Gewerbestrasse 11, 6330 Cham, Switzerland

I dedicate this book to the murder victims of the Zong, *the 208 survivors—including the man who survived by laying hold of a rope to save himself—and all Jamaicans, who embody his spirit of fortitude today.*

PREFACE AND ACKNOWLEDGEMENTS

I discovered Granville Sharp's two-part manuscript missive to the Lords Commissioners of the Admiralty at the British Library in May of 2015 while performing research for an article of literary criticism, my usual focus as a professor of Romantic-era literature at the University of Manitoba (Canada) and Visiting Fellow at Northumbria University (UK). I had only a passing knowledge of the history of slavery and abolition then, but it was enough to recognize the significance of the names "Granville Sharp" and "the *Zong*." My colleague at the University of Manitoba, Dana Medoro, had told me about the *Zong* massacre some years before—and, like so many others who hear this history, I was so shaken that it was seared into my memory and I sought out more information about it. Thanks to this experience, I recognized the significance of the mysterious manuscript I held in my hands at the British Library that day.

After finding the Sharp manuscript at the British Library, I became nearly obsessed with it and the history of the *Zong*. I felt like a sleuth as I slowly traced the document's strange provenance—and, like the Wedding Guest in S. T. Coleridge's *The Rime of the Ancient Mariner*, I felt "sadder and wiser" the more I learned about the horrors of the *Zong* massacre and the injustices of the court case that followed. As a Romanticist, I knew that slavery was a major aspect of the spirit of revolution and discussion of human rights that imbued the age, but I had not considered its influence so deeply before. I threw myself into my research with a verve I had not felt previously. Here was my personal invitation from the past—or, rather, the manuscript *demanded* that I take responsibility for it, learn more about the *Zong*'s place in the history of slavery and abolition, and tell the story of Sharp's mysterious manuscript as well as I could.

My resulting publications have led to outcomes that I could not have imagined. My scholarly article on Sharp's manuscript letter to the Admiralty at the British Library in *Slavery & Abolition* reached over seven hundred views online within a year, while a story about it in my University's newspaper, *UM Today*, made it as far as Jamaica.[1] There, Evelyn Smart read it and brought it to the Honourable Donna Parchment Brown, the Political Ombudsman of Jamaica, on account of the latter's interest in the *Zong* episode. Parchment Brown contacted me about working with her and Vivian Crawford, Executive Director of the Institute of Jamaica, on a project to commemorate the *Zong* and I enthusiastically accepted. My resulting research trip to Jamaica in May of 2017 was a whirlwind of exciting and emotionally moving events. I lectured on three occasions in Jamaica, the first as the main presenter at the *Zong* memorial in Black River, where the *Zong* landed in late 1783; for the second event, I presented a paper on my research into Sharp's *Zong* missive at the University of West Indies in Kingston; the third event was my presentation at the Institute of Jamaica, also in Kingston, during which I also launched the exhibition on the BL document that I created for the Institute of Jamaica. The exhibition traveled to Black River in October 2017 for Jamaican Heritage Month. Two national television interviews and a talk-radio interview rounded out my incredible trip to Jamaica.

Many people from several countries have encouraged me to write this book through their interest in and support for the project. I want to thank all of those who showed an early and enduring interest in this project, several of whom helped my research for it materially. James Walvin,

---

[1]Michelle Faubert, "Granville Sharp's Manuscript Letter to the Admiralty on the *Zong* Massacre: A New Discovery in the British Library," *Slavery & Abolition* 38, no. 1 (2016): 1–18. Some of the research in this book appears in the *Slavery & Abolition* article. Sean Moore, "Professor Finds Lost 232-Year Old Letter Condemning Slave Massacre," *UM Today*, http://news.umanitoba.ca/professor-finds-lost-232-year-old-letter-condemning-slave-massacre/, 19 August 2015, unpag.

author of *The Zong: A Massacre, the Law & the End of Slavery* (2011)—
the seminal monograph on the *Zong* case—has been hugely generous
in advising me via e-mail and telephone conversations. Others include:
James Basker, Sean Moore, Liesl Smith, Gad Heuman, Tim Lockley,
Lyle Ford, Salvy Trojman, Andrew Lyall, Clark Lawlor, Alan Vardy,
Chris Brown, Jenny Sharpe, Joel Faflak, Caroline Piotrowski, Marcus
Closen, Anita King, Tom Schmid, Bob O'Kell, and Elyssa Warkentin.
Most notably, Suzie Park and Charles Wharram, of Eastern Illinois
University, invited me to present on the *Zong* massacre and my discovery
of Sharp's missive to the Admiralty for the 27th Annual Lecture of the
Phi Beta Kappa Society in November of 2017. At Palgrave Press, I want
to thank Megan Laddusaw and Christine Pardue, as well as the anonymous readers of the manuscripts, whose comments and suggestions
improved the book immensely. Allan Ingram read a draft of this monograph; he caught several typos and responded enthusiastically to it, which
gave me the boost of confidence I needed to finish my task. As ever,
Allan, I am deeply grateful to you for your support. Finally, Shoshannah
Bryn Jones Square contributed to this book in multiple ways, not least
of which was by helping me to copyedit it as part of her work for me
as a Postdoctoral Fellow for my Social Science and Humanities Research
Council of Canada Insight Grant (2015–2020). I cannot thank her
enough for her great attention to detail and scholarly professionalism.
Any remaining errors are my own.

I also owe a huge debt of gratitude to the British Library, which so
generously allowed me to reproduce their images of the Sharp manuscript free of charge in this volume for the Appendix (© British Library
Board General Reference Collection T.35.(2), folios 1–15). Many
knowledgeable and helpful staff members at the BL helped my investi-
gation immeasurably, but I offer special thanks to Sandra Tuppen (Lead
Curator of Modern Archives and MSS 1601–1850, British Library).
I also want to thank the archivists and other employees at the various
archives I consulted, including Graham Thompson (Archives Assistant,
National Maritime Museum); George Hay (Military records specialist,
Advice & Records Knowledge Department, The National Archives);
Andrew Parry (Archives Assistant at the Gloucestershire Archives); Kirsty
Farthing (Archives Assistant, York Minster Historic Collections Team);
and others at the Wellcome Library and the Medical Society of London.
I am moreover grateful to so many people in Jamaica who made my
trip there the incredible success that it was: Donna Parchment Brown,

Vivian Crawford, and everyone at the Institute of Jamaica, including Sir Roy Augier. At the University of West Indies, I owe thanks to Michael Bucknor, Matthew Smith, Paulette Kerr, Verene Shepherd, Kim Robinson-Walcott, and James Robertson. Thanks are also due to all of those who attended or also presented at the multiple presentations in Jamaica, including students from the Black River Primary School—and their teachers, Roschelle Sheriff and Crisana Banton-Smith—the Junior Centre Drummers, representatives from Scotiabank at Black River, the Mayor of Black River Derrick Sangster, Canadian High Commissioner to Jamaica Sylvain Fabi, and so many others. Jamaican members of the media have helped to spread the word about the *Zong* episode, as well as my presentations on it, for which I am hugely thankful; they include Earl Moxam, Garfield Myers, and the television staff and interviewers from CVM at Sunrise and Smile Jamaica.

I am grateful to the University of Manitoba, as I developed a substantial portion of this monograph during a half-sabbatical in 2017. I offer a special note of thanks to the Social Science and Humanities Research Council of Canada (SSHRC): I made my discovery of the Sharp letter at the British Library and funded the trip to Jamaica through their generous award of a SSHRC Insight Grant (2015–2020).

Finally, none of this work could have advanced without the love and support of my mom, Yvonne Faubert, and my husband, Javier Uribe, who was a tireless, curious, and excited audience for my endless rambling on this topic—and who played driver, security guard, and techie for the trip to Jamaica. Thanks, Javi.

Winnipeg, Canada   Michelle Faubert

CONTENTS

1   Introduction   1
    1   *The Discovery of Granville Sharp's Letter to the Lords*
        Commissioners of the Admiralty on the Zong *in the*
        British Library: A Hidden Treasure Found   1
    2   *Overview*   6

2   Equiano, Sharp, Mansfield, and the *Zong* Massacre:
    History and Significance   13
    1   *The* Zong *Massacre: A Primer*   14
    2   *Olaudah Equiano*   22
    3   *Granville Sharp Versus Judge Mansfield*   27
    4   *The* Zong *Case: A Debated Legacy*   44

3   The Provenance of the British Library Document   59

4   The British Library Document: The Definitive Version
    of Sharp's Letter on the *Zong* to the Lords
    Commissioners of the Admiralty   75

5   The Historical Significance of the British Library
    Document   99
    1   *The Burial of the British Library Document and the*
        Truth of the Zong   100
    2   *(Re)Writing History*   106

6 Conclusion: Revisiting the History of Abolition 117

Correction to: Equiano, Sharp, Mansfield, and the *Zong* Massacre: History and Significance E1

Appendix: Transcription and Images of Sharp's Missive to the Admiralty on the *Zong* at the British Library 123

Index 159

EPIGRAPH

"Your writings, Sir, are not of trivial matters, but of great and essential things. ... Therefore, we wish, for ourselves and others, that these valuable treatises ... may be preserved and established as a monument or beacon to guide and to warn men, lest they should depart from the paths of justice and humanity; and that they may ... restrain the avaricious invaders of the rights and liberties of men, whilever the human race inhabits this earth below."[2]

From the Sons of Africa to Granville Sharp

[2] Quoted in Hoare, *Memoirs*, 374.

NOTE ON THE TEXT (APPENDIX)

Appendix: Transcription and images of the BL document, Sharp's manuscript of his letter to the Lords Commissioners of the Admiralty.

All oddities of grammar, spelling, and format are Sharp's. I do not note these instances with a "sic"; nor do I attempt to replicate special formatting, such as flourishes and unusually large writing, but I do replicate extra spacing and unusual page orientation, such as centring, when possible. At the end of many lines in this document, Sharp includes a long dash to fill in the remaining space before the edge of the page, but these marks serve a merely aesthetic purpose; I only include dashes that function as punctuation. Another oddity of this manuscript is that, in keeping with the formatting style typical of publications in this period, Sharp includes quotation marks at the beginning of each new line of quoted words, rather than simply a single opening and closing set of quotation marks, as is typical today. Because I do not replicate each line length in my transcription, I use today's method of marking off quotations. I strike through words so marked for deletion by Sharp (or apparently so, when it is done in the same ink as the rest of the document). Where marks or text have been added in pencil or different ink from the main text, I include this information through a footnote. Notably, such insertions are often difficult to read, but I provide my best estimation of them.

I enclose in square brackets all of my own additions to the main text, which I include only when necessary for sense. I indicate when the square brackets are Sharp's own. All Biblical references and other such contextual information I have adumbrated in footnotes in the transcription.

The British Library (BL) document does not have page numbers, but I begin my own numbering of the document with the first full page of the cover letter (1) and end it with the last page of the detailed document (15). I provide these numbers (in addition to the regular numbering of this monograph) in bold, marking the beginning of a new page with brackets and a slash ([/ **page number**]); in all of my references to the BL document in my discussion of the text, I refer to these numbers, rather than the page numbers of this monograph. Incidentally, the NMM document *is* numbered: the first page of the cover letter is 95 and the last page of the detailed account is 110. In my in-text references to the NMM document, the page numbers accord with the document's own numbers (95–110).

I am grateful to Shoshannah Bryn Jones Square's invaluable assistance in aiding me in the creation of the transcription of the BL document.

CHAPTER 1

Introduction

Abstract The introduction details the circumstances of my discovery of Granville Sharp's letter in the British Library, provides evidence that the British Library did not know of its presence there, and establishes the importance of both the *Zong* massacre and Sharp's letter for the history of slavery and abolition. It then provides an overview of the monograph.

Keywords Manuscript · Fair copy · *Zong* massacre · Granville Sharp Archival discovery · Slavery and abolition

1 THE DISCOVERY OF GRANVILLE SHARP'S LETTER TO THE LORDS COMMISSIONERS OF THE ADMIRALTY ON THE *ZONG* IN THE BRITISH LIBRARY: A HIDDEN TREASURE FOUND

> ... the Necessity of putting an entire stop to the Slave Trade, lest any similar Deeds of Barbarity, occasioned by it, should speedily involve the whole Nation in some such tremendous Calamity as may unquestionably mark the avenging hand of God, who has promised "to destroy the Destroyers of the Earth"!

M. Faubert, *Granville Sharp's Uncovered Letter and the* Zong *Massacre*,
https://doi.org/10.1007/978-3-319-92786-2_1

1

Granville Sharp

Old Jewry

2.[d] July 1783.[1]

The above passage on the last page of manuscript I held at the British Library (hereafter the "BL") in May of 2015 attested to the special nature of the handwritten document that I had inadvertently borrowed. Oddly, though, it was in a volume surrounded by printed eighteenth-century pamphlets of much less historical value. "Granville Sharp" was the famous name that appeared on the document. I recognized it as belonging to the great, early British hero of abolition. And here, apparently, was his letter from 1783 about "putting an entire stop to the Slave Trade." Sharp's intensity fairly jumped off the page through the frequent underlining and exclamation marks in the manuscript, which presented the author in his most enraged, impassioned mood. But to whom had Sharp written, and on what occasion? I reasoned that the first page of the handwritten document would tell me. Flipping quickly through the preceding pages—fifteen in all—I read the words at the top of the first page of the manuscript. They confirmed its historic significance:

Old Jewry London—2.[d] July 1783

My Lords

As the cognizance and right of enquiry concerning all Murders committed on board British Ships belongs properly to the Admiralty Department, I think it my Duty to lay before your Lordships two Manuscript Accounts wherein are stated from unquestionable authority the circumstances of a most inhuman and barbarous murder committed by Luke Collingwood the Master, Colonel James Kelsall, the Mate, and other persons, the Mariners or Crew of the Ship Zong or Zurg a Liverpool Trader freighted with Slaves &c. from the Coast of Africa; which Master, Mate, and Crew, on pretence of necessity lest there should be a want of water, wilfully and deliberately destroyed ... [132] poor Negro Slaves, by

---

[1] Granville Sharp, [BL document, copy of a letter to Lords Commissioners of the Admiralty] "Paper by Glanville [sic] Sharp on the Case of 132 Murdered Negroes," in *Tracts 35* (Old Jewry London, MS: n.p., July 2, 1783), 1. Here and in all references to the unpaginated manuscript at the British Library (hereafter the "BL document"), the cited page numbers accord with those in this volume's Appendix, my transcription of the missive. In every quotation from the Sharp missive, all emphases and other oddities of punctuation, spelling, formatting, and grammar are Sharp's.

casting them <u>alive</u> (as it is deposed) into the Sea with their hands bound or
fetter'd, to deprive them of all possibility of escaping!²

The missive concerns the case of the infamous *Zong* slave ship, from
which 132 enslaved Africans were thrown or forced overboard to their
deaths, an incident that has become emblematic of the horrors of the
slave trade. Sharp (1735–1813) wrote the letter to request that the
Admiralty prosecute the crew of the *Zong* for the murders. As the BL catalogue contained no record of this document, I suspected immediately
what I would soon determine to be the truth: the Library was not aware
that it owned this precious manuscript. In what follows, I will establish
several significant conclusions about the BL document: that it is the only
known fair copy of Sharp's letter to the Admiralty; that it passed through
several hands before ending up at the BL; that the only other extant copy
(at the National Maritime Museum, or NMM) is a working draft that
should be treated as ancillary to the BL letter; and, most importantly, that
Sharp meant to publish it. I also include images and a transcription of the
BL document (Sharp's two-part missive to the Admiralty) as an appendix to this volume. My investigation into the provenance of Sharp's letter
in the BL has led to several other discoveries of great importance to the
history of abolition, too, such as who was included in Sharp's group of
correspondents regarding the *Zong* case, and that Sharp's interest in publishing on slavery did not end in 1777, as scholars have hitherto assumed.

Sharp's missive to the Admiralty on the *Zong* massacre is crucially
important. The *Zong* case has been recognized as an incitement for the
nascent British abolition movement, while F. O. Shyllon describes Sharp
as "England's first abolitionist."³ The discovery of this manuscript in
the BL provides critical information about Sharp's contributions to the
abolition of slavery. Most histories present Sharp's anti-slavery activities
as rather tame and limited; these include his practical engagement in
the legal cases of Jonathan Strong, Thomas Lewis, and James Somerset
(sometimes spelled Somersett or Sommersett), formerly enslaved men
pursuing their freedom in England; his membership in the Society for
the Abolition of the African Slave Trade, founded in 1787, and his

²Sharp, BL document, 1.

³Robert Weisbord, "The Case of the Slave-Ship *Zong*, 1783," *History Today* 19, no. 8
(1969): 561–7, 566–7; F. O. Shyllon, *Black Slaves in Britain* (London and New York:
Oxford University Press, 1974), ix; and G. M. Ditchfield, "Sharp, Granville (1735–1813),"
Oxford Dictionary of National Biography (Oxford: Oxford University Press, 2004, 2012),
unpag., accessed June 16, 2015, https://doi.org/10.1093/ref:odnb/25208.

contributions to the African Institution, founded in 1807; his presence at the *Zong* hearing in May and private correspondence with influential Britons regarding the case; and his involvement in the establishment of Sierra Leone, a colony for formerly enslaved people that Sharp created with Thomas Clarkson, William Wilberforce, and others.[4] The BL document adds a radical element to Sharp's image, as it provides a glimpse of his dissidence and willingness to use anti-establishment tactics to advance the abolitionist cause. The manuscript in the BL reveals Sharp's intention to publish his correspondence with the Lords Commissioners of the Admiralty about the *Zong* case and thereby announce to all Britons that the mass murder of enslaved Africans was officially sanctioned and even rewarded.[5] Sharp's letter to the Admiralty at the BL at once embodies the silence surrounding slavery in the period and reframes the story of

---

[4] Weisbord, "Case," 566; Shyllon, *Black Slaves*, ix.

[5] There are surprisingly few publications devoted to Sharp alone, as Brycchan Carey's bibliography of secondary sources confirms (Brycchan Carey, "Granville Sharp (1735–1813)," unpag., page last updated March 3, 2014, accessed May 15, 2016, http://www.brycchancarey.com/abolition/sharp.htm). Carey lists the Hoare memoir and Walvin monograph I cite in this book, as well as a small biographical entry by Albert Frederick Pollard, and an early twentieth-century work on Sharp by Edward Charles Ponsonby Lascelles. (Prince Hoare, *Memoirs of Granville Sharp, Esq. Composed from His Own Manuscripts, and Other Authentic Documents in the Possession of His Family Authentic Documents in the Possession of His Family and of the African Institution* (London: Henry Colburn, 1820), *Google eBooks*, accessed June 25, 2015–August 30, 2017, https://books.google.ca/books?id=PrUEAAAAIAAJ; James Walvin, *The Zong: A Massacre, the Law & the End of Slavery* (New Haven and London: Yale University Press, 2011); Albert Frederick Pollard, "Granville Sharp," *The Dictionary of National Biography* (London: Smith, Elder & Co. 1885–1900), 1339–42; Edward Charles Ponsonby Lascelles, *Granville Sharp and the Freedom of the Slaves in England* (London: Humphrey Milford, 1928)). Two of the most thorough treatments of Sharp's anti-slavery activities are by F. O. Shyllon (*Black Slaves in Britain* (1974)) and David Brion Davis (*The Problem of Slavery in the Age of Revolution, 1770–1823* (Oxford: Oxford University Press, 1999)). Older sources include those by Ruth Anna Fisher ("Granville Sharp and Lord Mansfield," *The Journal of Negro History* 28, no. 4 (1943): 381–9) and Charles Stuart (*A Memoir of Granville Sharp* (New York: American Anti-Slavery Society, 1836), *Google eBooks*, accessed June 17, 2015, https://books.google.ca/books?id=eNxeks9xld4C). Sharp is often mentioned in publications on the *Zong* case, too. Aside from the publications that I cite elsewhere in this book, additional contemporary critical sources on the topics of both Sharp and the *Zong* include those by P. E. Lovejoy ("Autobiography and Memory: Gustavus Vassa, alias Olaudah Equiano, the African," *Slavery & Abolition* 27, no. 3 (2006): 317–47); Stephen J. May (*Voyage of the Slave Ship: J. M. W. Turner's Masterpiece in Historical Context* (Jefferson:

Sharp's abolitionist efforts. It "reset[s] the boundaries for the study of British abolition."[6]

The singularity of the fifteen-page BL document—consisting of a letter and detailed account of the events on the *Zong*—first attracted my attention to it. It is a beautifully handwritten manuscript in a volume containing around twenty printed pamphlets from the eighteenth century; these publications are mostly on medical matters, such as inoculation and contagious disease, which was the focus of my research when I borrowed the volume in the Rare Books & Music Reading Room at the BL. Knowing the rules of the Library well after over fifteen years working there as a scholar specializing in British Romantic-era literature, I was aware that manuscripts—especially old ones by famous people, such as the one I had inadvertently borrowed—were lent out under much stricter conditions than were even the rare books that I had so often consulted. And, yet, I was viewing Sharp's handwritten missive under non-manuscript conditions. The BL, I suspected immediately, did not know that it owned this treasure, and the Library later confirmed this conjecture to be accurate.[7] I had discovered a previously unknown, handwritten copy of Sharp's missive to the "Right Honorable Lords Commissioners of the Admiralty," as he specifies at the bottom of the three-page cover letter. To this letter Sharp adds another twelve pages, containing, as his own description announces, "An Account of the Murder of 132 Negro Slaves on board the Ship Zong, or Zurg, with some Remarks on the Argument of an eminent Lawyer in Defence of that

McFarland & Co., Inc., 2014)); and R. Burroughs ("Eyes on the Prize: Journeys in Slave Ships Taken as Prizes by the Royal Navy," *Slavery & Abolition* 31, no. 1 (2010): 99–115).

[6] I would like to thank the anonymous reader of my article "Granville Sharp's Manuscript Letter to the Admiralty on the *Zong* Massacre: A New Discovery in the British Library" in *Slavery & Abolition* for this fine turn of phrase, which aptly summarizes the significance of my find (38, no. 1 (2016): 1–18).

[7] A thorough catalogue search of the terms that would lead an interested researcher to this letter substantiated that there was no corresponding catalogue record for the letter. Sandra Tuppen, of the BL, confirmed via e-mail that there was no trace of the manuscript in their records and added later that the Library had been unaware of its existence in their collections until I informed them of it (Sandra Tuppen, e-mails to the author from the British Library, June 18, 29, July 1, 2015). The BL added a catalogue record of the document after I told them of it.

inhuman Transaction."[8] Together, these documents form one of the first detailed accounts of the infamous *Zong* case.

2   OVERVIEW

How rare, how valuable, was the manuscript by Sharp I had accidentally borrowed? Since very few primary sources on the *Zong* massacre exist, what is available is treasured by scholars of abolition. Noting that the historical paper trail connected to the *Zong* case, such as Captain Luke Collingwood's log book, has disappeared, Jane Webster bemoans the lack of documentary sources on the *Zong* and describes "Sharp's transcript" of the hearing in the NMM as "nothing less than an artefact of the beginning of the end of the slave trade."[9] James Oldham and Andrew Lewis recognize that it was a great boon to scholarship when Martin Dockray discovered the sworn affidavit for the Exchequer by James Kelsall, the first mate of the *Zong*.[10] The same may be said about the BL document. The fair-copy manuscript of Sharp's missive to the Admiralty at the BL is a carefully handwritten plea by one of the first anti-slavery activists in Britain, a record of his efforts to achieve justice for the murders committed on the *Zong*, and a delineation of the case that would eventually help to turn the tide of public opinion about slavery to end the brutal practice.[11]

However, scholars of slavery and abolition disagree about the significance of both the *Zong* case and Sharp for the history of British abolition. Thus, in this monograph, I examine the reception and historiography of the *Zong* case, as well as the contributions of Sharp, Olaudah Equiano, Lord Mansfield, and other major actors concerned with the episode. Today, the *Zong* incident is iconic of the horrors of slavery, one

---

[8] Sharp, BL document, 4.

[9] Jane Webster, "The *Zong* in the Context of the Eighteenth-Century Slave Trade," *Journal of Legal History* 28, no. 3 (2007): 285–98, 295.

[10] James Oldham, "Insurance Litigation Involving the *Zong* and Other British Slave Ships, 1780–1807," *Journal of Legal History* 28, no. 3 (2007): 299–318, 316; and Andrew Lewis, "Martin Dockray and the *Zong*: A Tribute in the Form of a Chronology," *Journal of Legal History* 28, no. 3 (2007): 357–70, *Taylor and Francis*, accessed July 17, 2015. Lewis further notes that the Kelsall affidavit is in The National Archives: Public Record Office (PRO) E 112/1528/173 (357 n2).

[11] Weisbord, "Case," 567.

of the most famous cases in the long history of the trade in human flesh. However, some historians contend that the lack of immediate response to it in eighteenth-century popular media and the courts renders the *Zong* case inconsiderable for the mobilization of abolitionist sentiment. I argue, on the contrary, that the *Zong* case had a decisive effect on the abolition movement because it inspired anti-slavery leaders to fight for the cause. The case was not well known to the average Briton during the abolitionist years—roughly 1787, when the Society for the Abolition of the African Slave Trade was established, to 1833, the year when Parliament passed the Slavery Abolition Act—but it was infamous among the most influential abolitionists. In the cases of Thomas Clarkson and the Quaker abolitionists who started the popular movement, for example, the *Zong* massacre was vital in spurring them into action.

Similarly, scholars disagree about whether Sharp deserves to be known as the father of British abolitionism or is a deservedly forgotten soldier in the battle against slavery. I contend that Sharp's influence on abolitionism was considerable in the eighteenth century and should be better recognized today. Like the *Zong* case itself, Sharp was not popularly known, but he inspired prominent abolitionists. Via his legal efforts on behalf of formerly enslaved Africans in England in the 1770s, his publications from that decade, and his dissemination of information about the *Zong*, Sharp paved the way for the anti-slavery activists who came after him—those who established the abolitionist movement that he did not succeed in starting himself.

Crucially, too, Sharp's decades-long, and sometimes conflicted, relationship with one of the best-known slave-memoirists, Olaudah Equiano (c. 1745–1797), is often overlooked, even though it reveals a personal side of the abolitionist movement—including that genuine friendships formed between the white and black British anti-slavery activists. This consideration is important because it undercuts the view of the abolitionist movement as a band of heroic white people saving helpless black victims, a perspective that is reinforced pictorially in the official logo of the Society for the Abolition of the African Slave Trade: the famous Wedgwood abolitionist medal features a kneeling and chained African begging to be recognized as "a man and a brother." Notably, Equiano—then a Briton—instigated the efforts to achieve justice for the victims of the *Zong* by bringing a news story on the trial to Sharp, with whom he had worked on anti-slavery cases in the 1770s. It is reasonable to conclude that the *Zong* massacre and case would have been lost to history were it not for their pre-existing relationship and Equiano's initial efforts to achieve justice for the murdered Africans. Their friendship, and the genuine influence of Sharp and the *Zong* case on abolitionism, require greater examination.

In considering Sharp's efforts to advance the cause of abolition in legal cases from the 1770s, I also discuss the role of Lord Mansfield (1705–1793), the Chief Justice of Britain from 1756 to 1788. A fascinating story of David-and-Goliath proportions emerges from this past, wherein Sharp challenged one of the most prominent members of the British legal establishment on the fine points of British law, commanding him at one point to do his duty as a magistrate and decide in favour of setting legal precedents to advance the abolition of slavery in Britain. In tracing this complex history, I also reveal how it has been distorted by widespread accounts of Mansfield's heroic contributions to the anti-slavery movement of the eighteenth century, such that the popular view of Mansfield today is as a champion of enslaved Africans and one who bravely advanced the cause with all the might of his influential position. The truth is that—despite Sharp's published demands that Mansfield decide in accordance with already established tenets of British law regarding the sanctity of the person in key cases concerning slavery—the judge repeatedly and cannily avoided decisions that would set a legal precedent to undermine the slave trade. I will consider historical and recent texts not only on Mansfield, but also on the *Zong*, Sharp, and Equiano, in order to determine the role of each in the course of the abolition of slavery. In that way, I hope to elucidate these complicated and conflicted histories.

The inadvertent nature of my discovery of the Sharp manuscript in a major archive raises important questions about the history of slavery and abolition. When Jane Austen famously writes in *Mansfield Park* (1814) of the "dead silence" with which the subject of the slave trade meets in polite conversation, she is also pointing to the cultural censorship that allowed the brutal practice of slavery to continue for hundreds of years in Britain—rendering this silence *deadly*, too.[12] The loss of Sharp's manuscript in the BL for roughly two centuries exemplifies such silence. To trace its provenance, I ask how and why it was preserved, as well as who owned it. To whom was it initially sent? And how did this important manuscript end up bound between obscure printed pamphlets on

---

[12] Jane Austen, *Mansfield Park*, ed. Jane Sturrock (Peterborough, ON: Broadview Press, 2001), 212.

medicine? Its earliest handlers did not preserve and catalogue it in the manner demanded by an important historical artefact—yet, they did not destroy the letter, either, and it was eventually placed in one of the world's safest, best-controlled collections, the BL. After the abolition movement began in earnest in 1787, British officials—such as parliamentarians and church leaders—sought to publicize the worst offences of the slave trade as a means of achieving their goal, but, in 1783, the anti-slavery movement was in its nascent stages and many wished for it to flounder. Was the BL document therefore suppressed? My investigation into the provenance of Sharp's letter in the BL has led to several other discoveries of great importance to the history of abolition, too, such as who was included in Sharp's circle of correspondents regarding the *Zong* case and that Sharp intended to publish the letter. The discovery of this letter and its intended fate encourages us to consider what was lost to history when the BL document remained unpublished, as well as how its wide distribution might have changed the course of abolition, including Sharp's contributions to it. The BL document represents the early failures of the abolitionist project in Britain, since it is the physical manifestation of Sharp's failed attempt to bring the *Zong* murderers to legal justice.

I am not the first to contemplate the historical significance of Sharp's unacknowledged missive to the Admiralty. Ian Baucom uses Sharp's missive to the Admiralty at the NMM as the anchor of his monograph, *Specters of the Atlantic: Finance Capital, Slavery, and the Philosophy of History* (2005), which he describes as "a history of that unacknowledged letter, the events it recounts, the appeal it makes, the business the Lords Commissioners left unfinished in not responding to it, the silence it writes into the histories of empire and the modern."[13] It is worth noting, however, that the Admiralty may not have received the letter or have had a chance to respond to it. Baucom comments, "There is ... no contemporaneous record that the letter was ever opened or read in the

---

[13] Ian Baucom, *Specters of the Atlantic: Finance Capital, Slavery, and the Philosophy of History* (Durham and London: Duke University Press, 2005), 4. The complete document contains both a kind of cover letter and a detailed account concerning the *Zong* murders, which I often call a "missive" to refer to both documents. The word "letter" is somewhat inaccurate because the detailed account of the *Zong* murders is not in letter-format, and, yet, Sharp sent both documents to the Admiralty, much as letters are sent; the word "missive," therefore, expresses most accurately what Sharp sent to the Admiralty, but I also use the word "letter" sometimes for stylistic variety.

surviving log of correspondence to and from the Commissioners assid-
uously kept by the Admiralty's clerks, nor in the equally fastidious minutes of the Commissioners daily meetings."[14] Thus, we must consider
that the missive may have become lost in the mail system or was otherwise intercepted before it reached its addressees, who therefore may
not have received it, rendering their lack of response to it unintentional.
Regardless, the "silence" to which Baucom gestures is real and it is even
deeper than he could have known it was. The newly discovered BL
manuscript reveals that Sharp's missive was silenced twice—once by the
Lords Commissioners of the Admiralty in failing, for whatever reason, to
answer it, and again by the early handlers of the BL manuscript.

I examine this silence as parallel to and contiguous with the warped
historiography of the *Zong*. For well over a century, and as recently as
2006, historians have sometimes misreported the facts of the case, such
as by reframing the *Zong* trial in heroic and positive terms. For example, some writers have incorrectly stated that justice was served for the
murders (it was not), or that Sharp himself instigated the trial (instead
of merely attending the hearing for an appeal), while others have mis-
counted the number of murder victims or claimed that Collingwood
returned to England (he died in Jamaica). I examine these errors as part
of an invented history of eighteenth-century Britain as characterized
by its devotion to liberty and opposition to tyranny—the same mythology that presents Mansfield as an abolitionist hero. In kind, but with no
obfuscation, I imagine an alternative history of abolition by considering
what would have happened if Sharp had been successful in publishing the
BL letter.

To reveal the power of Sharp's letter to the Admiralty and aid in
future scholarship on this topic, I include a useful appendix in this book
containing images and a detailed transcription of Sharp's two-part missive to the Lords Commissioners of the Admiralty in the BL. These copies of the BL document are the only ones available and are augmented
by detailed footnotes. Until the publication of Andrew Lyall's transcription of the NMM document in *Granville Sharp's Cases on Slavery*
(2017), the only published source of Sharp's missive to the Admiralty
was Prince Hoare's transcription of the NMM document in *Memoirs of
Granville Sharp* (1820). Accordingly, scholarship on the *Zong* case has

---

[14] Baucom, *Specters*, 3.

often relied on Hoare's text.[15] Hoare's publication does not meet contemporary scholarly standards, though, and it misrepresents many aspects of the source-text. Moreover, the NMM document is a draft of Sharp's missive, while the BL document is a fair copy of it, intended for publication, and likely the closest to the original document that Sharp sent to the Admiralty. I argue that future scholarship on Sharp's letter to the Admiralty on the *Zong* should use the BL document as the most reliable source.

The present study is the only overview of the primary and secondary materials on the *Zong* to clarify the known facts of the case. It is the first not only to examine closely all of the newly available primary materials about the *Zong* (including my recent discovery, the BL document), to adumbrate the information they provide definitively, and to delineate their provenance clearly, but it also provides an up-to-date scholarly transcription of Sharp's manuscript missive to the Admiralty in the BL. It is time to set the record straight about this vitally important episode in the history of abolition, and this examination does so.

[15] Hoare, *Memoirs*, 242–4, xvii–xxi.

CHAPTER 2

Equiano, Sharp, Mansfield, and the *Zong* Massacre: History and Significance

Abstract This chapter provides a short recapitulation of the history of the *Zong*, especially the terrible events of 1781 aboard the slave ship and those that followed the massacre, including the insurance trial initiated by the Gregson syndicate (the slave-traders) and Sharp's efforts to use the information from the hearing for an appeal of the trial decision to instigate a murder trial. With reference to a broad range of scholarship on the *Zong* incident, this chapter also clarifies several ambiguities about it, such as the ship's name and the number of victims from the massacre. Sharp learned of the *Zong* insurance trial in 1783 from Olaudah Equiano, whose legacy and long relationship with Sharp is outlined briefly. This chapter also details Sharp's abolitionist efforts in the years before the *Zong* case in 1783, which Judge Mansfield oversaw, and Sharp's repeated efforts in the 1770s to force Judge Mansfield to advance the cause of abolition in the British courts. The chapter ends with a consideration of the disputed influence of the *Zong* case on the history of abolition.

Keywords *Zong* massacre · *Zong* trial · Granville Sharp · Abolition Olaudah Equiano · Lord Mansfield

The original version of this chapter was revised: Post-publication correction has been updated. The correction to this chapter is available at https://doi.org/10.1007/978-3-319-92786-2_7

1   THE *ZONG* MASSACRE: A PRIMER

A summary of details concerning the *Zong* massacre will help to convey the BL document's significance. In 1781, the Liverpool syndicate, Gregson and partners, sent a slave ship called the *William* to the Cape Coast of Africa (present-day Ghana). While the crew of the *William* waited for the ship to be loaded up with kidnapped Africans, a process that often took several months, a unique opportunity presented itself: a Dutch ship called the *Zorgue*, or *De Zorg*, was for sale. Already loaded with 244 Africans, the *Zorgue* had been seized by a ship called the *Sally and Rachell* on behalf of the British government under the authority of a Letter of Marque, issued by the Vice-Admiralty Courts, which afforded British ships the right to seize other European slave ships as reparation for attacks on their own vessels.[1] The Dutch had recently committed such an offence, and Richard Hanley, captain of the *William*, bought the *Zorgue* on behalf of the Gregson syndicate. "This change of ownership was followed by a change of name," James Walvin writes: "henceforth the ship was known as the *Zong*."[2]

As the ship's story has been passed down through history, it has been called the "*Zong*" almost exclusively because the terrible events that occurred on it happened under British ownership, but that is not the only name used for the ship after the massacre of 1781, even in a British context. The issue of the name of the ship is important to a discussion of the BL document because Sharp refers to it as "the Zong or Zurg" many times in his letter to the Admiralty. Lewis writes, "It has long been supposed that *Zong* is a misreading of *Zorg*, a shortened form of the Dutch name *Zorgue*."[3] In her poetic reimagining of the *Zong* case, M. NourbSe Philip claims, "The name of the ship was the *Zorg*, meaning [ironically] 'care' in Dutch. An error was made when the name was repainted" on

---

[1] Jane Webster, "The *Zong* in the Context of the Eighteenth-Century Slave Trade," *Journal of Legal History* 28, no. 3 (2007): 285–98, 288; James Walvin, *The Zong: A Massacre, the Law & the End of Slavery* (New Haven and London: Yale University Press, 2011), 69; and Andrew Lyall, *Granville Sharp's Cases on Slavery* (Oxford and Portland, OR: Hart Publishing, 2017), 335 n271.

[2] Walvin, *Zong*, 69.

[3] Andrew Lewis, "Martin Dockray and the *Zong*: A Tribute in the Form of a Chronology," *Journal of Legal History* 28, no. 3 (2007): 357–70, 364 n16, *Taylor and Francis*, accessed July 17, 2015.

the ship.[4] To confuse matters further, in Hoare's transcription of Sharp's missive, the memoirist calls the ship "*Zung*" instead of Sharp's "*Zurg*." In recent commentaries, I have found almost no references to the ship as the "*Zurg*," with the exception of an article by Anita Rupprecht, who cites the documents by Sharp at the NMM as her source; my examination of the NMM documents confirms that Sharp refers to the ship as the "Zong or Zurg" in them, as he does in the parallel BL document.[5] Two historical writers call the ship the "Zurg," as well. One is George Gregory, who acknowledges his information on the *Zong* case in his volume of essays from 1785 as coming from a "Gentleman" who fits the description of Sharp closely.[6] The other is Thomas Cooper, an American Quaker, who provides an account of what he calls the "Zong or Zurg, Luke Collingwood, master" in *Letters on the Slave Trade* (1787); Cooper acknowledges Gregory's text as his source, suggesting that Sharp himself provided this information for both Gregory and Cooper.[7] Finally, Lewis comments that the crew may have given the ship's name as the *Zorgue*, its original Dutch name, when it landed at Jamaica; perhaps this circumstance explains why the Jamaican *Cornwall Chronicle* called it the "*Zorgue*" in a 5 January 1782 article about the ship's precarious state upon landing at Black River, Jamaica, with 208 survivors.[8] Notably, though, Lyall reports that "the name of the ship was changed when she arrived at Jamaica, first to the *Richard of Jamaica* and then to the

[4] M. NourbeSe Philip, *Zong! As Told to the Author by Setaey Adamu Boateng* (Toronto: The Mercury Press, 2008), 208.

[5] Anita Rupprecht, "'A Very Uncommon Case': Representations of the *Zong* and the British Campaign to Abolish the Slave Trade," *The Journal of Legal History* 28, no. 3 (2007): 329–46, 336. Sharp mentions the "Zong, or Zurg" on the first page of the NMM manuscript, numbered 95 (Granville Sharp, [NMM document] "Copy of a Letter to Lords Commissioners of the Admiralty," Old Jewry London, MS, 2 July 1783, repographic scan provided by the National Maritime Museum (NMM; REC/19), downloaded July 14, 2015).

[6] George Gregory, *Essays Historical and Moral* (London: J. Johnson, 1785), 304n. Walvin agrees that this "Gentleman" must be Sharp (Walvin, *Zong*, 172). See discussion on page 48, note 115, for more on this passage.

[7] Thomas Cooper, *Letters on the Slave Trade: First Published in Wheeler's Manchester Chronicle* (Manchester: C. Wheeler, 1787), 15–16, *Gale: The Making of the Modern World*, accessed June 20, 2017.

[8] Lewis, "Dockray," 364 n16.

Richard."[9] The crew may have provided these alternate names to create confusion about the identity of the ship and thereby distance themselves from the murderous events that recently occurred upon it. This supposition also clarifies why Sharp mentions both names of the ship in his missive: so that his reader knows that the "Zong or Zurg" is the same ship.

The *Zong* required a captain and crew before it could sail for Jamaica, which it did five months after being acquired by Hanley with an additional 196 Africans, for a staggering total of 459 people on board.[10] The overcrowded ship was manned by Captain Collingwood, formerly the surgeon on the *William* and a first-time captain; James Kelsall, first mate; crew members assembled from the *William* and sailors at the Cape Coast; and, strangely, one passenger, Robert Stubbs, the disgraced former Governor of Anomabu (spelled "Anamaboe" by Sharp), the slave-trading fort on the Cape Coast of Africa.[11] Although the motivation for the murders is ambiguous, as is the number of victims, the crimes that occurred during the *Zong*'s voyage to Jamaica are undisputed by historians.[12] As Sharp writes in his missive to the Admiralty in the BL,

> I am inform'd by M.ʳ Stubbs himself, as also by a Memorandum from the Deposition of <u>Kelsall</u> the Chief Mate. (one of the Murderers) that <u>54</u> persons were actually thrown overboard <u>alive</u> on the 29.ᵗʰ Nov.ʳ and <u>42</u> more were also thrown overboard on the 1.ˢᵗ Dec.ʳ:. … [and they] <u>cast 26 more human persons alive into the Sea</u>. … whose hands were also fettered, or bound; & which was done, it seems, in the sight of many other unhappy Sufferers, that were brought up upon the Deck for the same detestable purpose, whereby 10 of these poor miserable human Creatures were driven to the lamentable <u>Necessity of jumping overboard</u> … to avoid the fettering

[9] Lyall, *Cases*, 364.

[10] Verene A. Shepherd, "Jamaica and the Debate Over Reparation for Slavery: An Overview," in *Emancipation and the Remaking of the British Imperial World*, ed. Catherine Hall, Nicholas Draper, and Keith McClelland (Manchester: Manchester University Press, 2014), 223–50, 228; Webster, "Context," 291; and Lyall, *Cases*, 263.

[11] Walvin, *Zong*, 69; Granville Sharp, [BL document, copy of a letter to Lords Commissioners of the Admiralty] "Paper by Glanville [sic] Sharp on the Case of 132 Murdered Negroes," in *Tracts 35* (Old Jewry London, MS: n.p., July 2, 1783), 2, 7.

[12] Sharp, BL document, 1. Sharp calls the slavers' claim that they were low on water a "pretence," while Kelsall claimed in his evidence given in November 1783 in the Exchequer that the murdered Africans had been chosen "without Respect to sick or healthy," and all were "marketable slaves" (Sharp, BL document, 10; Lyall, *Cases*, 343).

or binding of their hands, & were <u>likewise drowned</u>! [¶] Thus 132 [X] innocent human persons were wilfully put to <u>a violent death</u>.[13]

Sharp's footnote marker "[X]" gestures to the following note: "133 were
ordered to be thrown over ... but one Man was saved by catching hold
of a Rope which hung over board."[14] Stubbs narrated these events not
only to Sharp directly, but also, more officially, as the only witness called
in court, since Collingwood died upon landing in Jamaica in 1781.
Kelsall gave his evidence after the trial as an affidavit in the Exchequer
in November.[15] Stubbs and Kelsall—eyewitnesses to and, likely, actors in
the massacre—stated the facts of the case simply and individually, since
they had little to fear in their reportage of the events. The case in question concerned not murder, after all, but insurance: the owners of the
Zong, the Gregson syndicate, were suing their insurers for the compensation of their jettisoned "cargo" of 132 Africans.

Notably, the number of victims from the *Zong* massacre is in question.
Sharp attests clearly in the BL document that "no less than 133 of the
unhappy Slaves on board the Zong were inhumanly doomed to be cast
into the Sea":

> 122 ... were cast <u>alive</u> ... into the Sea with their hands fettered; also
> <u>10</u> poor Negroes, who, being terrified with what they had seen of the
> unhappy fate of their Countrymen, jumped overboard in order to avoid
> the fettering or binding of their hands, <u>and were drowned</u>; and <u>one</u> Man
> more that had been <u>cast overboard alive</u>, but escaped, it seems, by laying
> hold of a Rope which hung from the Ship into the Water, and thereby,
> without being perceived, regained the Ship, secreted himself, and was
> saved.[16]

According to Sharp's account of the murders, then, the crew threw 123
people overboard, one of whom saved himself, but Sharp attributes an
additional ten deaths to the crew to account for the ten people who
jumped overboard and died, for a total of 132 victims. After all, Sharp

---

[13] Sharp, BL document, 8–9.

[14] Sharp, BL document, 9.

[15] Walvin, *Zong*, 87; James Oldham, "Insurance Litigation Involving the *Zong* and Other
British Slave Ships, 1780–1807," *Journal of Legal History* 28, no. 3 (2007): 299–318, 316.

[16] Sharp, BL document, 2.

reasons, these last ten people jumped in order to avoid being thrown over while in shackles—in an attempt to escape being murdered by the crew—making the latter responsible for these deaths, too.[17] The crime committed against the one African who escaped must be considered to be attempted murder.

To add to the numerical confusion, the historical record on the *Zong* differs widely regarding the number of victims. The way in which historians have calculated—or have refused to account for—the total number of deaths adds to the mystery of the number of Africans killed. For instance, Dave Gunning claims incorrectly that the total number of murders should be counted as 131.[18] Undoubtedly because the tally of *Zong* victims differs between various accounts of the case, too, some historians report the massacre in roundabout terms: for example, Oldham writes that "approximately 130" Africans were murdered, and that the number of victims was "130-plus slaves."[19] Problematically, though, such roundabout reportage risks implying that individual lives are less valuable when murder is perpetrated in large numbers. Indisputably, as NourbSe Philip comments, "The exact number of African slaves murdered remains a slippery signifier of what was undoubtedly a massacre."[20]

Period texts further complicate the matter of the number of murder victims from the *Zong*. The Gregson vs. Gilbert insurance trial report from 22 May 1783 records that the crew of the *Zong* threw 150 Africans overboard, but this figure is almost never cited in histories of the incident, which generally agree on 132 as the correct number of murder victims, following Sharp's account of the case.[21] Crucially, though, other period evidence suggests that the number of Africans killed in the *Zong* incident may, in fact, be closer to the little-cited number of 150. Lyall's transcription of "James Kelsall's Answer" from the Documents

---

[17] Sharp, BL document, 8.

[18] Dave Gunning, *Race and Antiracism in Black British and British Asian Literature* (Liverpool: Liverpool University Press, 2010), 46.

[19] Oldham, "Insurance," 300, 312.

[20] Philip, *Zong!*, 208 n3.

[21] Anon., "Gregson vs. Gilbert Trial Report, 1783," *Common LII English Reports Decisions* for May 1783, 629–30, 629, accessed May 24, 2016, http://www.commonlii.org/uk/cases/EngR/1783//85.pdf. An exception to this rule is Lewis' article, in which he cites Kelsall's higher number, given below ("Dockray," 364).

in the Exchequer and filed 12 November 1783—several months after the original trial, the hearing in May, and the date of the letter in the BL—states that the number of murdered Africans is 143.[22] Kelsall's testimony (given in November 1783) sheds greater light on the *Zong* incident in other ways, too. Kelsall—called "this Defendant" in the "Answer"—reportedly stated "that Ten other Slaves who were upon Deck fearing they might suffer the unhappy Fate of those destroyed spied Opportunities at different Times when unobserved of leaping overboard and leapt from the said Ship into the Sea and were drowned so that the Outside Number of Slaves so drowned amounted to One Hundred and forty two," ten more than 132, the number of victims given in Sharp's letter and most discussions of the *Zong*.[23] Yet, even 142 may not be the maximum number of murder victims in this massacre: the Kelsall "Answer" also includes the odd and shocking statement that the first "Slaves so thrown overboard as aforesaid were Women and Boys but none of them Infants save one (not reckoned in the Number of good and valuable Slaves)," which suggests that, counting this infant, 143 Africans were murdered.[24] The grammatical shell-game that is the expression "none of them [were] Infants save one"—instead of saying, more directly, "one infant was drowned"—expresses well the monstrous perspective of the murderers, who denied not just the humanity of their victims, but their very existence if they were not "valuable Slaves."

---

[22] Lyall, *Cases*, 335; Walvin, *Zong*, 225 n25. Both Lyall and Walvin list this source as the "Answer" of James Kelsall and locate it in The National Archives, E112/1528; Lyall adds "173" to this cataloguing number. Like the letter I found in the British Library, Kelsall's "Answer" was found by the late Martin Dockray in TNA (Webster, "Context," 291; Oldham, "Insurance," 316). There may be yet other undiscovered documents by Kelsall that could provide additional information about the *Zong* murders, too, since Lyall comments that the Kelsall affidavit has "not been traced" yet in the same book in which he provides a transcription of the Kelsall answer, suggesting that the affidavit is different from the "answer" (Lyall, *Cases*, 274 n227). Moreover, Oldham states, "Apparently another version of Kelsall's story was prepared before the motion for a new trial in the King's Bench was heard, as counsel for the owners claimed to have in hand during the 21–22 May proceedings in the King's Bench what they described as a sworn affidavit by Kelsall that fully confirmed Stubbs's testimony" (Oldham, "Insurance," 316). The other "version of Kelsall's story" might be what Sharp refers to as "a Memorandum from the Deposition of Kelsall the Chief Mate" in the BL document, but this "Memorandum" has not been located, either, to the best of my knowledge (Sharp, BL document, 7).

[23] Lyall, *Cases*, 342.

[24] Lyall, *Cases*, 343.

Such was the reasoning of the Atlantic slave trade, which viewed people as merchandise and machines. The infant was "not reckoned in the
Number of good and valuable Slaves" because he or she was too small to
work.

Such reasoning also provides a partial explanation for why the crew
committed the *Zong* murders: because they were too ill to be "reckoned ... good and valuable Slaves," the victims were less than worth-
less to the *Zong* crew, for they still required sustenance and space on
board the crowded ship until they landed at Black River. More critically,
though, the Africans were literally worth more dead than alive to the
murderers. The plan, evidently, was to collect insurance on the drowned
Africans, who would have fetched a poor price, if any, on the slave mar-
ket in Jamaica because they were likely all sick, Sharp points out.[25] This
reasoning also explains the mystery of how the crew "mistook Jamaica
for Hispaniola," as Sharp reports in the BL document.[26] That is to say,
the crew of the *Zong* did not make a navigational error at all, but they
intentionally steered the ship off course, thereby extending the trip so
that they could concoct their lie about fearing they would run out of
water. In his "Answer," Kelsall denies vehemently that the victims were
anything but "in Good Health and Condition none of them being sick
or weakly infirm or emaciated to this Defendants Knowledge or Belief [;
and ...] there was no infectious or other Disorder on board the said Ship
at that Time save that the Crew were much afflicted with the Scurvy."[27]
However, this claim may be dismissed as a base falsehood, told to coun-
ter the underwriters' accusation that the crew killed the Africans in order
to commit insurance fraud. After all, the Gregson syndicate (the *Zong*'s
owners) could collect insurance for the kidnapped Africans killed out of
"necessity"—the legal term underlying their case for why they had to
"jettison" them—but not for those who died of disease.

Knowing these rules well, the Gregson slave-trading syndicate publicized the details of the murders themselves by suing their insurers for the
loss of their human "cargo." As Sharp avers in the BL document,

> the Contest between the Owners and Insurers of the Ship, though a mere
> mercenary Business amongst themselves, about the pecuniary value (and

[25] Sharp, BL document, 5.
[26] Sharp, BL document, 5.
[27] Lyall, *Cases*, 340.

not for the <u>blood</u> of so many <u>human Persons</u> wickedly and unjustly put
to death) has nevertheless occasioned the disclosure of that horrible transaction, which otherwise; perhaps, might have been known only amongst
the impious Slave Dealers of Liverpool, and have never been brought to
light.[28]

Today, one may think that those intimately concerned with the slave
trade—the slave owners, crew, and insurers—were half-maddened
and their perceptions distorted by the cruel world in which they were
immersed, such that they foolishly publicized the horrendous crimes
they committed, unaware of the horrified reaction it would inspire in an
English court of law. Some people thought so in 1783, too: the anonymous writer of the only newspaper article devoted to the *Zong* case—
which appeared in the *Morning Chronicle and London Advertiser* on 18
March 1783—was present at the insurance trial and asserts, "The narrative seemed to make every person present shudder; and I waited with
some impatience, expecting that the Jury, by their foreman, would
have applied to the Court for information how to bring the perpetrator
of such a horrid deed to justice" for the murders.[29] After all, the *Zong*
insurance case was judged by a group of jurors who were all regular
Britons and not representatives of the slave trade. Given these circumstances, one might conjecture sensibly that, when the facts of the case
were stated in court, then the events aboard the *Zong* would be seen for
what they were: mass murder. However, the reality is that the court case
found *in favour of* the Gregson syndicate and the *Zong*'s owners were
thus owed the insurance money for the loss of their "cargo" of human
beings.[30]

The immediate reaction of the court to the insurance case was hardly
one of outrage. The case involved no "whistle-blowers" tearing the lid
off a secret, for there was no secret. It was not unheard of for Africans
to be killed on British slave ships, Jeremy Krikler attests; Walvin likewise comments that, well into the nineteenth century, many additional
Africans would be murdered during the Middle Passage by being thrown

---

[28] Sharp, BL document, 1–2.

[29] Anon., *Morning Chronicle and London Advertiser*, London, 18 March 1792, issue
7107, unpag., *Gale: 17th–18th Century Burney Collection Newspapers*, accessed June 20,
2017.

[30] There is no evidence that the Gregson syndicate was actually paid out.

overboard from slave ships, and James Robertson agrees.[31] Shyllon
asserts that "in 1796 another case of mass murder of African slaves was
brought before the Court of King's Bench," but this time it could be
fought with an act passed in 1794 that guarded against insurance claims
for "loss by throwing overboard of slaves on any account whatsoever."[32]
During the hearing for an appeal of the *Zong* insurance case in May of
1783, which Sharp attended, the underwriters attempted to claim that
humans could not be treated as property. However, Rupprecht explains,
"That line of argument could not be pursued. ... Lord Chief Justice
Mansfield quashed it, asserting that insurance law defined slaves as commodities and not human beings."[33] The semantic and ideological, not to
mention moral, error of seeing humans as disposable and remunerable
property was thus proven to be culture-wide and written into British law.
The murders of at least 122 people—plus ten cases of manslaughter and
one case of attempted murder—were officially, legally sanctioned and the
slavers were to be compensated for them.

2   Olaudah Equiano

Given the outcome of the trial and proof of the immense power of
the West India slavers in Britain—supported by King, Parliament,
courts, and commoners—a formerly enslaved man living in England
in 1783 could be excused for losing faith in his new society, which, it
appeared, saw him as less than human. Could justice be found in a place

---

[31] Jeremy Krikler, "A Chain of Murder in the Slave Trade: A Wider Context of the *Zong*
Massacre," *International Review of Social History* 57, no. 3 (2012): 393–415, 395; Walvin,
Zong, 104, 200–1; and James Robertson, Review of *The Zong: A Massacre, the Law and
the End of Slavery*, by James Walvin, *The Historian* 75, no. 3 (2013): 640–1, 641. Notably,
however, Webster claims that jettisoning slaves was not common ("Context," 292).

[32] Shyllon, *Black Slaves*, 206. Other slave-owning countries added to the body-count,
too. For example, Robert Walsh writes about his experiences in 1828–1829 regarding a
Portuguese ship that he boarded to seize the kidnapped Africans destined to be slaves:
"She had taken in, on the coast of Africa, 336 males, and 226 females, making in all 562,
and had been out seventeen days, during which she had thrown overboard fifty-five"
(Robert Walsh, *Notices of Brazil in 1828 and 1829* (London: F. Westley and A. H. Davis,
1830), vol. 2, 479, *Google eBooks*, accessed July 28, 2017, https://books.google.ca/
books?id=or7vAQAACAAJ.

[33] Anita Rupprecht, "'A Limited Sort of Property': History, Memory and the Slave Ship
Zong," *Slavery & Abolition* 29, no. 2 (2008): 265–77, 274.

where his fellows were called "cargo" and their murders termed "jetti-soning"—the Africans having been thrown overboard in three so-called "*parcel*[s]"?[34] Despite official evidence to the contrary, Equiano did not believe that his British brethren were so monstrous. When the insurers asked for a retrial, Equiano read about the case in the 18 March 1783 edition of the *Morning Chronicle and London Advertiser* and brought the matter to Sharp. Sharp's account of his meeting with Equiano in the letter to the Admiralty appears, in retrospect, like the momentous encounter of heroes: "Having been earnestly solicited and called upon by a poor Negro, for my assistance to avenge the blood of his mur-dered Countrymen," writes Sharp, "I thought it my duty to spare nei-ther labour nor expence in collecting all the information concerning this horrible transaction that I could possibly procure."[35] This "poor Negro" would become one of eighteenth-century Britain's most influen-tial writers about slavery. Equiano, sometimes known by his slave-name, Gustavus Vassa, wrote one of the best-known slavery narratives to date, *The Interesting Narrative of the Life of Olaudah Equiano, or Gustavus Vassa, the African, Written by Himself* (1789). Although Equiano had lit-tle power in March of 1783, he trusted that Sharp—a white man, known agitator for the rights of the enslaved in England, and devoted anti-slavery activist since the late 1760s—would take up his cause, and he was correct.

The occasion of the *Zong* trial was neither the first time that Sharp and Equiano had met, nor the first that Sharp had attempted to secure legal justice for enslaved Africans. Equiano reports in *Interesting Narrative* that his efforts to help a man named John Annis to escape recapture by his slave-owners in England led him to Sharp's doorstep in 1774:

> I proceeded immediately to that philanthropist, Granville Sharp, Esq. who received me with the utmost kindness, and gave me every instruction that was needful on the occasion. I left him in full hope that I should gain the unhappy man his liberty, with the warmest sense of gratitude towards Mr. Sharp for his kindness; but, alas! my attorney proved unfaithful; he took

[34] Prince Hoare, *Memoirs of Granville Sharp, Esq. Composed from His Own Manuscripts, and Other Authentic Documents in the Possession of His Family Authentic Documents in the Possession of His Family and of the African Institution* (London: Henry Colburn, 1820), *Google eBooks*, accessed June 25, 2015–August 30, 2017, https://books.google.ca/books?id=PrUEAAAAIAAJ, 238.

[35] Sharp, BL document, 1.

my money, lost me many months employ, and did not do the least good in the cause.[36]

Despite the poor conclusion of this intervention, as well as that of the *Zong* case, Equiano maintained his faith in and gratitude for Sharp's support of the anti-slavery cause. When he formed the abolitionist society called the "Sons of Africa" in 1787—along with others, such as formerly enslaved African and abolitionist writer in England, Ottobah Cugoano (c.1757–1791)—Equiano signed a moving letter of thanks to Sharp that includes a commentary on the significance of the latter's many publications on the topic of slavery:

> Your writings, Sir, are not of trivial matters, but of great and essential things of moral and religious importance, worthy the regard of all men. …
> Therefore, we wish, for ourselves and others, that these valuable treatises may be collected and preserved, for the benefit and good of all men, and.
> … as a monument or beacon to guide and to warn men, lest they should depart from the paths of justice and humanity; and that they may more and more become a means of curbing the vicious violators of God's holy Law, and to restrain the avaricious invaders of the rights and liberties of men.[37]

The religious piety and focus on resistance to oppression in this letter were not only designed to appeal to Sharp, who promulgated such principles throughout his writings, but they also reflect Equiano's personal interests: Seymour Drescher reports that Equiano applied for the position of missionary to Africa in 1779, showing Equiano's early interest in promoting Christianity in areas linked to the slave trade.[38]

These interests would resurface in *Interesting Narrative* from 1789, in which Equiano describes his life-experiences from 1755 to 1787, from having been kidnapped from Africa as a child to being enslaved on ships in the Middle Passage, and then becoming an Englishman, among other

---

[36]Olaudah Equiano, *The Interesting Narrative of the Life of Olaudah Equiano, or Gustavus Vassa, the African, Written by Himself,* 1789, ed. Angelo Costanzo (Peterborough, ON: Broadview Press, 2001), 196.

[37]Quoted in Hoare, *Memoirs,* 374; I also provide part of this passage as an epigraph to the present monograph.

[38]Seymour Drescher, "The Shocking Birth of British Abolitionism," *Slavery & Abolition* 33, no. 4 (2012): 571–93, 573.

experiences, including his conversion to Methodism—much to the displeasure of one of his most famous reviewers, Mary Wollstonecraft, who complained of these religious sections as "tiresome."[39] Read in the context of Equiano's abolitionist efforts, though, these passages gain great significance because his anti-slavery efforts were a natural outcome of his religious principles, as was the case with his friend Sharp. Nor should Equiano's role in advancing the cause of abolition be understated. While he had an influential audience for his efforts to achieve freedom for African slaves before *Interesting Narrative* was published—and, in fact, he petitioned Queen Charlotte to help end the slave trade in 1788—he managed to reach a far wider audience through his 1789 publication. By 1827, Equiano's *Interesting Narrative* had gone into seventeen editions and been translated into Dutch and German, while the author had travelled all over the British Isles to promote the book, including at abolitionist meetings.[40]

In contrast with Equiano's claims in the *Interesting Narrative*, historian Vincent Carretta argues that Equiano was not born in Africa, but South Carolina, in *Equiano, the African: Biography of a Self-Made Man.*[41] Carretta also asserts that Equiano went by the name of "Gustavus Vassa" until 1789, when he published the *Interesting Narrative*, a deduction that is confirmed by Sharp's identification of him as "Gustavus Vasa" in his diary.[42] I use the African name "Olaudah Equiano" to refer to him because the name "Gustavus Vassa" was forced

---

[39] W. [Mary Wollstonecraft], Review of *The Interesting Narrative of the Life of Olaudah Equiano, or Gustavus Vassa, the African. Written by Himself*, in *The Analytical Review, Or History of Literature, Domestic and Foreign, on an Enlarged Plan* (London: J. Johnson, 1789), vol. 4, 27–9, 27, *Google ebooks*, accessed February 25, 2013, https://books. google.ca/books?id=2O4vAAAAYAAJ&pg=PA27&dq=The+Analytical+Review+equiano+J.+Johnson,+1789&hl=en&sa=X&ved=0ahUKEwiWxIWh7qLWAhUh_4MKHeHoDj8Q6AEINjAD#v=onepage&q=The%20Analytical%20Review%20equiano%20J.%20Johnson%2C%201789&f=false.

[40] F. O. Shyllon, *Black People in Britain 1555–1833* (London: Oxford University Press, 1977), 221, 235.

[41] Vincent Carretta, *Equiano, the African: Biography of a Self-Made Man* (Athens: University of Georgia Press, 2005), e.g. 319. A shorter summary of Carretta's argument regarding Equiano's name and birthplace appears in the article "Olaudah Equiano or Gustavus Vassa? New Light on an Eighteenth-Century Question of Identity" (*Slavery & Abolition* 20, no. 3 (1999): 96–105, accessed August 19, 2017, https://doi.org/10.1080/01440399908575287).

[42] Carretta "New Light," 104; Sharp qtd. in Hoare, *Memoirs*, 236.

on him during his slavery, rendering it a tool of linguistic violence. This name signified that he had no power over the most basic aspects of his existence, such as his identity, that he was under others' total control, and that he was essentially and existentially a "slave" (a word I use mindfully here, as opposed to "enslaved," which I use elsewhere throughout this monograph). To call Equiano by his slave-name even after his manumission would be to suggest that he could never be free, even when he had no so-called "master"—that he was ontologically a "slave." Although it may be that Equiano did not refer to himself by his African name until 1789, he clearly identified himself as an African years before that time, since Sharp begins the BL document by noting that he promised to help Equiano "avenge the blood of his murdered Countrymen," specifically the African victims of the *Zong*.[43] Finally, in the fifth edition of *Interesting Narrative*, Equiano vehemently opposes the assertions of those who questioned his African identity as a way of undermining his integrity and, by extension, his anti-slavery arguments.[44] Given the powerful implications of (re)naming in the colonial slave trade, I adhere to Equiano's clear wishes in the case of his name, which is so closely tied to his African identity.

Notably, Sharp appears in the subscription list for the first edition of *Interesting Narrative* as a purchaser of two copies. The lasting—if not always smooth—friendship between the two men is also evident in correspondence from the period. In a letter from Sharp to his brother, John Sharp, dated 23 June 1787, Sharp comments on the advancement of the Sierra Leone project, to which Equiano contributed: "I had the pleasure of hearing this day of the safe arrival of the African settlers at Madeira islands; and that all the jealousies and animosities between the Whites and the Blacks had subsided, and that they had been very orderly ever since Mr. Vasa and two or three other discontented persons had been left on shore at Plymouth."[45] Clearly, the men remained friends, though, despite their disagreements: in a letter of introduction for Equiano to present on his travels, Thomas Digges claims to have met Equiano in the company of Sharp in 1791. Finally, in a letter to his niece, Sharp himself describes having visited Equiano in his last illness in 1797: "He was a

---

[43] Sharp, BL document, 1.
[44] Carretta, "New Light," 98.
[45] Quoted in Hoare, *Memoirs*, 312–13.

sober, honest man—and I went to see him when he lay upon his death bed, and had lost his voice so that he could only whisper."[46] These abolitionists' desire to work together for the cause of justice began before and extended long beyond the *Zong* case of 1783.

3   GRANVILLE SHARP VERSUS JUDGE MANSFIELD

Equiano had good reason to revisit Sharp in 1783 to ask for help in achieving justice for the *Zong* victims. Sharp has long been considered by many to have been Britain's first abolitionist, or the "father of abolition," and his efforts for the cause were well recognized in his day.[47] Moved by Equiano's visit, Sharp writes in his diary of the illustrious people whom he approached on 21 March 1783 to begin his campaign for justice on behalf of the victims of the *Zong*—"the Bishops of Chester [Beilby Porteus] and Peterborough [John Hinchcliffe], and General Oglethorpe, and Dr. Jebb"—but these visits were far from introductory, as he had lobbied these powerful men to advance the cause of abolition in the decade before.[48] Christopher Leslie Brown reports that Sharp had visited no fewer than twenty-two prelates in 1779, including "bishops to introduce an abolition bill ..., when the House of Commons established a committee to investigate the administration of the African trade."[49] Perhaps most notably, in 1772, Sharp wrote Lord North, then the Prime Minister, asking him to take action against "the present miserable and deplorable slavery of Negroes ... in our colonies," calling the cause "a point of considerable consequence to this kingdom."[50] Sharp's status as the first British anti-slavery activist was recognized in his time, and not least by Clarkson (1760–1846) himself, who wrote the following

---

[46] Shyllon, *Black People*, 237; Sharp quoted in Shyllon, *Black People*, 238.

[47] Christopher Leslie Brown, *Moral Capital: Foundations of British Abolitionism* (Chapel Hill: University of North Carolina Press, 2012), 160, 172; F. O. Shyllon, *Black Slaves in Britain* (London and New York: Oxford University Press, 1974), ix, 189; Gomer Williams, *History of the Liverpool Privateers and Letter of Marque: With an Account of the Liverpool Slave Trade* (London: W. Heinemann, 1897), 568; and G. M. Ditchfield, "Sharp, Granville (1735–1813)," *Oxford Dictionary of National Biography* (Oxford: Oxford University Press, 2004, 2012), unpag., accessed June 16, 2015, https://doi.org/10.1093/ref:odnb/25208.

[48] Quoted in Hoare, *Memoirs*, 236.

[49] Brown, *Moral*, 194.

[50] Quoted in Hoare, *Memoirs*, 79, 78.

encomium regarding the circumstances that gave birth to the abolition
movement:

> first, they produced that able and indefatigable advocate, Mr. Granville
> Sharp. ..., both a writer and an actor in the cause. In fact, he was the first
> labourer in it in England. By the words "actor" and "labourer," I mean,
> that he determined upon a plan of action in behalf of the oppressed
> Africans, to the accomplishment of which, he devoted a considerable por-
> tion of his time, talents, and substance.[51]

Clarkson goes on to relay the various instances upon which Sharp fought
for the rights and freedom of Africans in England, which began in the
1760s and continued up to and beyond the *Zong* case in 1783. After the
Zong case, Sharp became the Chair of the Society for the Abolition of
the African Slave Trade—one of only three Anglicans in a committee of
twelve dominated by Quakers—and he devoted himself to the establishment of Sierra Leone, a project that was fraught with problems almost
from the beginning, but which abolitionists intended as an African
homeland where the enslaved who were kidnapped from all parts of
Africa could establish a free and democratic community.[52]

Others would attempt to crown themselves with the laurel of being
the first abolitionist writer. Of his anti-slavery verse from 1782, the poet
William Cowper famously wrote "to Lady Hesketh in February 1788, ...
'I was one of the earliest, if not the first of those who have in the present
day, expressed their detestation of the diabolical traffic,'" Brycchan Carey

---

[51] Thomas Clarkson, *The History of the Rise, Progress, and Accomplishment of the Abolition
of the African Slave-Trade, by the British Parliament*, 2 vols. (London: Longman, Hurst,
Rees, and Orme, 1808), vol. 1, 67, *Online Library of Liberty*, accessed August 28, 2017,
http://oll.libertyfund.org/titles/clarkson-the-history-of-the-abolition-of-the-african-
slave-trade-vol-1.

[52] Brown states that Sharp refused to be the Chair of the Society for the Abolition of
the African Slave Trade, but several others, such as Shyllon and Williams, comment that
Sharp was indeed its Chair (Brown, *Moral*, 198; Shyllon, *Black People*, 231; and Williams,
Liverpool, 568). Sharp also signs himself as "Chairman" of the Society in a letter quoted
in an anonymous period article in *Felix Farley's Bristol Journal* (Anon., *Felix Farley's
Bristol Journal*, December 22, 1788, issue 2043, unpag., *Gale: 17th–18th Century Burney
Collection Newspapers*, accessed June 16, 2017). In another anonymous article from the
same newspaper, Sharp is again called the "Chairman" of the Society (Anon., *Felix Farley's
Bristol Journal*, September 12, 1788, issue 2081, unpag., *Gale: 17th–18th Century Burney
Collection Newspapers*, accessed June 16, 2017).

notes; but, he adds, "John Bicknell and Thomas Day's *The Dying Negro* [from 1773] precedes Cowper's anti-slavery verse by almost a decade and, even if he had missed that poem, it is inconceivable that Cowper was not aware of Granville Sharp's ... work against slavery."[53] For years, Sharp was virtually alone in agitating for abolition, *A Representation of the Injustice and Dangerous Tendency of Tolerating Slavery* appearing in 1769 like a voice crying in the wilderness. Very few writers then wished to join him in the anti-slavery cause—until the abolitionist movement became established in the late 1780s, when an explosion of abolitionist writing appeared.[54]

From the mid-1760s to the 1780s, Sharp focused much of his energy on the abolitionist cause, but, admittedly, he was not the leader of the popular movement of the late 1780s that resulted in the passing of the Parliamentary acts against the slave trade (1807) and slavery in the colonies (1833).[55] Sharp's earliest involvement with the anti-slavery cause may be traced through three major legal cases: that of Jonathan Strong, Thomas Lewis, and James Somerset, all of whom were formerly enslaved men living in England when they met Sharp. His abolitionist work began in 1765 with the case of Jonathan Strong, who had been brought to England from Barbados by his master David Lisle, a lawyer, who beat the youth so badly that he was on the point of death and lame in both legs.[56] Lisle had turned Strong out into the street as useless in his near-death condition, whereupon Sharp found him outside the house of his brother, William Sharp, a physician who treated the poor for free. Two years after the brothers helped Strong, who had spent about a month in the hospital recovering (and would later die at the age of 25 from his injuries), Lisle met Strong in the street. Impressed by Strong's apparent good health, Lisle seized him to sell him to James Kerr, who intended to

---

[53] Bryccham Carey, *British Abolitionism and the Rhetoric of Sensibility: Writing, Sentiment and Slavery, 1760–1807* (New York: Palgrave Macmillan, 2005), 98.

[54] See, especially, Carey's *British Abolitionism and the Rhetoric of Sensibility* and James Basker's *Amazing Grace: An Anthology of Poems About Slavery, 1660–1810* (New Haven: Yale University Press, 2002) for more information about anti-slavery writing.

[55] Brown, *Moral*, 160.

[56] Information for the story of Strong has been taken from Walvin, *Zong*, 169; David Brion Davis, *The Problem of Slavery in the Age of Revolution, 1770–1823* (Oxford: Oxford University Press, 1999), 392; Ditchfield, "Sharp," unpag.; Shyllon, *Black Slaves*, 18–39; and Clarkson, *History*, 67.

use Strong for forced labour in Jamaica. Sharp again intervened, and this time legally: "Sharp took up Strong's case, [and] secured his release from prison when Lisle obtained his arrest as an escaped slave."[57] However, Sharp was far from satisfied with Lord Chief Justice James Mansfield's decision that freed Strong because it also directed that "no slave could claim freedom merely as the result of being in England"; Mansfield would repeat this decision, which was based on a 1729 opinion by Attorney-General Philip Yorke and Solicitor General Charles Talbot, in several other cases, too.[58] The Strong decision formed Sharp's approach to abolition. He thereafter immersed himself in the study of law and generated several influential abolitionist texts to fight it, focusing first on secular and then religious laws against slavery. Lisle challenged Sharp to a duel, which the latter refused; and, with Kerr, Lisle filed a lawsuit against Sharp and his brother James (not William, for some unknown reason) for "trespass" against their property in Strong. However, Sharp fended off this case by circulating his earliest text on the illegality of slavery in Britain, *A Representation of the Injustice and Dangerous Tendency of Tolerating Slavery* (1769), informally among the lawyers, even though it was then still in manuscript. It was so convincing that his persecutors were discouraged from pressing their case.[59] Sharp had carried his point substantively, if not legally.

Sharp wrote several important abolitionist texts in the 1770s on the basis of his legal research. Significantly, though, in Sharp's own words, he had "never opened a lawbook (except the Bible)" in his life before this period.[60] This comment introduces Sharp's *oeuvre* on slavery succinctly, as it demonstrates his view that religious and secular laws are commensurate and inseparable. The first two texts, *A Representation of the Injustice and Dangerous Tendency of Tolerating Slavery* and *An Appendix to the Representation of the Injustice and Dangerous Tendency* (1772), give thorough, authoritative, and convincing legal arguments regarding why slavery was already illegal in Britain—rather than reasons

---

[57] Ditchfield, "Sharp," unpag.

[58] Shyllon, *Black Slaves*, 25–6; Davis, *Problem*, 392.

[59] Kathleen Chater, "Strong, Jonathan (c.1747–1773)," *Oxford Dictionary of National Biography* (Oxford: Oxford University Press, 2012), unpag., accessed June 16, 2015, https://doi.org/10.1093/ref:odnb/100415; Davis, *Problem*, 392; and Shyllon, *Black Slaves*, 31.

[60] Shyllon, *Black Slaves*, 22.

for why it should be declared unlawful—and it had an almost immediate effect in British courts. While the first text convinced Lisle and Kerr's lawyers to drop their case against the Sharps, the 28-page appendix to that work was even more momentous. It was linked to two important cases on slavery, those of formerly enslaved Africans Thomas Lewis and James Somerset.

Sharp was moved to write the *Appendix* of 1772 after the Rex v. Stapylton case of 1771 concerning Lewis, who had been enslaved in the West Indies and was in Chelsea in 1770 when his former master, Robert Stapylton, tried to sell him back into slavery in Jamaica. Sharp rescued Stewart from this fate by presenting a writ of Habeus Corpus moments before the ship was set to sail overseas from the River Thames, forcing the captain to free the kidnapped man. Despite this positive outcome, Sharp was again displeased with the verdict: he lamented in a letter that the judge "Lord Mansfield avoided bringing the question to issue, by discharging the Negro on some other pretence"—specifically the issue of whether Stapylton could produce written evidence of his owner-ship of Lewis (he could not)—and Sharp further accused Mansfield "of 'open contempt of the principle of the Constitution' and the laws of England."[61] In short, Sharp would settle for nothing less than an official declaration in a British court of the illegality of slavery, and Mansfield refused to provide it, being wary of the detrimental effects of such a declaration for the British economy, not to mention the social effects: Mansfield would later express his fear that a positive ruling in favour of the freedom of enslaved people in Britain would result in the release of "fourteen to fifteen thousand slaves throughout the land" and wreak havoc in the streets.[62] The degree of Mansfield's reticence about the legality of slavery in Britain is clear from his decision in the Lewis case: "it is much better that it should never be discussed or settled. I don't know what the consequences may be, if the masters were to lose their property by accidentally bringing their slaves to England. I hope it never will be finally discussed."[63] Far from wishing to advance the freedom of enslaved people, Mansfield hoped that the issue would never come to court. He encouraged the silence about slavery that is emblematized,

[61] Quoted in Shyllon, *Black Slaves*, 53.
[62] James Oldham, *English Common Law in the Age of Mansfield* (Chapel Hill: University of North Carolina Press, 2004), 305, 320.
[63] Shyllon, *Black Slaves*, 53.

I argue, by BL document, which was likely already buried in the archives in the years before the abolition movement began in 1787.

This silence is also reflected in the misrepresentation of Mansfield in popular culture. He is widely viewed as an early and influential propo-nent of abolition by supposedly "freeing the slaves in England through his decision in the *Somerset* case," but modern scholarship has revealed that these claims are baseless.[64] Nevertheless, heroic status is conferred upon Mansfield in popular culture, such as through the contemporary film *Belle* (2014), which presents the Chief Justice as a champion of enslaved people in Britain, one who condemned the Gregson slave-trading syndicate through his judgment against the slavers in the *Zong* case, thus delivering the death-blow to slavery itself through these means.[65] The reality is that the jury's decision found in favour of remunerating the slavers for the murders of the Africans aboard the *Zong* and Mansfield did nothing to intervene. *Belle* also presents Mansfield as a devoted guardian to his bi-racial niece, Dido Elizabeth Belle (1761–1804), who lived with him and was a beneficiary of his will, but the same will reveals Mansfield's hypocrisy: Shyllon reports that "There is a copy of Lord Mansfield's Will in the Probate Records section of the Public Record Office, which shows that the man canonized for emancipating black slaves in England in 1772 [in the Somerset case], was a slave-owner himself until his death twenty-one years later."[66] Mansfield would suf-fer financial losses if slavery were to be declared illegal under British law. As such, it should come as no surprise that, in every major case relat-ing to slavery with which Sharp was involved and over which Mansfield presided (those concerning Strong, Lewis, Somerset, and the *Zong*), Mansfield evaded the opportunity to advance the anti-slavery cause.

Sharp commented that he did not want to publish his *Appendix* "until there be an absolute necessity for disclosing it," and this necessity attended the Somerset case, which was decided by Mansfield in 1772, over six months after it first came to court in late 1771.[67] Somerset was a formerly enslaved African living freely in England, having been brought

---

[64] James Oldham, *The Mansfield Manuscripts and the Growth of English Law in the Eighteenth Century* (Chapel Hill: University of North Carolina Press, 1992), vol. 2, 1221.

[65] *Belle*, directed by Amma Asante (2014; Buckinghamshire, UK: Pinewood Studios), film.

[66] Shyllon, *Black Slaves*, 234.

[67] Shyllon, *Black Slaves*, 126; Oldham, *Manuscripts*, 1226.

there from Boston in America by Charles Stewart. Stewart recaptured Somerset in order to sell him back into slavery in Jamaica, but Sharp worked to free Somerset from this fate, enlisting several attorneys to argue the case. The official decision for the trial was that enslaved people could not be transported overseas into slavery in the colonies upon reaching Britain, another instance of Mansfield's desire to avoid passing absolute judgment on the question of whether people could ever be property under British law.[68] The outcome of the trial benefited Somerset, but the legal outcome for slavery, in general, was limited.

Although Somerset gained his freedom through Mansfield's decision, the judge failed to recognize the legal argument that Sharp delineates in *A Representation of the Injustice and Dangerous Tendency of Tolerating Slavery*, in which he demonstrates explicitly that, under current British law, one could only enslave oneself by an explicit and written contract of agreement between the two parties, the owner and the enslaved.[69] As David Brion Davis notes, "Lord Mansfield reluctantly ruled that no positive law entitled a slaveholder to detain a slave forcibly in England or transport him out of the country. What alarmed Sharp the most was Mansfield's advice that West Indian merchants appeal to Parliament for a legislative remedy."[70] This solicitous guidance for the slave-owners sits uncomfortably with some anti-slavery statements Mansfield made during the trial. Ruth Paley reports, "Lord Mansfield declared the return [of Somerset to the West Indies] unlawful, stating that 'Slavery is so odious that it must be construed strictly' and derive from positive law."[71] Mansfield seems to have been of two minds regarding slavery. One wonders how the same man can call slavery "odious" and, in the same trial, advise slavers to protect themselves through Parliamentary means—or, for that matter, own enslaved people himself until the end of his life.

Mansfield's refusal to decide upon the larger questions underlying slavery pushed Sharp into action: Sharp's greatest historian, Shyllon, comments, "He not only published his censure of Mansfield, but sent

---

[68] E.g. Oldham, *Manuscripts*, 1221, 1229.

[69] Granville Sharp, *A Representation of the Injustice and Dangerous Tendency of Tolerating Slavery* (London: Benjamin White, and Robert Horsfield, 1769), e.g. 9, 21.

[70] Davis, *Problem*, 393.

[71] Ruth Paley, "After Somerset: Mansfield, Slavery and the Law in England, 1772–1830," *Law, Crime and English Society, 1660–1830*, ed. Norma Landau (Cambridge: Cambridge University Press, 2002), 165–84, 165.

copies to the judges of the Court of King's Bench, and had Mansfield's copy delivered by none other than James Somerset."[72] Although Sharp does not mention Mansfield by name in the texts, the *Appendix* takes aim at the Lord Chief Justice in no uncertain terms:

> Therefore when a Notorious Outrage and Breach of the Peace is committed under the pretence of any such groundless claim of service, the Magistrate who neglects to relieve the person oppress'd, and to punish the Offenders, is certainly a partaker of their Guilt; and no upright and conscientious Judge (who does not set up his own will above the laws of the Land) can possibly entertain any doubt in his mind about the punishment of such Offenders.[73]

Sharp invested great effort into the Somerset trial, as he was certain that Mansfield would not be able to evade the question of the legality of slavery under British law in this case. Despite his devotion to the case, though, Sharp denied himself the satisfaction of witnessing the outcome in person: he conscientiously avoided the court during the Somerset decision, knowing that his very presence in the room was likely to annoy Mansfield and could negatively influence the result of the trial.[74] Once Mansfield passed his decision, however, Sharp would go unnoticed no longer. A mere clerk in the Ordnance Office, Sharp levelled his dressing-down to the most influential legal personage in Britain by distributing his *Appendix*. Sharp's boldness in speaking truth to power was an ethical stance, as is clear from his correspondence:

> Although I am a placeman, and indeed of a very inferior rank, yet I look on myself to be perfectly independent, because I have never yet been afraid to do and avow whatever I thought just and right, without the consideration of consequences to myself: for, indeed, I think it unworthy of a *man* to be afraid of the world; and it is a point with me, never to conceal my

[72] Shyllon, *Black Slaves*, 126.

[73] Granville Sharp, *An Appendix to the Representation: (Printed in the Year 1769,) of the Injustice and Dangerous Tendency of Tolerating Slavery, Or of Admitting the Least Claim of Private Property in the Persons of Men in England* (London: Benjamin White and Robert Horsefield [sic], 1772), 19.

[74] Shyllon, *Black Slaves*, 80.

sentiments on any subject whatever, not even from my superiors in office, *when there is a probability of answering any good purpose by it.*[75]

This philosophy also explains Sharp's eagerness to challenge the legal and military establishment in the *Zong* case almost a decade later.

Sharp was dissatisfied with the Somerset decision, but, oddly, the popular misunderstanding of it answered Sharp's wishes for the case to a greater extent than he could have hoped. As is still often the case today, many people at the time believed that the Somerset decision freed the enslaved in Britain, and they acted accordingly.[76] In spite of the encomia heaped upon Mansfield by popular history for his supposed liberation of enslaved Africans upon reaching Britain, the judge would later clarify that his decision in the Somerset case directed merely that they could not be sold back into slavery away from Britain.[77] Even before the eighteenth century was through, however, British newspapers reported the outcome of the trial as advancing the abolitionist cause much more decisively. For example, the anonymous writer of an article from 29 to 31 January 1788 in *St. James's Chronicle or the British Evening Post* asserts,

> In the Case of Sommerset, the Negro, it was determined by the Court of King's Bench, that Slavery could not exist in England; but as this was a constitutional Question, did not the Determination virtually extend to the whole Empire? In Ireland the Judges held that it did.—If by the Constitution Slavery cannot exist in England, how can it properly exist in its Dependencies[?][78]

This writer argues that the supposed freedom of enslaved people in Britain after the Somerset case must be expanded to the colonies. Through such means, "the misleading publicity given to *Somerset* meant that some black slaves benefited from the resultant confusion and found themselves *de facto* free," Paley comments, such that the Somerset "mythology did slowly turn into reality" and not only for enslaved

---

[75] Hoare, *Memoirs*, 100, emphasis in original; also in Shyllon, *Black Slaves*, 120.

[76] Oldham, *Manuscripts*, 1221; Oldham, *Common Law*, 305, 322; Shyllon, *Black Slaves*, 85; and Paley, "Somerset," 165.

[77] Oldham, *Manuscripts*, 1221, 1229.

[78] Anon., *St. James's Chronicle or the British Evening Post*, January 29–31, 1788, issue 4213, unpag., *Gale: 17th–18th Century Burney Collection Newspapers*, accessed June 16, 2017.

people and the wider British populace: a substantial number of judges also "believed that *Somerset* had indeed abolished slavery in England."[79] Particularly in America, many legal minds interpreted Mansfield's decision to mean that slavery was illegal "*unless* specific legislation authorized it."[80] Sharp seems to contribute to the misapprehension of the Somerset decision in a text from 1776, *The Just Limitation of Slavery: In the Laws of God, Compared with the Unbounded Claims of the African Traders and British American Slaveholders*, in which he declares, "But it is not enough, that the Laws of England exclude Slavery merely from this island, while the grand Enemy of mankind triumphs in a toleration, throughout our Colonies, of the most monstrous oppression to which human nature can be subjected!"[81] By stating that "the Laws of England exclude Slavery ... from this island," Sharp appears to promote the misunderstanding that no one could be enslaved while in Britain, but his point is that slavery was already against British law—even if the Lord Chief Justice refused to recognize this fact in a decision that would set a legal precedent and alter the way in which the law was interpreted in subsequent trials. In other words, the historical outcome of the Somerset trial was more positive for the abolitionist cause than was the official outcome. This pattern would repeat itself with respect to the *Zong* case in 1783: it ended in a crying injustice and was not reported widely in contemporary newspapers, but the case advanced the historical march towards abolition significantly by influencing the leaders of the abolitionist movement.

After the Somerset trial of 1772, Sharp published texts on abolition with great zeal, reflected not only in terms of the number of texts he produced, but also in terms of his passionate tone in them. Most of these works seek to demonstrate the illegality of slavery in Britain as a Christian nation and advance the view that God's laws are, in fact, more binding than are secular laws because offenders are doomed to eternal punishment for breaking them. These texts include *An Essay on Slavery: Proving from Scripture Its Inconsistency with Humanity and*

[79] Paley, "Somerset," 182.

[80] William R. Cotter, "The Somerset Case and the Abolition of Slavery in England," *History* 29, no. 255 (1994): 31–56, 32.

[81] Granville Sharp, *The Just Limitation of Slavery in the Laws of God, Compared with the Unbounded Claims of the African Traders and British American Slaveholders* (London: B. White, and E. and C. Dilly, 1776), 2.

Religion (1773), *The Law of Passive Obedience, Or Christian Submission to Personal Injuries* (1776), *The Law of Liberty: Or, Royal Law, by Which All Mankind Will Certainly Be Judged!* Earnestly Recommended to the Serious Consideration of All Slaveholders and Slavedealers (1777), and *The Law of Retribution* (1776), the subtitle of which exemplifies Sharp's increasing focus on divine justice as the reason to outlaw British slavery: *A Serious Warning to Great Britain and Her Colonies, Founded on Unquestionable Examples of God's Temporal Vengeance Against Tyrants, Slave-holders, and Oppressors.* On the first page of this text, Sharp denounces the African slave trade as having been

> publicly supported and encouraged by *the Legislature of this Kingdom* for near a century last past [sic]; so that the *monstrous destruction of the Human Species* ... may certainly be esteemed a *National Crime* of the most aggravating kind, which (according to the usual course of God's Providence in the World) will probably draw down some exemplary vengeance upon the unrepenting Inhabitants of this Island![82]

Sharp's increasing focus on the danger of divine retribution in response to British slavery was both earnest and calculated. There can be no doubt that this devoted man of faith believed strongly that God would punish Britain for its "iniquity," one of Sharp's favourite words to describe the slave trade, but this emphasis also suggests a considered rhetorical effort to achieve greater change for the cause of abolition. In his hard-won legal knowledge and soundly argued early texts, Sharp's goal was to force the British courts to recognize the illegality of slavery under secular British law in at least one decision, but he had been denied that satisfaction time and again. His increasing focus on divine retribution effectively declared to his opponents that they could not deceive God with their chicanery, nor could it help them to circumvent their ultimate fate under divine law.

Sharp demonstrates that, no matter how unjust the arbiters of secular laws were, justice would nevertheless be served to the supporters of the slave trade—including judges and other legislators—by a higher judge, God himself. Crucially, Sharp located their punishment in this world, rather than focusing on the afterlife for the period of God's retribution.

[82] Granville Sharp, *The Law of Retribution; or, A Serious Warning to Great Britain and Her Colonies* (London: W. Richardson, 1776), 1.

He seeks to augment the reader's panic in *The Law of Retribution* by arguing that the American Revolution was evidence that God's wrath over slavery was already being visited on Britons:

> a speedy Reformation is absolutely necessary (as well with respect to the *African Slave-trade*, encouraged in this Kingdom, as the *Toleration of Slavery* in the British American Dominions) if we mean to entertain the least hope of escaping a severe *National Retribution*, which (if we may judge by our present Civil Dissentions and horrid *mutual* Slaughters of *National Brethren*) seem ready to burst upon us![83]

In this line of argument about the immediacy of Divine punishment, which was increasingly common in texts written after the great Lisbon earthquake of 1755, Sharp seeks to inspire fear in the most worldly of sinners and inject a sense of urgency into the abolition debate.

In his day, Sharp was sometimes described as naïvely idealistic and the puppet of more savvy agitators for abolition, such as in an anonymous article from 15 to 17 September 1789 in *St. James's Chronicle or the British Evening Post*.[84] However, Sharp shows his canny understanding of his audience when he writes, "I am well aware, indeed, how very unfashionable it is, now-a-days, to quote *Scripture*, when matters of *Law, Politics*, or *Trade* are called in question."[85] Arguably, Sharp's later texts on abolition have been virtually ignored by contemporary scholars for the same reason, but by being so dismissive of these works we miss a greater point about his evolving anti-slavery tactics in the eighteenth century. Seeing the glacial pace at which British law was moving to eradicate slavery—despite his logically sound and irreproachable legal arguments—Sharp wished to inspire fear in individual readers and a sense of personal responsibility for what he dubbed a "national crime" that had yet to be recognized as such on the national stage. In *Law of Liberty*, Sharp warns, "The horrible Guilt therefore, which is incurred by *Slave-dealing* and *Slave-holding*, is no longer confined to the few hardened *Individuals*,

---

[83] Sharp, *Retribution*, 3.

[84] Anon., *St. James's Chronicle or the British Evening Post*, September 15–17, 1789, issue 4432, unpag., *Gale: 17th–18th Century Burney Collection Newspapers*, accessed June 16, 2017. Also, Davis, *Problem*, 391; Ditchfield, "Sharp," unpag.; and Hoare, *Memoirs*, 175, 198–9.

[85] Sharp, *Retribution*, 3.

that are immediately concerned in those baneful Practices, but alas! the Whole British Empire is involved!"[86] Sharp warns that every Briton was responsible for eradicating slavery, and that ignoring evil would not change its nature or defer its inevitable consequence: Divine punishment.

Since these texts from the 1770s were Sharp's final and most voluminous publications on anti-slavery, most historians treat them as his most significant writings on the topic. However, I contend that his missive on the *Zong* to the Admiralty at the BL should be considered alongside these important texts, particularly because he intended to publish it. From this perspective, the similarities between Sharp's missive to the Admiralty and his earlier publications on anti-slavery come into clearer view. For example, Sharp uses the above rhetorical tactic of warning his fellow Britons about the visitation of divine vengeance for slavery several times in the Admiralty missive: he warns that the "whole Nation" will be destroyed by the "avenging hand of God" if the *Zong* murderers are not brought to justice.[87] Sharp wrote the letter after attending the May hearing for an appeal of the insurance case, inspired by Equiano's entreaty to help him obtain justice for the murdered Africans.[88] Sharp's attempt to bring murder charges against the crew of the *Zong* via his missive to the Admiralty failed, as these naval officials apparently never responded to his pleas and the murderers from the *Zong* were never tried for their crimes. Yet, Sharp's missive to the Admiralty remains an important would-be publication by the father of abolition, and the only one by him from the 1780s.

The *Zong* case brought the old combatants, Mansfield and Sharp, together again—and, once more, as in the Strong, Lewis and Somerset cases, Mansfield refused this opportunity to advance the cause of abolition. Echoing many historians, Srividhya Swaminathan notes that "Lord Mansfield famously remarked, 'the case of the slaves was

---

[86] Granville Sharp, *The Law of Liberty, or, Royal Law* (London: B. White, and E. and C. Dilly, 1777), 49.

[87] Sharp, BL document, 15, 2.

[88] As Sharp notes in the letter to the Admiralty, he "spare[d no] ... expence" for a single, costly transcription of the proceedings, a transcription that he calls the "Vouchers" in the BL document, the only manuscript copy of which is at the NMM (Sharp, BL document, 1). To be clear, the NMM document is a transcription of the hearing for an appeal in May, not the original March trial. Lord Mansfield presided over both and granted a new trial as a result of the May hearing, but there exists no evidence that the appeal ever occurred.

the same as if horses had been thrown overboard,'" a quotation that is sometimes provided as evidence of his callous attitude towards the murdered Africans.[89] However, the full quotation of Mansfield's words ameliorates this infamous statement somewhat:

> The Matter left to the Jury was, whether it was from necessity for they had no doubt (though it shocks one very much) the Case of Slaves was the same as if Horses had been thrown over board[.] it is a very shocking Case. The Question was, whether there was an Absolute Necessity for throwing them overboard to save the rest, the Jury were of opinion there was—We granted a Rule to shew Cause from the Novelty of the Case. I don't know the Ground they went upon.[90]

Mansfield seems at pains to convey his personal reaction of dismayed "shock" over the barbarity of the crew's actions and the grounds of the case by mentioning the word twice. What should be more notorious, therefore, is another comment that Mansfield made at the May hearing in which he does not proclaim his "shock" in response to the cruelty of the incident:

> Since the trial I was informed if they die a Natural Death they do not pay but in an Engagement if they are attacked & the Slaves are killed they will be paid for them as much as for Damages done for goods &c it is frequently done, just as if Horses were killed, they are paid for in the Gross, just as well as for Horses killed but you don't pay for Horses that die a Natural death.[91]

Mansfield neither introduces nor follows these words with a commentary on the cruelty of the slavers' mercenary attitude towards the murdered Africans or the absurd and inhumane treatment of them as though they were farm animals. Although Mansfield's *blasé* attitude here surely enraged Sharp, he, uncharacteristically, does not express his indignation at Mansfield's words.

Another odd lacuna in the historical record of the *Zong* trial has helped to bolster Mansfield's undeserved reputation as an anti-slavery

---

[89] Srividhya Swaminathan, "Reporting Atrocities: A Comparison of the *Zong* and the Trial of Captain John Kimber," *Slavery & Abolition* 31, no. 4 (2010): 483–99, 484.

[90] Mansfield quoted in Lyall, *Cases*, 245.

[91] In Lyall, *Cases*, 255.

agitator: it is well known that Mansfield oversaw the May hearing for an appeal, but the "fact that Lord Mansfield was himself the [original March] trial judge seems not to have been known, or at least that fact went unremarked," Oldham comments.[92] The historian queries why Mansfield's involvement with the case has gone unnoticed: "Given Sharp's anger about the way Mansfield conducted earlier cases involving slavery, the Somerset case and R. v Stapylton [the Lewis case], it is surprising that Sharp was silent about Mansfield's having presided over a jury that rendered a verdict wholly favourable to the owners of the *Zong* for the loss of 130-plus slaves at £30 each."[93] Here, Oldham implies that Mansfield might have intervened in some way or mitigated the outcome of the verdict if he had so desired to do so—and other scholars of eighteenth-century law confirm this possibility. Gregory Smith remarks,

> Mansfield did not have the individual power to set aside a verdict with his own opinion. However, he could have reserved his judgement on the verdict (juries declare the verdict, judges sentence based on the verdict) and sent the case to the ... [twelve] Judges, a kind of supreme appeal court that convened the nation's top ... judges to consider particularly complex or novel cases where the law itself was challenged by the facts of a case.[94]

As the Chief Justice of Britain at the time, Lord Mansfield had the power to do more to resolve the legal problem at the heart of the *Zong* case. The legal claims of the owners were in direct opposition to those of the murdered Africans, described by Sharp as "The property of these poor injured Negroes in their own Lives."[95] Some may claim that, by allowing the hearing for an appeal in May of 1783, Mansfield did intervene thus, but it amounted to nothing in the cause of justice. Although the option was open to him, Mansfield never recommended the *Zong* case to a higher court, where it would be accorded the attention that it deserved and perhaps even have resulted in achieving justice for the murder victims.

Nevertheless, Sharp's very presence at the hearing reminded the court that, as much as they wished to frame the case as "a mere pecuniary

[92] Oldham, "Litigation," 312.
[93] Oldham, "Litigation," 312.
[94] Gregory Smith, e-mail to the author, June 19, 2017.
[95] Sharp, BL document, 13.

claim," to use Sharp's phrasing, what was really at stake was much more meaningful: the treatment of human beings as disposable property, the very basis of slavery.[96] Nor did the defense appreciate Sharp's introduction of this focus to the case. Solicitor General John Lee represented the *Zong*'s owners in the hearing for an appeal, as he had done at the original trial in March; quoting from Sharp's manuscripts, Hoare mentions in the *Memoirs* that Sharp's

> presence at the trial [sic: hearing] did not escape the notice of the pleaders employed on the part of Collingwood:—"At the trial respecting the ship *Zong*, an eminent counsel for the owners (J. Lee, of Yorkshire, Esq.) violently exclaimed to the Judges, that a person was in Court (at the same time turning round and looking at me) who intended to bring on a criminal prosecution for murder against the parties concerned: 'but,' said he, 'it would be madness: the Blacks were property.'"[97]

Lee's angry recognition of Sharp's presence in the court and the view he represented shows that Sharp clearly disturbed the "learned Advocate for Liverpool iniquity," as Sharp calls Lee.[98] Here, the lawyer voluntarily mentions Sharp's demand for murder charges, which was extraneous to the concerns of the hearing and could only undermine his own case.

Such indirect evidence of Sharp's influence is typical. Brown comments that Sharp "would have a decisive impact on the crystallization of antislavery impulses in certain circles within the Church of England," but he adds that Sharp's overall responsibility for the success of the abolition movement was subtle: although "Sharp raised consciousness, he did not start a movement."[99] The man considered to be the "father of abolition" by many is in some ways a marginal figure with respect to the popular movement that ended slavery, but some early abolitionists blamed wider British society, rather than Sharp, for his rather solitary position as an early anti-slavery activist: James Ramsay asks in 1784, "Why, then, hath the active zeal of the benevolent Mr. Granville Sharp, and a few others, in the business that we now agitate, hitherto made the unfeeling indifference of our age, and nation, but the more

---

[96] Sharp, BL document, 14.

[97] Hoare, *Memoirs*, 240.

[98] Sharp, BL document, 12.

[99] Brown, *Moral*, 195.

conspicuous?"[100] Ramsay implies that, if Sharp was unable to engage his fellow Britons in the abolitionist cause, then their heartlessness was to blame, not any failing of Sharp's.

Sharp had little public support for his radical approach to abolition. Brown reports that his "tireless cajoling of the bishops produced few genuine converts. Most had no desire to take a public position on a question of commercial policy."[101] Nor did the Quakers, who spearheaded the popular movement to abolish slavery in the 1780s, support Sharp's uncompromising methods. They sought to work with the establishment, rather than to antagonize it, and they focused first on gradual emancipation and abolishing the slave trade, rather than on abolishing West Indian slavery as a whole, reasoning that they would advance the cause with greater success in this moderate way.[102] Since the Quakers succeeded where Sharp did not, their approach appears superior in retrospect, but it is impossible to fault Sharp on an ideal level; as nobody should have, he could not countenance tolerating slavery for another day. A man of great and unwavering principles, Sharp believed that anything less than striking at slavery itself would be to accept its existence and essentially condone it. An illustration of Sharp's courageous impracticality on this matter is in Hoare's memoirs, where he provides Clarkson's account of how Sharp addressed the Society for the Abolition of the African Slave Trade in its early days:

> Of ten persons who were present, Granville stood singly for including the abolition of slavery in the title of the Society. "As *slavery*," he asserted, "was as much a crime against the Divine laws as the *Slave Trade*, it became the Committee to exert themselves equally against the continuance of both; and he did not hesitate to pronounce all present *guilty before God*, for shutting those, who were then slaves all the world over, out of the pale of their approaching labours." He delivered this his protest against their proceedings in the energetic manner usual to him, when roused on the

---

[100] James Ramsay, *An Essay on the Treatment and Conversion of African Slaves in the British Sugar Colonies* (London: James Phillips, 1784), 105.

[101] Brown, *Moral*, 195.

[102] Drescher, "Shocking," 575. For a thorough history of the Quaker's involvement with abolition, see Brycchan Carey's monograph, *From Peace to Freedom: Quaker Rhetoric and the Birth of American Antislavery, 1657–1761* (New Haven: Yale University Press, 2012).

subject,—with a loud voice, a powerful emphasis, and both hands lifted up towards Heaven.[103]

Unsurprisingly, Sharp failed to convince other abolitionists to adopt his approach by shouting at them that their method made them *"guilty before God."* Such vignettes suggest yet another reason why Sharp is not more celebrated in the history of anti-slavery: his personal characteristics may have detracted from his lasting legacy. Davis comments, "Sharp's associates respected his saintlike *naïveté*, but recognized him as an eccentric. And the role of eccentric allowed him to expose the moral compromises of his society without being branded as a rebel," although it doubtless also undermined his authority as a potential leader of abolition.[104] In his eccentricity, Sharp may have alienated others who were on his side in the fight to stop slavery. He was so strict and steadfast in his (excellent) principles that he appears to have been lacking in diplomacy at times. This characteristic could not have won Sharp many admirers who wished to sing his praises to the ear of history.

4   THE *ZONG* CASE: A DEBATED LEGACY

Just as Sharp has sometimes been viewed as tangential to the history of abolition, so has the *Zong* massacre been regarded thus at times, but period writings show that it was a catalyst for the popular abolition movement. Drescher asserts that "The reaction to the *Zong* case was significant precisely for its lack of immediate resonance" in the public sphere, while Swaminathan comments, "Though this insurance case did have a profound influence among anti-slave-trade organisers and become [sic] iconic in abolitionist literature, there was almost no immediate impact on the public consciousness," particularly because there existed very little newspaper reportage of the event.[105] Elsewhere, Swaminathan continues,

---

[103] Hoare, *Memoirs*, 415, Hoare's emphasis; I have been unable to find this passage in any edition of Clarkson's texts.

[104] Davis, *Problem*, 391.

[105] Seymour Drescher, *Capitalism and Antislavery: British Mobilization in Comparative Perspective* (New York: Oxford University Press 1987, 1986), 204 n30; Swaminathan, "Atrocities," 483.

Some present-day historians have noted that the *Zong* incident did not have much of an impact at the time. Linda Colley states that the case "passed almost without notice" and ... Drescher asserts that the case became important "only in retrospect, after the emergence of popular abolitionism [in 1787]." Both analyses rely on the legal implication of the case, of which there were admittedly none.[106]

While most agree that the legal ramifications of the *Zong* trial were minimal, various commentators differ regarding the popular awareness of it. Beginning with Clarkson in 1808, many writers claim wrongly that newspaper articles on the *Zong* were published widely in response to the trial. Since Clarkson is one of the most famous of all abolitionists, his inaccurate statement regarding the considerable influence of news articles about the *Zong*—and Sharp's contribution to them—has had a wide-ranging effect. In *The History of the Rise, Progress, and Accomplishment of the Abolition of the African Slave-Trade, by the British Parliament* (1808), Clarkson reports on Sharp's agitation for justice on behalf of the *Zong* victims: "But though nothing was done by the persons then in power, in consequence of the murder of so many innocent individuals, yet the publication of an account of it by Mr. Sharp in the newspapers, made such an impression upon others, that new coadjutors rose up."[107] Similarly, Hoare claims that Sharp "sent an account of the whole transaction to the news-papers" in 1820 and, in 1861, W. O. Blake—whose source appears to be Clarkson, since he repeats his phrasing exactly at some points—echoes the claim that Sharp himself published newspaper articles on the *Zong*.[108] The subtitle of Cooper's *Letters on the Slave Trade* suggests possible news-sources on the *Zong*: *First Published in Wheeler's Manchester Chronicle; and Since Re-printed with Additions and Alterations*. However, I have been unable to trace the relevant articles by Cooper in this publication. Among contemporary historians, Shyllon and Weisbord are the only writers I have discovered who assert that Sharp wrote newspaper accounts of the *Zong*, but they

[106] Srividhya Swaminathan, *Debating the Slave Trade: Rhetoric of British National Identity, 1759–1815* (Burlington: Ashgate, 2013), 97.

[107] Clarkson, *History*, 97.

[108] Hoare, *Memoirs*, 245–6; W. O. Blake, *The History of Slavery and the Slave Trade, Ancient and Modern*. (Columbus, OH: H. Miller, 1861), 166.

are far from the only ones who claim that period newspapers published other writers' commentaries on the incident.[109]

   I have discovered no primary evidence to support the claims that information on the *Zong* was widely available through period newspapers. My advantage at this point in scholarly history is that I have access to a wide range of digitized historical sources on the case, including the monumental database the *17th- and 18th-Century Burney Newspapers Collection*, available through Gale resources. However, even in the broad digital universe, I have found no articles devoted solely to the *Zong* incident by Sharp or anyone else, besides the original article from 18 March 1783 in the original *Morning Chronicle and London Advertiser* newspaper that Equiano brought to Sharp, and which appears to have been the original source of textual information about the event for both men. In fact, I have located only one mention of the *Zong* case in a popular publication: an article in *The Gentleman's Magazine* from 1783. It provides a brief discussion of the events of the *Zong* massacre, followed by a footnote on Sharp: "We rejoice to hear ... that a true patriot, a true christian [sic], has nobly stepped forth, and, at his own expence, instituted a criminal process against those workers of wickedness; the event of which, we hope will *put away this evil among us*."[110] In the phrase "instituted a criminal process," this writer seems to refer to the fact that Sharp "Ordered Messrs. Heseltine and Lushington to commence a prosecution" against the murderers from the *Zong* "in the Admiralty court," as Sharp puts it in his diary.[111] (In the official reports provided in *The Parliamentary Debates* from 1812, James Heseltine is termed "the king's proctor" and his partner, Stephen Lushington, an "East India director," who, together, helped to commence a claim in the "British High Court of Admiralty"; given that Sharp sent his letter to the Lords Commissioners of the Admiralty, it is reasonable to assume that these are the same men

---

[109] Shyllon, *Black Slaves*, 197, 206; Weisbord, "Case," 566; Rupprecht, "'Uncommon,'" 336; Brown, *Moral*, 284; and Dwight A. McBride, *Impossible Witnesses: Truth, Abolitionism, and Slave Testimony* (New York: New York University Press, 2001), 27.

[110] Anon., "136. *Bishop of* Chester's *Sermon Before the Incorporated Society for the Propagation of the Gospel in Foreign Parts, on* Friday, February 4, 1783," *The Gentleman's Magazine* 53, no. 2 (1783): 859, *Google eBooks*, accessed August 31, 2017, https://books.google.ca/books?id=ONc_AQAAMAAJ&dq=The+Gentleman%27s+Magazine:+1783,+nobly+stepped+forth&source=gbs_navlinks_s. Also cited in Walvin, *Zong*, 106; Shyllon, *Black People*, 228; and Drescher, *Capitalism*, 204 n30.

[111] Quoted in Hoare, *Memoirs*, 236.

to whom Sharp refers in his diary.)[112] Although this criminal prosecution was never successfully "instituted," the comment that Sharp did so "at his own expence" may show the writer's knowledge of Sharp's expensive "Vouchers"—his expensive transcription of the hearing for an appeal, which accompanies the copy of the document parallel to the BL document in the NMM.[113] As such, this reference in *The Gentleman's Magazine* comes tantalizingly close to discussing Sharp's missive to the Admiralty.

A few notable early monographs mention the *Zong* massacre and Sharp's involvement with the case. The earliest publication of this sort is the English translation of Clarkson's first-prize winning essay for Cambridge University, *An Essay on the Slavery and Commerce of the Human Species, Particularly the African*, published in English in 1786 and originally written in Latin in 1785. Clarkson highlights Sharp's abolitionist efforts with reference to the *Zong* in the first pages of his preface:

> Nor did he [Sharp] interfere less honourably in that cruel and disgraceful case, in the summer of the year 1781, when *an hundred and thirty two negroes*, in their passage to the colonies, were thrown into the sea alive, to defraud the underwriters; but his pious endeavours were by no means attended with the same success [as in the Somerset case]. To enumerate his many laudable endeavours in the extirpation of tyranny and oppression, would be to swell the preface into a volume.[114]

In this case, Clarkson's reportage of the matter does not lead to a misinterpretation of how influential Sharp and the *Zong* case were for the history of abolition, but, rather, it *is* the likely source of their influence, for Clarkson's essay is reckoned one of the most persuasive, ground-breaking works in early abolitionism. An account of Sharp's efforts for the *Zong* victims also appears in Gregory's *Essays Historical and Moral*

---

[112] Anon., *The Parliamentary Debates from the Year 1803 to the Present Time*, ed. T. C. Hansard (London: Longman, Hurst, Rees, Orme, and Brown, 1812), vol. 23, 777, *Google eBooks*, accessed April 23, 2018, https://books.google.ca/books?id=twlAAQAAMAA-J&printsec=frontcover&source=gbs_ge_summary_r&cad=0#v=onepage&q&f=false.

[113] See page 82 in Chapter 4 for more on the cost of Sharp's transcription of the May hearing.

[114] Thomas Clarkson, *An Essay on the Slavery and Commerce of the Human Species, Particularly the African, Translated from a Latin Dissertation, Which Was Honoured with the First Prize, in the University of Cambridge, for the Year 1785, with Additions* (London: J. Phillips, 1786), xiv, *Online Library of Liberty*, accessed August 28, 2017, http://oll.libertyfund.org/titles/1070.

(1785), Cooper's source for his discussion of the *Zong*.[115] Gregory provides a long account of the incident that is so close to Sharp's letter to the Admiralty in terms of diction and organization that Gregory's—and therefore Cooper's—accounts seem to reproduce Sharp's letter in some places. This similarity—as well as the fact that Gregory is the only writer besides Sharp to refer to the ship as the "Zong, or Zurg"—suggests that Gregory's source may well have been Sharp's letter to the Admiralty, or, at least, one of the letters on the *Zong* that he sent to other influential people in 1783. Gregory does not mention Sharp by name, but he certainly refers to him when he writes, "For the principal materials of the following narrative, the author acknowledges himself indebted to a Gentleman, whose unremitting endeavours in the cause of humanity demand the sincere thanks of every friend of liberty, justice, and religion."[116] Since Gregory's account was published only four years after the *Zong* insurance trial and was the source for other discussions of the case in influential abolitionist works, it is evident that the massacre and Sharp's writing on it were indeed important for the early history of abolition.

One of the most influential early abolitionist works that mentions the *Zong* is Ramsay's *An Essay on the Treatment and Conversion of African Slaves in the British Sugar Colonies* from 1784, published by the prolific Quaker printer James Phillips only one year after the *Zong* trial. Without naming the ship, the captain, or any of the people connected to the *Zong*, Ramsay's influential abolitionist text provides a detailed description of the event that leaves no uncertainty as to its identity. The account begins, "In the month of March 1783, the following circumstances came out in the trial of a case of insurance at Guildhall. An ignorant master of a slave-ship had overshot his port, Jamaica, and was

---

[115] Thomas Cooper, *Letters on the Slave Trade: First Published in Wheeler's Manchester Chronicle* (Manchester: C. Wheeler, 1787), 14–15, *Gale: The Making of the Modern World*, accessed June 20, 2017.

[116] Gregory, *Essays*, 304n. A major difference between Gregory's and Sharp's treatments of the *Zong* massacre is their treatment of Collingwood, however. According to Shyllon, in another venue Gregory defends Collingwood as a decent man who was nevertheless "'deeply infected by the callousness of the iniquitous traffic,'" which regarded Africans "'as an inferior race of beings, whom we are entitled to treat as we please'" (Shyllon, *Black Slaves*, 193 n1; see also Walvin, *Zong*, 173). I have been unable to locate this quotation in a text by Gregory.

afraid of wanting water before he could beat up again to the island."[117] The emotional description of the massacre that follows clearly seeks to fill the reader with horror—and not only of the crew's actions, but also of the British legal system for rewarding the murderers: "Can humanity imagine that it was meant, in any possible circumstances, to submit the fate of such numbers of reasonable creatures to the reveries of a sick monster [Collingwood]; or that his brutal instrument [Kelsall] should dare to boast of his obedience, and even do it with impunity, in the highest criminal court of the best informed people of Europe?"[118] As important as Ramsay's text is for our consideration of early popular knowledge about the *Zong* case and Sharp's influence on abolition, it contains a flaw that is worth noting here: Ramsay repeats the slavers' lie that they accidentally steered the ship off course and murdered the Africans out of the "necessity" to jettison some people on board so that they would not be short of water for everyone else. Ramsay thereby confirms the slavers' defence, even though he also recognizes the absurdity of their claim when he acknowledges that the ship "brought into port 480 gallons of water" at Black River, Jamaica.[119] Most interpretations of the case accord with that of Sharp, who contends that the slavers' plea of "necessity" was a fabricated story created to claim insurance on the murder victims fraudulently.[120] In his letter to the Admiralty, Sharp delineates the most probable reason for why the *Zong* crew murdered the Africans:

> a great number of the remaining Slave[s] on the day last mentioned were sick of some disorder or disorders & likely to die or not, live long. ... the Dead & dying Slaves would have been a dead loss to the Owners (and, in some proportion, a loss also to the persons employed by the Owners) unless some pretence or expedient had been found to throw the loss upon the Insurers ... as in the case of Jetsam or Jetson i:e: a plea of Necessity to cast overboard some part of a Cargo to save the rest.[121]

Incidentally, Sharp reports that the *Zong* came into port at Jamaica with less water than does Ramsay—"at least 200 Gallons of fresh water

[117] James Ramsay, *Treatment*, 35–6n.

[118] Ramsay, *Treatment*, 35–6n.

[119] Ramsay, *Treatment*, 35–6n.

[120] *Eg*. Gregory, *Essays*, 305.

[121] Sharp, BL document, 5–6.

by their own confession," Sharp states, as opposed to Ramsay's "480 gallons"—but both figures undermine the credibility of the Gregson claim, for the ship was manifestly not short on water and, according to the slave traders' own evidence, no one on board was ever put to half-rations of water in anticipation of greater need.[122] (Oddly, some contemporary historians have also accepted the Gregson syndicate's account of why they committed the murders, thereby undermining the historical narrative as one about insurance fraud, as well as mass murder.)[123] More pertinent to the present discussion about the historiography of Sharp and the *Zong* case, though, is Ramsay's statement about the early influence of Sharp on abolitionist writers: he recognizes the "active zeal of the benevolent Mr. Granville Sharp" in the cause of abolition, and at a time when very few were willing "to obey the call of humanity [,] ... relieve the sufferings of the wretched [, and] ... boldly encounter the oppressor's rage, or offer up selfish interest at the altar of mercy."[124] Sharp was thus viewed as a hero of the abolitionist cause as early as 1784, one year after he attended the *Zong* hearing.

A few other monographs from the 1780s mention the *Zong* case, and they, too, give rise to additional questions about the details of the massacre while providing evidence of popular access to knowledge about it. *Remarks on the Slave Trade, and the Slavery of the Negroes. In a Series of Letters* (1788) by Africanus—identified in some sources as William Leigh[125]—is unusual in providing such precise details as the number of victims, Collingwood's name, the dates of the murders, and the motivation for them:

> It is a fact, which came out in evidence in the course of the trial at the Court of King's Bench, Guildhall, sometime in March 1783, that the

[122] Sharp, BL document, 9. Notably, the 18 March 1783 article on the *Zong* in the *Morning Chronicle and London Advertiser* states that the ship brought 420 gallons of water into port (Anon., *Morning Chronicle*, unpag.).

[123] Eg. Christine A. Sears, Review of *The Zong: A Massacre, the Law and the End of Slavery*, by James Walvin, *Journal of World History* 27, no. 4 (2013): 890–2, 892.

[124] Ramsay, *Treatment*, 105.

[125] Jack P. Greene, *Evaluating Empire and Confronting Colonialism in Eighteenth-Century Britain* (Cambridge: Cambridge University Press, 2013), 328; the "notes" for the *ECCO* entry for this text also identify Africanus as William Leigh. Incidentally, Africanus's *Remarks* was published by James Phillips, the famous Quaker printer of abolitionist texts.

people on board this ship had not been put on short allowance [of water]: the excuse which the Mate of the ship, who gave the evidence, made for this conduct was, that if the Slaves, who were then sickly had died a natural death, the loss would have been the owners; but as they were thrown alive into the sea, it would fall upon the underwriters.[126]

Intriguingly, Africanus states that the "Mate of the ship," who was Kelsall, gave "evidence," but it should be noted that Kelsall only gave evidence as an affidavit in the Exchequer in November of 1783, considerably after both the trial in March, the hearing for an appeal in May, and the composition of Sharp's letter to the Admiralty in early July. Stubbs, officially a passenger on the ship, was the only person aboard the *Zong* to give evidence for the trial, as both Lewis and Walvin note.[127] Africanus may refer to what Sharp calls Kelsall's "Memorandum" from his "Deposition" for the March trial when he refers to the first mate's "evidence," but Africanus' terminology suggests that his source of information on the *Zong* was the 18 March 1783 article on it in *The Morning Chronical and London Advertiser*, which also claims that the "Mate ... gave the evidence" in the trial (an inaccuracy also noted by Oldham).[128] Perhaps the anonymous writer of the news article believed that Stubbs was the first mate, which both Lewis and Walvin suggest may actually have been the case temporarily: there is evidence that Collingwood argued with Kelsall and, being too ill to command the ship himself, Collingwood appointed Stubbs to take over at the time of the massacre.[129] Lewis confirms this interpretation as a possibility, first quoting from period manuscripts of cases in the King's Bench: "'One witness only was examined, a person who was a passenger but took the command towards the end of the voyage when the captain was exhausted and disabled.' It is a possible meaning that Stubbs, the only witness examined at the King's Bench trial, was in charge towards the end of the Atlantic

---

[126] Africanus, *Remarks on the Slave Trade, and the Slavery of the Negroes. In a Series of Letters* (London: J. Phillips, 1788), 33n, *Eighteenth Century Collections Online*, accessed June 21, 2017, tinyurl.galegroup.com/tinyurl/4xT9v1.

[127] Lewis, "Dockray," 364 n16; Walvin, *Zong*, 87.

[128] Sharp, BL document, 7; Anon., *Morning Chronicle*, unpag.; and Oldham, "Litigation," 312.

[129] Lewis, "Dockray," 362; Walvin, *Zong*, 96–7.

voyage until the missed sighting of Jamaica on 27/28 November."[130] However, Stubbs claimed that he only witnessed—rather than partook in—the throwing over of the Africans, and then only from his cabin, rather than from the ship's deck, as is revealed in the shorthand account of the trial for which Sharp paid and calls one of his "Vouchers" in the letter to the Admiralty.[131] Thus, the newspaper article's report that "the mate acknowledged he himself had thrown them overboard by the Captain's orders" is yet more mysterious, since Stubbs apparently made no such claim.[132] Moreover, in Kelsall's affidavit from November, which was never presented in a trial or published until very recently (by Lyall), he denies repeatedly that the Africans were killed because they were ill. Africanus agrees with Sharp and others that the murders were committed in order to commit insurance fraud, but he did not obtain this information from the *Morning Chronicle and London Advertiser* article, which accepts that the murders were perpetrated for want of water. The source of Africanus' report that a "Mate," whether Kelsall or Stubbs, admitted that the crew committed murder in order to commit insurance fraud remains unknown.

What *is* clear from Africanus' 1788 text is that Sharp had earned his reputation as the "father of abolition" by this point in history. Africanus dedicates *Remarks on the Slave Trade* to "Grenville [sic] Sharp, Esq. Chairman of the Society" for "the abolition of the Slave-Trade" in a passage that leaves no doubt as to Sharp's influence on the cause:

> Every friend to freedom and humanity has beheld ... the progress of your benevolence. We see ... that he who first claimed the impartial protection of the British laws for Somerset, and proved the mischiefs arising from the want of such protection in the case of Collingwood, now stands foremost in the general cause of justice and freedom: ... and the persevering benevolence of Mr. Sharp becomes a subject of emulous imitation.[133]

Not only does Africanus credit Sharp with motivating others to join in the cause of abolition, but he also recognizes the importance of the *Zong* case for the anti-slavery movement by mentioning "the case of

[130] Lewis, "Dockray," 364 n16.
[131] Lyall, *Cases*, 263–4.
[132] Anon., *Morning Chronicle*, unpag.
[133] Africanus, *Remarks*, unpag.

Collingwood," the captain of the *Zong*. Some historians today claim that neither Sharp nor the *Zong* case played a major role in abolishing slavery, but historical writers who contributed to the cause with their own pro-abolitionist texts clearly assert otherwise.

Other monographs that mention the *Zong* massacre provide less specific details about the event than does Africanus, but they nevertheless seek to advance the abolitionist cause by appealing to the reader's sympathy for the victims. Only four years after the *Zong* trial, Ottobah Cugoano—a formerly enslaved African living in England who is sometimes called by his slave-name John Stuart, and, with Equiano, one of the Sons of Africa—published a moving account of the case in *Thoughts and Sentiments on the Evil and Wicked Traffic of the Slavery and Commerce of the Human Species, Humbly Submitted to the Inhabitants of Great-Britain* (1787). Without naming the ship, captain, or crew, Cugoano provides a comprehensive description of the massacre. Quickly dispensing with the Gregson argument of the "necessity" of killing the Africans to preserve water as a fabrication, Cugoano reports that "These poor creatures, it seems, were tied two and two together when they were thrown into the sea, lest some of them might swim a little for the last gasp of air."[134] The unusual detail that the victims were tied in pairs—mentioned only by Cugoano in period writings, according to my research—and the sympathetic tone of this passage that is augmented by the emotive adjectives and consideration of the individual victims' last moments reveal Cugoano's deft mingling of fact with emotional rhetoric.[135] Similarly, in *Thoughts upon the African Slave Trade* (1788), John Newton (1725–1807)—a former slave-ship captain and the composer of the beloved hymn "Amazing Grace"—also discusses the massacre in emotive terms. Yet, Newton does so without mentioning any specific identifiers, such as names. He introduces the *Zong* case as

[134]Ottobah Cugoano, *Thoughts and Sentiments on the Evil and Wicked Traffic of the Slavery and Commerce of the Human Species, Humbly Submitted to the Inhabitants of Great-Britain* (London: n.p., 1787), 111–12.

[135]Contemporary historian Shyllon also mentions that the victims of the *Zong* were tied in pairs: "Chained two by two, right leg and left leg, right hand and left hand, each slave had less room than a man in a coffin" (Shyllon, *Black Slaves*, 184). McBride mentions that the "Africans [were] chained together and thrown overboard" (McBride, *Impossible*, 26). Most commentators mention that the victims were chained or otherwise fastened, but they do not specify if they were tied singly, in pairs, or in a group.

a melancholy story, too notoriously true to admit of contradiction, of more than a hundred grown slaves, thrown into the sea, at one time, from on board a ship, when fresh water was scarce; to fix the loss upon the Underwriters, which otherwise, had they died on board, must have fallen upon the Owners of the vessel. These instances are specimens of the spirit produced, by the African Trade, in men, who, once, were no more destitute of the milk of human kindness than ourselves.[136]

Newton usefully turns the massacre into the spur for British soul-searching by commenting that the crew of the *Zong* was composed of fellow Britons, not monsters whom the readers can pretend are essentially different from themselves. Similarly, Cugoano encourages readerly sympathy with the racial "other"—enslaved Africans—and, in particular, the victims of the *Zong* by writing an emotionally moving and authoritative text in English, while identifying himself as a formerly enslaved African. Metaphorically and literally, Cugoano speaks the readers' language. Through this textual common-ground, Cugoano demonstrates that he and, by extension, all Africans are similar to the mainly white British audience of his text, who should therefore sympathize with the victims of the slave trade.[137] Such writing about the *Zong* massacre serves to suggest that all Britons must take responsibility for slavery and the travesties associated with it.

Despite these important abolitionist publications, the average Briton could not have known much about the *Zong* massacre before the popular anti-slavery movement began in 1787 because newspapers, the main source of information for such readers, published little on the event.[138] Abolitionist monographs were an important source of information on the case, but they were not as widely distributed as were newspapers. Another avenue of information about the *Zong* was even less accessible: Oldham comments that "the fullest printed account of the case before 1820 was that given by James Allan Park in his treatise on insurance, first published in 1787," but the audience for such a text was quite

[136] John Newton, *Thoughts Upon the African Slave Trade* (London: J. Buckland and J. Johnson, 1788), 15.

[137] See Brycchan Carey's *British Abolitionism and the Rhetoric of Sensibility* for more on Cugoano's—and Equiano's—use of sentimental rhetoric in their slavery narratives (e.g. 140).

[138] Swaminathan, "Atrocities," 485.

limited.[139] The newspaper article in the *Morning Chronicle and London Advertiser* from 18 March 1783 that Equiano brought to Sharp stands virtually alone in providing information about the *Zong* to a broad readership. This significant document is worth quoting at length in light of its influence on later writers. The anonymous writer of the article begins by noting that she or he had recently heard a sermon that suggested an increasing spirit of humanity would be shown in the African slave trade. (Significantly, the sermonizer was Beilby Porteus; he would be a recipient of one of Sharp's letters on the *Zong* after Equiano's visit.)[140] Any such hope raised by the sermon was undermined, however, by the *Zong* insurance trial, which the writer attended:

> The Jury, without going out of Court, gave judgment against the Underwriters; the mate acknowledged he himself had thrown them overboard by the Captain's orders, which he thought was to him a sufficient warrant for doing any possible thing, without considering whether it was criminal or not. ... A greater aggravation of the crime is, that it is said, the Captain, who died sometime after, was in a delirium, or fit of lunacy when he gave the orders. That there should be bad men to do bad things in all large communities, must be expected; but a community makes the crime general, and provokes divine wrath, when it suffers any member to commit flagrant acts of villainy with impunity.[141]

This passage fairly pulsates with the contradictions between the writer's expectations—that justice for the murders would prevail, that the average person is horrified to learn of the brutality of the slave trade—and the facts of the trial, which the jury decided quickly and in favour of rewarding the killers. The article clearly disturbed many of its readers, including Sharp, and they were thus moved to express their outrage in writing.

I have demonstrated that the *Zong* is mentioned in several major abolitionist monographs that were published by 1788, and it is reasonable to assume that some of the writers of these texts obtained information about the massacre from the above news article. Others obtained their information about the *Zong* from Sharp himself. By publishing on the murders before 1788, all of these writers helped to keep the memory of

[139] Oldham, "Litigation," 310.
[140] Shyllon, *Black Slaves*, 187; Swaminathan, "Atrocities," 486.
[141] Anon., *Morning Chronicle*, unpag.

the *Zong* massacre alive in the British consciousness and provided the basis for the subsequent use of the event as a catalyst for the abolition of slavery. In short, the little that was published on the *Zong* before 1788 was nevertheless vital for the history of anti-slavery.

Many historians consider the *Zong* to be the pre-eminent example of the horrors of slavery, an iconic event that signifies beyond its own terrible facts to reveal the attitude that undergirds slavery, one that views humans as commodities, and the nightmarish situations to which it leads. Rupprecht contends that "the narrative helped to shape the archive of abolitionism, and thus it became iconic within the cultural memory of slavery. As both event and emblem, the *Zong* continues to resonate far beyond the confines of an abstract legal debate concerning 'pecuniary value.'"[142] Still others claim that the *Zong*'s influence on abolition was more direct. Swaminathan argues that "The awareness of the *Zong* incident created a powerful and growing feeling of discontent amongst antislavery activists," while Brown attests, "The incident … would be remembered by later antislavery campaigners as crucial to exposing the horrors of the slave trade."[143] Information about the *Zong* may not have been widely available before the advent of the popular abolition movement, but it clearly influenced some of the most prominent leaders of it, such as Clarkson, Ramsay, Newton, the American Quaker William Dillwyn, and Sharp himself—several of whom were founding members of the Society for the Abolition of the African Slave Trade, formed in London in 1787, and ground-zero for the popular abolitionist movement in Britain.[144] Clarkson makes this claim in *The History of the Rise, Progress, and Accomplishment of the Abolition of the African Slave-Trade, by the British Parliament*:

> I must … go back to the year 1783, to record an event, which will be found of great importance in the present history [of abolition]. … [T]he Society [of Friends, i.e. the Quakers] … had sent a petition to Parliament in this year, praying for the abolition of the Slave-Trade. It had also laid the foundation for a public distribution of the books as just mentioned,

[142] Rupprecht, "Uncommon," 330; see also Ian Baucom, *Specters of the Atlantic: Finance Capital, Slavery, and the Philosophy of History* (Durham and London: Duke University Press, 2005), 220.

[143] Swaminathan, *Debating*, 97 n25; Brown, *Moral*, 284.

[144] Brown, *Moral*, 426.

with a view of enlightening others on this great subject. The case of the ship *Zong*, which I have before had occasion to explain, had occurred this same year. A letter also had been presented ... by Benjamin West, from Anthony Benezet ... to our Queen, in behalf of the injured Africans, which she had received graciously. These subjects occupied at this time the attention of many Quaker families. ... [who] frequently conversed upon them. They perceived, as facts came out in conversation, that there was a growing knowledge, and hatred of the Slave-trade, and that the temper of the times was ripening towards its abolition. Hence a disposition manifested itself among these, to unite as labourers for the furtherance of so desirable an object.[145]

Clarkson attests that the *Zong* case was one of the most significant episodes in the history of abolition, for it motivated the Quakers to launch their successful campaign to end the slave trade. Our view of this complex history may be distorted somewhat at this late date, leading us to question the extent of the impact of the *Zong* episode on abolition, but this passage—by one of the key members of the popular movement, and in a text from 1808, the year in which the slave trade was officially abolished through an act of Parliament—demonstrates that the *Zong* case was vital to its success.

Prince Hoare notes that Sharp moved away from his long-time address on Old Jewry in 1783, which must have been at some point after he sent his letter to the Admiralty in that year, as he inscribes it from that address.[146] As such, the Society for the Abolition of the Slave Trade's address on Old Jewry could not have been the same as Sharp's, as the Society was formed in 1787. Through his written efforts to bring the murderers to justice, Sharp helped to make the *Zong* case emblematic in the historiographical record, particularly since his published letters on the case have been the most detailed accounts of it available until

---

[145] Clarkson, *History*, 122–4.

[146] Prince Hoare, *Memoirs of Granville Sharp, Esq. Composed from His Own Manuscripts, and Other Authentic Documents in the Possession of His Family Authentic Documents in the Possession of His Family and of the African Institution* (London: Henry Colburn, 1820), *Google eBooks*, accessed June 25, 2015–August 30, 2017, https://books.google.ca/books?id=PrUEAAAAIAAJ, 383.

recently.[147] Equiano and Sharp failed to bring the *Zong* murderers to justice, but their efforts highlighted both the perversity of the British legal system that would remunerate murderers for their crimes and the guilt of the entire British nation for supporting slavery. These efforts may have been circumscribed in their immediate effect, but their influence was powerful and lasting.

[147] For transcriptions of the court proceedings, see Lyall's text.

CHAPTER 3

The Provenance of the British Library Document

Abstract This chapter details the complex, difficult investigation into the provenance of the British Library document and provides the first examination of the relationship between different pieces of primary evidence relating to Sharp's writing on the *Zong* case. This chapter delineates who was the intended recipient of the British Library document (as opposed to the letter's addressees, the Lords Commissioners of the Admiralty), and who owned it (it passed between at least three libraries in a few decades). This chapter also considers who was included in Sharp's circle of correspondents regarding the *Zong* case, that Sharp intended to publish the letter to the Admiralty in the British Library, and that the British Library document was sent to an unaccounted-for person whom we have yet to recognize as playing a part in this vital episode in the history of abolition.

Keywords Fair copy · Publication · Provenance · Archives · National Maritime Museum · Granville Sharp · Libraries

The BL document is Sharp's fair-copy manuscript of his missive to the Admiralty on the *Zong* murders. The historical record reveals that Sharp mailed letters on the *Zong* case to several influential people who could conceivably bring the murderers to justice: Bishop Porteus, Bishop

Hinchcliffe, and the Duke of Portland, who may also have received a copy of the Admiralty missive.[1] In my investigation into the provenance of the BL document, I sought to discover whether any of these references to Sharp's letters, especially the earliest ones, refer to the BL document, and whether the letter that Sharp finally sent to the Admiralty still exists. In the course of my research, I not only resolved these queries, but I also uncovered new information about documents relating to the *Zong* case, both published and in various archives, as well as evidence to show that Sharp sent the BL document to someone whom we have yet to recognize as an actor in this crucial episode in the history of abolition.

One of the first steps of my research was to ascertain whether the BL document could be the original missive that Sharp actually sent to the Admiralty. The surest evidence that it is not the original missive is that it contains the word "copy"—almost cut off, apparently during the binding of the volume—at the top of two of its pages. Yet, the BL document is not just any copy. Clearly, it is a fair copy: it has few deletions and the handwriting is extraordinarily neat, much more so than other specimens of Sharp's handwriting to which I have compared it.[2] To whom was this

---

[1] See, for example, Anita Rupprecht, "'A Very Uncommon Case': Representations of the *Zong* and the British Campaign to Abolish the Slave Trade," *The Journal of Legal History* 28, no. 3 (2007): 329–46, 336; Prince Hoare, *Memoirs of Granville Sharp, Esq. Composed from His Own Manuscripts, and Other Authentic Documents in the Possession of His Family Authentic Documents in the Possession of His Family and of the African Institution* (London: Henry Colburn, 1820), 241, 246, *Google eBooks*, accessed June 25, 2015–August 30, 2017, https://books.google.ca/books?id=PrUEAAAAIAAJ.

[2] I compared Sharp's handwriting in the BL document with examples available online, such as: "Original 1803 autograph letter signed by the famous English slave trade abolitionist, Granville Sharp" (Granville Sharp, "Original 1803 autograph letter signed by the famous English slave trade abolitionist, Granville Sharp," *The Sierra Leone Web*, accessed July 14, 2015, http://www.sierra-leone.org/Postcards/SLARTIFACTS31962.jpg; page updated 2016); Granville Sharp, Letter by Granville Sharp to Richard How on Sierra Leone (1790) (Granville Sharp, Letter by Granville Sharp to Richard How, March 17, 1790, Bedford Borough Council: Sierra Leone, accessed July 14, 2015, http://bedsarchives.bedford.gov.uk/ExploreYourArchive/Africa/SierraLeone.aspx); and examples available online in Yale University's The Taussig Collection: Granville Sharp (Granville Sharp, "Argument in the Case of James Sommersett a Negro (1772), with Granville Sharp's handwritten notes," *The Taussig Collection: Granville Sharp*, Yale Law School: Lillian Goldman Law Library, accessed August 29, 2017, http://library.law.yale.edu/news/taussig-collection-granville-sharp). Granville Sharp, [BL document, Copy of a Letter to Lords Commissioners of the Admiralty] "Paper by Glanville [sic] Sharp on the Case of 132 Murdered Negroes," in *Tracts 35* (Old Jewry London, MS: n.p., July 2, 1783).

polished copy of Sharp's missive to the Admiralty sent? Was the owner of the volume in which it is bound also the intended recipient of the letter? The most definitive evidence that demonstrates the provenance of the BL document does not appear within its pages; rather, the pages that introduce this letter in the volume reveal its background and ownership. The title-sheet before the letter and table of contents at the start of the volume, both handwritten (although evidently not by Sharp), reveal the BL document's provenance.

The BL document is bound in a volume labelled simply as *Tracts 35* on the spine. Determining its owner was the first step I took in uncovering the likely identity of the letter's intended recipient, but I learned early on in my research that Sharp did not send his letter to the owner of *Tracts 35*. Hints that it originates from the collection of one John Coakley Lettsom are that the table of contents lists the title "Lettsom on General Inoculation," while the following handwritten text faces the initial page of Sharp's cover letter to the Admiralty: "Dr Lettsom Basinghall Street Plan of a Portable vapour Bath." Two mentions of the name "Lettsom" on separate items in the volume suggest strongly that they refer to its owner. The address "Basinghall Street" moreover demonstrates that this owner was physician John Coakley Lettsom (1744–1815), as the *Oxford Dictionary of National Biography* (hereafter *ODNB*) provides this address as his own.[3] Plenty of other evidence in *Tracts 35* suggests that it belonged to Lettsom, too. For example, other items in the volume hint that its owner was a physician with an interest in inoculation, and indeed Lettsom was so: he supported the vaccination movement and Edward Jenner when the latter introduced his groundbreaking method to much opposition in the late eighteenth century. In fact, Lettsom's *A Letter to Sir Robert Barker, Knt., F. R. S. and George Stacpoole, Esq.*;

---

[3] J. F. Payne, "Lettsom, John Coakley (1744–1815)," revised by Roy Porter, *Oxford Dictionary of National Biography* (Oxford: Oxford University Press, 2004, 2015), unpag., accessed August 7, 2015, https://doi.org/10.1093/ref:odnb/16527. Unless otherwise noted, all of the biographical information about Lettsom I provide is from this *ODNB* entry.

Upon General Inoculation (1778) brought him into conflict with other doctors of his day; this document is the same one that appears later in *Tracts 35* and to which the handwritten table of contents refers with the shortened phrase, "Lettsom on General Inoculation." Also notable is that the title "Inoculation at Liverpool" appears in the table of contents, as Lettsom had Liverpudlian connections: in a letter from Lettsom to Reverend J. Plumptre, the doctor writes, "The Anniversary of the General Sea-Bathing Infirmary was well attended, with Lord Eardley in the chair. The Earl of Liverpool, our President, had engaged to favour us with his company; but, alas! Just as he was leaving the House of Lords, the assassination of Mr. Perceval was perpetrated."[4] This reference to the "General Sea-Bathing Infirmary," to which Lettsom evidently belonged (he writes of "*our* President"), points to the fact that Lettsom was also a keen supporter of sea-bathing for health.[5] The title "Plan of a Portable Vapour Bath," denoting the text that appears before the Sharp document, shows that the owner of this volume was interested in this topic, too.

That the volume *Tracts 35* includes not only the Sharp letter, indicative of the collector's interest in anti-slavery, but also one of the most famous abolitionist poems of the day—"The Wrongs of Africa" by William Roscoe (1787)—further supports the supposition that this volume was Lettsom's because, in keeping with his Quaker principles, he was decidedly against slavery. Unlike Mansfield, who claimed to be uneasy about slavery and yet owned enslaved people to the end of his life, the good doctor lived in accordance with his stated principles: in 1767, upon the death of his father, Lettsom inherited a plantation complete with enslaved Africans in the West Indies, but he immediately gave them manumission, despite having no other fortune at the time.[6]

I conclude confidently, then, that *Tracts 35* was Lettsom's. The BL's surmise regarding the ownership of *Tracts 35* accords with mine. Sandra Tuppen of the BL writes,

[4]Thomas Joseph Pettigrew, *Memoirs of the Life and Writings of the Late John Coakley Lettsom: With a Selection from His Correspondence*, 2 vols. (London: Nichols, Son, and Bentley, 1817), 166, *Google eBooks*, accessed July 7, 2015, https://books.google.ca/books/about/Memoirs_of_the_Life_and_Writings_of_the.html?id=MIpmAAAAMAA-J&redir_esc=y.vol.2.

[5]Ibid., my emphasis; Payne, "Lettsom," unpag.

[6]Payne, "Lettsom," unpag.

The volume was acquired by the British Museum library (our predecessor body) before 1827. We know this because of the type of British Museum ownership stamp inside it. Because there is just one stamp at each end, we believe that the contents of the volume were already gathered together before we acquired it. If we had acquired the pamphlets separately and then bound them, we would have stamped each item as it was acquired. It is possible the items were collected together by Dr John Coakley Lettsome or Lettsom, whose name is written on a number of items. He died in 1815.[7]

In short, the BL deduced independently that Lettsom was the owner of *Tracts 35*. However, Lettsom was not the original recipient of Sharp's letter to the Admiralty in the BL.

The discovery that Lettsom was also a correspondent of Sharp's would seem to settle the case for identifying the founder of the London Medical Society as the recipient of the Sharp letter, and not just as the owner of *Tracts 35*, but such is not the case. To begin with, Lettsom appears not to have been an active abolitionist, so Sharp would have little reason to send him a fair copy of his missive to the Admiralty. Moreover, the two men only seem to have begun writing to each other three years after the 1783 date of the BL document. In 1786, Sharp writes quite formally to Lettsom, referring to himself in the third-person and apparently to thank Lettsom for a volume of writing: "Mr. Granville Sharp presents his respectful compliments to Dr. Lettsom, and sincerely thanks him for his valuable and obliging present; which is the more acceptable to G. Sharp, as it contains memoirs of no less than three of his particular friends, who are highly worthy of respectful remembrance."[8] The first phrase of this passage suggests that Sharp had not contacted Lettsom before this letter; the last part of it demonstrates that Lettsom and Sharp shared acquaintances. With this latter information, I deduced how the BL document came into Lettsom's possession, even though he was probably not its original recipient: Sharp sent it to an acquaintance, and Lettsom received it thereafter from that source.

Discovering the identity of the owner of *Tracts 35* and the intended recipient of the BL missive are different matters. Moreover, the BL

---

[7] Sandra Tuppen, e-mails to the author from the British Library, June 18, 29, July 1, 2015.

[8] Pettigrew, *Memoirs*, vol. 2, 234.

document is a manuscript *copy* of Sharp's missive to the Admiralty, meaning that the recipient of the BL document was not the addressee of the original missive, or, rather, the addressees: the "Lords Commissioners of the Admiralty." So, who was the recipient—or original owner—of the BL copy of the Admiralty missive? Upon concluding that Sharp and Lettsom did not correspond until 1786, as well as that they shared mutual acquaintances, I began to search for the recipient of the BL document among their common acquaintances.

One candidate for the missive's original intended recipient is suggested by the handwritten table of contents, which lists "Smeathman on Elocution and Polite Literature." Thomas Pettigrew's memoirs of Lettsom show that Henry Smeathman (1742–1786) and Lettsom had been correspondents since at least 1772.[9] Sharp and Smeathman were also correspondents. The Hoare *Memoirs* reproduces what appears to be the first contact between them, but this formal letter from Smeathman to Sharp is dated 1786, which discounts him as a possible recipient of the 1783 Admiralty letter, since we know that Sharp sent it soon after composing it.[10] The content of this 1786 letter pertains to the shared interest of Lettsom and Sharp, which the *ODNB* describes: "In 1786 Smeathman's plan of settlement for Sierra Leone was published. The Committee for the Relief of the Black Poor and Granville Sharp championed Smeathman's plan, which in May 1786 the Treasury agreed to finance. Smeathman himself was appointed agent for the enterprise."[11] As might be expected, the acquaintances that Sharp and Lettsom shared were also abolitionists.

Sharp and Lettsom had several abolitionist friends, such as the famous American doctor of the mind, Benjamin Rush (1746–1813), a Quaker and Founding Father of the United States. Rush wrote to Sharp from Philadelphia in 1773, ten years before the date of the BL document, making him a viable possibility as a recipient of it, but not a very

[9] E.g. Pettigrew, *Memoirs*, vol. 2, 262.

[10] Hoare, *Memoirs*, 268. Please see the discussion of all of the known recipients of letters by Sharp on the *Zong* case on pages 76–7 below. In a letter dated 18 July 1783 to the Duke of Portland, now at the NMM, Sharp himself notes that he had sent his missive to the Admiralty that same month. See page 76 for a discussion of this passage.

[11] Starr Douglas, "Smeathman, Henry (1742–1786)," *Oxford Dictionary of National Biography* (Oxford: Oxford University Press, 2005, 2013), unpag., accessed July 6, 2015, https://doi.org/10.1093/ref:odnb/93969.

likely one.[12] After all, Rush lived in America, meaning that the missive would have had to travel overseas and back to Britain again to end up in Lettsom's library. Lettsom was also friends with John Fothergill, a fellow Quaker-abolitionist-physician, whose work Lettsom edited as *The History of Coffee, by the late Dr. John Fothergill* (1809). Hoare's *Memoirs* shows that Sharp had been in touch with Fothergill since at least 1772, as well.[13] However, Fothergill died in 1780 (b. 1712), thereby precluding him as a recipient of the 1783 letter to the Admiralty. Most intriguingly, Lettsom and William Dillwyn, another Quaker, were both members of the Meeting for Suffering Committee on the Slave Trade (1783–1792) and— what is not recorded anywhere else in the literature on the *Zong*—Dillwyn apparently accompanied Sharp to the Court of Exchequer at Westminster to attend the hearing for an appeal of the *Zong* case, but it was deferred that day. Dillwyn notes in his diary for 19 April 1783: "After breakfast went thro' Rain with Geo. Harrison to Westminster Hall where met Granville Sharp. Were disappointed by a Negro Trial not coming on."[14] Given that the insurance trial for the *Zong* happened in March and was followed within that month by the newspaper article on it that Equiano brought to Sharp to inform him about the massacre, the "Negro trial" that Dillwyn mentions is likely the hearing for an appeal of the case, which finally took place in May. Therefore, Dillwyn was clearly in touch with Sharp about the *Zong* and knew Lettsom, too, making him a possible recipient of the BL document. However, an even better candidate surfaced soon after I made this discovery.

This method of searching for the recipient of the BL document among Lettsom and Sharp's mutual acquaintances led me at the end of one workday to a more probable candidate as the letter's recipient. Rereading the section of Hoare's *Memoirs* in which Sharp describes his actions in the days after learning about the *Zong* massacre from Equiano in March, I reasoned that one of the people he visited might be the recipient of the BL document: "MS. ... '21st.—Called on the Bishops of Chester [Porteus] and Peterborough, and General Oglethorpe, and

---

[12] Hoare, *Memoirs*, 113.

[13] Hoare, *Memoirs*, 82.

[14] William Dillwyn, *William Dillwyn Diaries*, unpag., Aberystwyth transcription by Richard Morris, accessed June 15, 2017, http://www.swansea.ac.uk/crew/researchprojects/dillwyn/diaries/williamdillwyndiaries.

Dr. Jebb.'"[15] The last of these people—Sir Richard Jebb (bap. 1729, d. 1787)—turned out to be a friend to Lettsom, too. Upon Jebb's death, Lettsom wrote,

> I loved that man, with all his eccentricity. ... and yet he was the unhappy slave of unhappy passions. His own sister is, and has long been, in a madhouse; the same fate attends his cousin; and a little adversity would have placed poor Sir Richard there also. There was an impetuosity in his manner, a wildness in his look, and sometimes a strange confusion in his head, which often made me tremble for the safety of the sensorium. He had a noble, generous heart, and a pleasing frankness among his friends; communicative of experience among the faculty; earnest for the recovery of his patients, which he sometimes manifested by the most impetuous solicitude. Those who did not well know him, he alarmed. Those who did, saw the unguarded and rude ebullition of earnestness for success.[16]

Jebb, it turns out, was the physician of the Prince of Wales in 1783 and a favourite of King George III.[17] Jebb had the ears of royalty. I reasoned that Sharp may have written to Jebb of the *Zong* murders as part of his calculated attempts to reach the most influential people in Britain with the story of the *Zong*, a supposition that would also explain the extraordinary neatness of the BL document; that is, if the letter was to be presented to the *eyes* of royalty, it had better be impressively polished. The fact that Sharp visited Jebb on 21 March 1783, only two days after Equiano's visit, made him a strong possibility as the recipient of the BL document. Moreover, Lettsom's admission that he "loved" the eccentric physician made him a likely candidate for inheriting the missive upon the death of the unmarried, childless man in 1787, had it belonged to Jebb. However, further research divulged that Lettsom did not inherit Jebb's library. As the following title indicates, Jebb's library was put up for sale, rather than bequeathed to a friend: *A Catalogue of the Genuine Library of the Late Sir Richard Jebb ... The Sale Will Begin on Friday, February 1, 1788, by Benjamin White, and Son* (1788). It remained conceivable that Lettsom bought the BL missive during this sale, but more concrete

---

[15] Hoare, *Memoirs*, 236.

[16] Quoted in Pettigrew, *Memoirs*, vol. 1, 126–7.

[17] Norman Moore, "Jebb, Sir Richard, first baronet (bap. 1729, d. 1787)," revised Michael Bevan, *Oxford Dictionary of National Biography* (Oxford: Oxford University Press, 2004), unpag., accessed July 2, 2015, https://doi.org/10.1093/ref:odnb/14684.

evidence as to the missive's recipient soon replaced this conjectural option.

The morning after I made these discoveries about Jebb, I received an e-mail that presented the best candidate to date as the recipient of Sharp's missive at the BL. It was from Andrew Parry, Archivist at the Gloucestershire Archives (hereafter GA), a response to my inquiry regarding the documents by Sharp on the *Zong* in their holdings, about which I learned from Walvin's great book *The Zong*.[18] I understood that the GA held Sharp's personal copy of the missive to the Admiralty, but Parry's e-mail changed my mind: "I can confirm that the only letter [in the GA] written by Granville Sharp mentioning the *Zong* incident is catalogued as reference D3549/13/1/B1. It was written on the 23rd May 1783 to William Lloyd Baker"; upon further inquiry from me, Parry revealed:

> The letter is ... two pages long (one sheet—written on both sides). The account of the *Zong* incident is written within the body of this one single letter. The reference D3549/13/1/B1 does actually refer to six documents written between Granville Sharp and William Lloyd Baker but I have checked the other letters catalogued under this reference and this is the only document that refers to it.[19]

This information revised many of my previous beliefs. The known holdings by Sharp on the *Zong* in the GA is not Sharp's own copy of the Admiralty missive, but only a single, two-page letter written on one sheet of paper, addressed to William Lloyd Baker. Further research on the GA website uncovered a partial transcription of the GA letter, and it is not parallel to the BL document. Sharp comments in it, "The contest between the owners and insurers of the ship is a mere mercenary business about the pecuniary value of the negroes; but I hope to obtain from it sufficient evidence to commence a criminal prosecution ... for

---

[18] Andrew Parry, e-mails to the author from the Gloucestershire Archives, July 3, 8, 16, 2015. Walvin notes that he consulted these documents, which he calls "Granville Sharp's own papers," when they were still in the possession of the Lloyd Baker family—that is, before they gave the documents to the GA in 1977 (James Walvin, *The Zong: A Massacre, the Law & the End of Slavery* (New Haven and London: Yale University Press, 2011), 216). In an e-mail to me, Walvin comments that he consulted the Sharp documents on the *Zong* (then in the possession of the Lloyd Baker family) in 1974 (James Walvin, e-mail to the author, 5 July 2015).

[19] Parry, e-mail, 3 July 2015.

murder."[20] Subsequently, I acquired a digital scan of the GA letter. Neither the foregoing passage nor any other in the GA letter appears in the BL document, the Hoare transcription, or the NMM document. In short, the GA's letter by Sharp on the *Zong* to William Lloyd Baker is not another copy of the Admiralty missive. This information suggests that William Lloyd Baker might have been the original recipient of the BL document, especially since the GA's holdings prove that Sharp wrote to him on the *Zong* in the first half of 1783. I wondered: Could he be the mutual acquaintance of Lettsom and Sharp for whom I had been searching?

The *ODNB* did not seem to promise much at the outset of my investigation into this lead, as Sharp is mentioned nowhere in the "William Baker" entry. Disappointingly, too, this name is listed in the *ODNB* minus the "Lloyd," but this person is the only "Baker" in the *ODNB* with dates (bap. 1742, d. 1785) that match my basic search parameters. The entry's final note about the dispersal of Baker's property set off alarm bells for me, though: "His library became the property of the physician and philanthropist Dr. J. C. Lettsom."[21] I reasoned that Sharp sent the BL document to Baker and it became mixed up with Lettsom's own library in *Tracts 35* sometime after he acquired Baker's library. I had no evidence that Lettsom bought Jebb's library, but here was reliable proof that he did obtain Baker's library.

To summarize, the conclusion that the BL document was originally sent to Baker (d. 1785) and thereafter acquired by Lettsom appeared to be the strongest of the theories about the provenance of the BL document because the most concrete evidence substantiated it. William Lloyd Baker received a document about the *Zong* from Sharp in the first half of 1783, and Lettsom, the owner of the BL document, acquired the library of one William Baker a few years later. I reasoned that Lettsom acquired the BL document as part of the Baker library. This connection promised tantalizing new information about the GA archives, too: since the GA owns a letter by Sharp to Lloyd Baker about the *Zong* that is not a copy

[20] Granville Sharp, scanned copy of "Letter from Granville Sharp to William Baker About the *Zong* Incident, 23 May 1783 [D3549 13/1/B1]," Gloucestershire Archives, disk received August 5, 2015, unpag.

[21] H. R. Tedder, "Baker, William (bap. 1742, d. 1785)," revised Arthur Sherbo, *Oxford Dictionary of National Biography* (Oxford: Oxford University Press, 2004, 2015), unpag., accessed July 3, 2015, https://doi.org/10.1093/ref:odnb/1144.

of the BL document, I theorized that Sharp originally sent the BL document as part of a three-part package to Lloyd Baker, which would have
been comprised of Sharp's letter to Lloyd Baker, now at the GA, and the
two-part BL document.

However, a serious problem plagues this theory: it turns out that the
"William Baker" listed in the *ODNB* is not the "William Lloyd Baker"
to whom Sharp wrote the *Zong* letter now in the GA, catalogued under
Sharp's name. The first hint that I was descending into a surreal world
of doubles was that the only match for the name "William Baker" in the
GA internal database is that of Reverend William Lloyd Baker (1752–
1830); these dates do not match those of the William Baker (d. 1785)
whose library Lettsom acquired. It had seemed that William Baker (d.
1785) could nevertheless be the recipient of the Sharp letter at the GA,
though, because several people on the subscriber's list in the Hoare
Memoirs are called simply "Baker" and not "Lloyd Baker," which suggests a lasting link between Sharp and the Bakers, not just with the Lloyd
Bakers.[22] And even the GA website refers to the recipient of the Sharp
letter as simply "William Baker" without the name "Lloyd," which suggests that "Lloyd" is sometimes legitimately dropped when mentioning
the family name.[23] However, in a subsequent e-mail, Parry confirmed
my fears that I was pursuing a promising-but-false lead: "I believe," he
wrote, "the William Lloyd Baker [who was] the recipient of Sharp's letter, was actually the Rev William Lloyd Baker (1752–1830) who is mentioned in the [record] D3549 Lloyd-Baker family of Hardwicke Court
collection from which the letter originates."[24] As much as I wanted to
resist it, this reliable information—supplied by an archivist at the GA, no
less—informed me that the recipient of Sharp's letter on the *Zong* in the

---

[22] Hoare, *Memoirs*, vii.

[23] Sharp, "Letter from Granville Sharp to William Baker About the *Zong* Incident, 23
May 1783 [D3549 13/1/B1]," unpag. Notably, too, "The purchase of Stoutshill in Uley
by the Rev William Lloyd Baker in 1785 marked the beginning of the family's connection
with Gloucestershire," which suggests that the lack of connection between the William Baker
(d. 1785) and Gloucestershire does not undermine his candidacy as a recipient of the Sharp
letter (Parry, e-mail, 8 July 2015). Interestingly—but not necessarily relevantly—Sharp comments on Jebb's replacement by one "George Baker" as physician to the King, a position that
Jebb had held since 1786 (Pettigrew, *Memoirs*, vol. 1, 128). I do not know if this "George
Baker" is any relation to either William Lloyd Baker or the William Baker (d. 1785), the latter of whom I am advancing as the most likely recipient of the BL document.

[24] Parry, e-mail, 16 July 2015.

GA was not William Baker (d. 1785), the man whose library Lettsom bought. This realization was a disappointment because it destroyed my most concrete conclusion: that the recipient of the GA letter was also the recipient of the BL document, and that the GA letter had once accompanied the BL document in a three-part package that had since been divided. This deduction was also eminently logical. I had reasoned: To how many William Bakers could Sharp have sent letters about the *Zong* in the first half of 1783? Almost unbelievably, it turns out that the answer is, "Two."

At this point in the investigation into the provenance of the BL missive, the following facts and probabilities were in play: Sharp sent a letter on the *Zong* to Rev. William Lloyd Baker (d. 1830) that is now at the GA; Lettsom owned the BL document, perhaps through his purchase of the older Baker's library in 1785 (further confirmed by Sylvanus Urban),[25] which explains why the BL missive is so different in subject matter from most of the other items in *Tracts 35* (i.e., they originated from two libraries); finally, Lettsom did not seem to know Lloyd Baker (d. 1830), which discounted the latter as a potential recipient of the BL document. I began to query why Sharp would have sent his missives to the two Bakers, and this line of questioning led me to my final discovery.

Sharp's reason for sending the GA letter to Lloyd Baker (d. 1830) was probably personal. He opens the letter with a reference to his own life and daily activities: "My time has been much taken up lately in endeavouring to obtain evidence against the master and crew of a Liverpool slave ship who cast overboard about 123 poor negro slaves alive into the sea with their hands fettered."[26] Sharp wrote to Lloyd Baker about the *Zong* hearing not to advance his political cause, it seems, but to inform his family about matters that were important to him; Lloyd Baker was, after all, family. As the GA online catalogue notes: "the Sharp line continued through the children of Mary Sharp, heiress of William Sharp [Granville's physician brother] and wife of Thomas J. Lloyd Baker

[25] Sylvanus Urban, "Dr. John Coakley Lettsom, M.D.," *The Gentleman's Magazine, and Historical Chronicle*, vol. 85, pt. 2, issue 114 (London: Nichols, Son, and Bentley, 1815), 469–73, 471, *Google eBooks*, accessed July 17, 2015, https://books.google.ca/books/about/The_Gentleman_s_Magazine.html?id=oiM3AAAAYAAJ&redir_esc=y.

[26] Sharp, scan of GA letter, 1. Here, Sharp excludes the 10 kidnapped Africans who jumped in this tally of the *Zong* murders, but he does include the man who saved himself by catching hold of a rope.

of Gloucestershire."[27] The particular date of Sharp's letter to Lloyd Baker—23 May 1783—suggests why Sharp was moved to write his relatives on that date: Sharp attended the 21 May 1783 hearing for an appeal of the *Zong* trial.[28] Sharp was likely disturbed by this experience and needed to unburden himself to sympathetic correspondents.

Yet, the elder Baker (d. 1785) did not appear to be Sharp's relative or friend. Why would Sharp have sent the BL document to him? I conducted additional research into the possible connections between this William Baker and Sharp and found only one—but it is a winner. Baker published several books by Sharp, including *An Account of the Ancient Division of the English Nation into Hundreds and Tithings* (1784), which Baker published only one year after Sharp composed the BL document. Noting that the book was published by "Galabin and Baker," I searched for evidence that the second of the publishers' names belonged to the Baker whose library Lettsom bought and located it in the *ODNB* entry for him: "When Kippax [Baker's former business partner] died, Baker took over the business, later moving to Ingram Court, Fenchurch Street, in the City of London and forming a partnership with John William Galabin."[29] The proximity of the date of the BL document (1783) and that of the publication of Sharp's book (1784) proves that Sharp published with Baker around this time. I would thereafter discover that, in fact, Sharp published no fewer than five publications with Galabin and Baker in 1780, although these were mostly on equal democratic representation, as is the case in *An Account of the Ancient Division of the English Nation into Hundreds and Tithings*.[30] Nonetheless, the text

---

[27] Anon., "Inhuman Traffic: Granville Sharp and the Sharp Family," *Gloucestershire Archives Online Catalogue*, unpag., accessed July 3, 2015, http://www.gloucestershire.gov.uk/archives/learning-for-all/online-exhibitions/inhuman-traffic/.

[28] Walvin, *Zong*, 231 n15.

[29] Tedder, "Baker," unpag.

[30] Sharp published several texts with Galabin and Baker in 1780: Granville Sharp, *The Legal Means of Political Reformation, Proposed in Two Small Tracts* (London: Galabin and Baker, 1780); Granville Sharp, *Declaration of the People's Natural Right* (London: Galabin and Baker, 1780); Granville Sharp, *Equitable Representation Necessary to the Establishment of Law, Peace, and Good Government* (London: Galabin and Baker, 1780); Granville Sharp, *Annual Parliaments, The Ancient and Most Salutary Right of the Commons of Great Britain* (London: Galabin and Baker, 1780); and Granville Sharp, *A Defence of the Ancient, Legal, and Constitutional, Right of the People, to Elect Representatives for Every Session of Parliament* (London: Galabin and Baker, 1780).

from 1784 is hardly devoid of discussion about slavery. Sharp inserts a tract on the Sierra Leone project as an appendix to the book, and he also includes footnotes that mention slavery at length: quoting from his earlier anti-slavery text, *A Representation of the Injustice and Dangerous Tendency of Tolerating Slavery*, Sharp comments with reference to the Somerset case that, under British law, enslaved people cannot "be divested of" their humanity nor that of their children, and therefore no person can be considered chattel.[31] Significantly, too, Sharp had advanced the abolitionist cause through publications with Galabin and Baker many years before, and on behalf of a most influential Quaker hero of the cause: Sharp mentions in *An Appendix to the Representation of the Injustice and Dangerous Tendency of Tolerating Slavery* that he "caused" Benezet's abolitionist text, *A Short Account of That Part of Africa, Inhabited by the Negroes*, "to be reprinted in 1768" by these publishers, demonstrating Sharp's knowledge that Baker was willing to publish texts on abolition.[32] Most likely, then, Sharp sent the BL document—a copy of Sharp's two-part missive to the Admiralty on the *Zong*—to Baker for publication. Sharp would have had to create a fair copy of his missive to the Admiralty for the printers if he did, indeed, wish it to be published by Baker—and the BL document is, without a doubt, a fair copy. To be sure, the neatness of the document and beauty of the penmanship are the characteristics that first drew my strong interest to it. In comparison with the BL document, the NMM document appears to be a draft for Sharp's personal use.

Intriguingly, a text from 1818 to 1819 confirms that Sharp intended to publish material on the *Zong*. In the fifth edition of Bryan Edwards' *The History, Civil and Commercial, of the British West Indies*, the

---

[31] Granville Sharp, *An Account of the Ancient Division of the English Nation into Hundreds and Tithings* (London: Galabin and Baker, 1784), 261, 46–7n, *Google eBooks*, accessed July 17, 2015, https://books.google.ca/books?id=Em-sPAAAAYAAJ&pg=PA1&dq=An+Account+of+the+Ancient+Division+of+the+English+Nation+into+Hundreds+and+Tithings.&hl=en&sa=X&ved=0ahUKEwjJsq_D6aLWAhUX84MKHSs6DPgQ6AEIJjAA#v=onepage&q=An%20Account%20of%20the%20Ancient%20Division%20of%20the%20English%20Nation%20into%20Hundreds%20and%20Tithings.&f=false.

[32] Granville Sharp, *An Appendix to the Representation: (Printed in the Year 1769) of the Injustice and Dangerous Tendency of Tolerating Slavery, or of Admitting the Least Claim of Private Property in the Persons of Men in England* (London: Benjamin White, and Robert Horsefield [sic], 1772), 18.

following statement appears about Sharp's efforts after the *Zong* hearing, misleadingly called a "trial" here:

> In 1783, he [Sharp] had an opportunity of producing a considerable effect upon the public mind, by making fully and extensively known the circumstances of an atrocious transaction, which had taken place on board the *Zong* slave-ship of Liverpool, commanded by Captain Collingwood. This transaction was the murder of a hundred and thirty-two slaves, who, being sickly, were thrown into the sea, by order of the captain, to enable his owners to claim the value of them from the underwriters. ... The pretext for this cold-blooded massacre was want of water, a pretext which was disproved by evidence. The underwriters resisted the claim upon them, and, the matter being brought to a trial, Mr. Sharp employed a shorthand writer, to take down the proceedings, which he afterwards *procured to be printed and widely circulated*. Copies were sent to the Lords of the Admiralty, and to the Duke of Portland, but they remained unnoticed.[33]

Significantly, this passage does not state that Sharp actually succeeded in publishing the court proceedings, but that he "procured" them in order "to be printed and widely circulated," leaving open the question of his success in doing so. This statement is notable as the only concrete evidence I have discovered to confirm my theory that Sharp intended to publish on the *Zong* trial. However, it cannot be attributed to Edwards, the nominal author of this text, because no previous edition of it contains information on the *Zong* and Edwards died in 1800.[34] Nor is it likely that Edwards would have approved of this anonymously authored addition of abolitionist sentiment to his text: as the *ODNB* entry for him points out, he owned 1500 enslaved people in Jamaica and strongly opposed William Wilberforce's efforts to advance the anti-slavery cause in Parliament.[35] Nevertheless, this passage is intriguing because it stands as yet another early instance of two beliefs about the aftermath of the

---

[33] Bryan Edwards, *The History, Civil and Commercial, of the British West Indies*, 5th ed., vol. 4 (London: G. and W. B. Whittaker, 1818–1819), 315–16, my emphasis, *World Scholar: Latin America & the Caribbean*, accessed June 16, 2017, http://worldscholar.tu.galegroup.com/tinyurl/4wmed0.

[34] Richard B. Sheridan, "Edwards, Bryan (1743–1800)," *Oxford Dictionary of National Biography* (Oxford: Oxford University Press, 2004), unpag., accessed June 16, 2017, https://doi.org/10.1093/ref:odnb/8531.

[35] Ibid.

Zong that have been questioned by more recent scholarship: it contends that the *Zong* case was "fully and extensively known" almost immediately after the 1783 trial and that Sharp himself made it so by publishing widely on it.

A similar sentiment appears in Hoare's *Memoirs* of Sharp from 1820. Hoare claims that Sharp was "unwearied in diffusing his powerful and unanswerable remarks on the flagrant enormity of the case, which had been so strenuously vindicated."[36] More recently, Oldham recognizes that Sharp's "unofficial" accounts of the *Zong* case that appear in Hoare's *Memoirs* "were prepared as ammunition for Sharp's bombardment of the government to achieve abolition."[37] The newly discovered BL document by Sharp appears to be a more official account of the *Zong* episode than the NMM draft from which Hoare worked, and it was undoubtedly also prepared in the cause of abolition. I conclude that Sharp sent the BL document to Baker with the intention of publishing it—in order to proclaim "his powerful and unanswerable remarks" on the *Zong* case further.[38]

---

[36] Hoare, *Memoirs*, 246.

[37] James Oldham, "Insurance Litigation Involving the *Zong* and Other British Slave Ships, 1780–1807," *Journal of Legal History* 28, no. 3 (2007): 299–318, 310.

[38] It seems that Sharp abandoned his plan to publish the missive to the Admiralty after Baker's death in 1785, as I have found no evidence that he published it elsewhere.

CHAPTER 4

The British Library Document: The Definitive Version of Sharp's Letter on the *Zong* to the Lords Commissioners of the Admiralty

Abstract This chapter provides detailed evidence to prove that the Sharp letter in the British Library is a fair copy—and therefore the most definitive version—of Sharp's letter to the Admiralty, while the National Maritime Museum copy is a draft. However, since the National Maritime Museum copy has been the only known manuscript of Sharp's Admiralty missive to this point, it has been treated as the most authentic version of it, if not the version actually sent to the Admiralty; several features of the National Maritime Museum document show that it is not the original missive, this chapter reveals. It also establishes the following original claims: that the letter Sharp actually sent to the Admiralty is now lost or destroyed, that Hoare's transcription is based on the National Maritime Museum draft, and that Hoare altered several aspects of Sharp's original draft.

Keywords Fair copy · Publication · *Zong* massacre · Granville Sharp
Transcription · Editorial choices

In this chapter, I provide detailed evidence to prove that the BL document is the only fair copy—and therefore the most definitive version—of Sharp's letter to the Admiralty on the *Zong* massacre. The only other extant manuscript (at the NMM) is a rough draft, which should be considered as secondary to the BL letter. However, since the NMM copy has been the only known manuscript of Sharp's Admiralty missive to this point, it has been treated as the most authentic version of it, and even as the version actually sent to the Admiralty, although several features of the NMM document show that it is not the original missive. In what follows, I also include the full proof for my other original claims about Sharp's letter to the Admiralty, including that the letter Sharp actually sent to the Admiralty is now lost or destroyed, that Hoare's transcription is based on the NMM draft, and, crucially, that Hoare altered several aspects of the NMM document, rendering the Hoare transcription an imprecise and misleading source for scholarly study.

The holdings at the NMM catalogued as "REC/19 - Documents relating a case in the Court of King's Bench involving the ship *Zong*" constitute the greatest number of manuscripts related to the *Zong* case. As part of these holdings, the NMM possesses a copy of Sharp's letter dated 18 July 1783 to the Duke of Portland, who was the Prime Minister of Britain in 1783; in it, Sharp writes, "I have inclosed the Copy of a Letter; which I sent to the <u>Lords of the Admiralty</u>, <u>in the beginning of the present Month</u>, with an Account of the Murder of <u>132 Negro</u> Slaves on board the Ship <u>Zong</u> or <u>Zurg</u>, <u>Liverpool</u> Trader. The original Vouchers are now at the <u>Admiralty</u>, & I have not yet received any Answer respecting them."[1] This comment suggests that Portland received a copy of the letter to the Admiralty, although it may only have been the cover letter (that is, without the detailed description, which, along with the cover letter, form the two-part, parallel documents I discuss as the BL and NMM missives to the Admiralty by Sharp). While Portland does not appear to have responded, Hoare's transcriptions of the replies of Dr. Hinchcliff (Bishop of Peterborough) and Dr. Porteus (Bishop of Chester) to Sharp reveal that Sharp also sent letters about

---

[1] Granville Sharp, Letter to the Duke of Portland, 18 July 1783, repographic scan of REC/19, National Maritime Museum, 111–14, 113, downloaded July 14, 2015. It is possible that the two-part Admiralty missive in REC/19 at the NMM (a transcription of which is in *Granville Sharp's Cases on Slavery* by Lyall) is what Sharp "inclosed" with his letter to Portland—meaning that the NMM's Admiralty missive is Portland's copy—but, given its rather messy editorial state, I argue that it was, rather, Sharp's personal draft of the missive. I purchased from the NMM a high-quality "repographic" scan of everything but the "Vouchers" in REC/19; my claims about these holdings are therefore based on solid evidence. Incidentally, REC/19, or the NMM's two-part missive to the Admiralty that parallels the BL document, is paginated; in my references to it, I cite these page numbers and term it the "NMM document."

the *Zong* to these two men.[2] However, as with the Portland letter, these responses do not indicate clearly whether Sharp sent Hinchcliff and Porteus both the cover letter and the detailed description: Hinchliffe thanks Sharp for sending him the "enclosed narrative of one of the most inhuman barbarities I ever read of" and Porteus thanks Sharp "for the copy of the letter you was so obliging as to send to me."[3] To summarize, then, the historical record reveals that Sharp sent letters on the *Zong* case to William Lloyd Baker, William Baker, Porteus, Hinchcliffe, and the Duke of Portland, as well as that Portland received a copy of (perhaps only the cover letter of) Sharp's missive to the Admiralty. The location of Portland's copy of the Admiralty letter is uncertain, and there is no evidence that the other letters (to Lloyd Baker, Baker, Porteus, and Hinchcliffe) are copies of Sharp's letter to the Admiralty now at the BL and the NMM.

Do any traces remain of the original missive that Sharp actually sent to the Admiralty? Since the transcription of the two-part document in Hoare's *Memoirs* was composed from Sharp's "own manuscripts," as Hoare's long title asserts (*Memoirs of Granville Sharp, Esq. Composed from his* [Sharp's] *own Manuscripts, and other Authentic Documents in the Possession of his Family and of the African Institution*), the memoirist could not have taken it from the missive that Sharp actually sent to the Admiralty: having sent it off, Sharp did not maintain it as part of his "own manuscripts" for Hoare to transcribe after Sharp's death in 1813.[4] The BL missive cannot be the one that Sharp sent to the Admiralty, either, since it is marked "copy" at the top of two pages. Its provenance also denies its candidacy as the original letter to the Admiralty. Finally, the messiness of the NMM document suggests that it is not the original letter: presumably, Sharp would have taken great care to write a fair copy version of the cover letter and detailed description for its powerful

[2] Anita Rupprecht, "'A Very Uncommon Case': Representations of the *Zong* and the British Campaign to Abolish the Slave Trade," *The Journal of Legal History* 28, no. 3 (2007): 329–46, 336; Prince Hoare, *Memoirs of Granville Sharp, Esq. Composed from His Own Manuscripts, and Other Authentic Documents in the Possession of His Family Authentic Documents in the Possession of His Family and of the African Institution* (London: Henry Colburn, 1820), 246, *Google eBooks*, accessed June 25, 2015–August 30, 2017, https://books.google.ca/books?id=PrUEAAAAIAAJ.

[3] Quoted in Hoare, *Memoirs*, 246.

[4] Hoare, *Memoirs*, 242–4, xvii–xxi.

addressees, but the NMM copy appears to be a draft in comparison with the BL document. Since no other copy of Sharp's manuscript letter to the Admiralty exists, the most logical conclusion is that the original letter that Sharp actually sent to the Admiralty is now lost or destroyed.

The present study focuses on the BL document, rather than the NMM document, but I would like to begin my comparison of the two with an observation about the NMM document. The handwriting in it is not only messy, but it does not even appear to be Sharp's, in comparison with other examples of his handwriting.[5] Moreover, since the handwriting in the NMM document (parallel to the BL document) appears to be the same handwriting as in the NMM's "Vouchers"—the transcription of the hearing that Sharp paid a shorthand writer to create, which I discuss hereafter—I suggest that the NMM document was copied out by the same shorthand writer. He (and it was most likely a man) may have worked from Sharp's oral recitation of the letter, but, given the great level of organization and detail in the document, he most likely transcribed the NMM document from a draft (now lost) provided to him by Sharp. In what follows, I will identify Sharp as the author of this NMM document, even though I do not believe it is written in his hand.

Until my discovery of the BL missive, the NMM document was the only extant manuscript of Sharp's Admiralty missive. Some have even treated it as the very missive that Sharp sent to the Admiralty. For example, Baucom identifies the Sharp manuscript holdings at the NMM as the "complete handwritten set of documents" that Sharp "sent to the Lords Commissioners of the Admiralty on July 2, 1783."[6] Several features of the NMM document indicate that it is not the original missive sent to the Admiralty, though. On the title page before the detailed account in the NMM document, the following note appears in faint and (unusually) sepia-toned ink: "NB The letters C & O over the References signify

---

[5] See Chapter 3, footnote 2, for the other examples of Sharp's handwriting to which I compared the NMM manuscript.

[6] Ian Baucom, "'*Signum Rememorativum, Demonstrativum, Prognostikon*': Finance, Capital, the Atlantic, and Slavery," *Victorian Investments: New Perspectives on Finance and Culture*, ed. Nancy Henry and Cannon Schmitt (Bloomington: Indiana University Press, 2008), 35 n4, 22; see also Ian Baucom, *Specters of the Atlantic: Finance Capital, Slavery, and the Philosophy of History* (Durham and London: Duke University Press, 2005), 335 n1. In his replication of Sharp's index of documents in the NMM, however, Baucom repeats Sharp's word "copy" before the first item in the packet: "Copy of a Letter to the Lords of the Admiralty" (Baucom, *Specters*, 125).

Copy and Original this being the Copy"; by "References," Sharp means the citations to the "Vouchers" that appear in parentheses throughout this document, which do, indeed, sometimes have a faint "o" or "c" over them.[7] Significantly, this statement suggests that Sharp uses the word "original" to refer to the final letter he sent to the Admiralty and the present document as "the Copy" (and I follow suit in this discussion).[8] Also, in a footnoted criticism of the defence lawyer, John Lee, Sharp mentions in the NMM copy that "This name was not inserted in the original Letter," which demonstrates both that the NMM copy is not "the original Letter" and that the letter finally sent to the Admiralty does not include the name "Lee" (which, incidentally, is basically true of the BL document, since Sharp crosses the name out).[9] Sharp clearly designates the two-part Admiralty missive in the NMM as a copy and not the original document that he sent to the Admiralty.[10]

Other evidence reveals that the NMM does not have the originals that Sharp sent to the Admiralty on the *Zong*. Graham Thompson of the NMM states as much in the following email to me: "REC/19 came into the Manuscripts collection as a purchase from a private owner in

[7] Granville Sharp, "Copy of a Letter to Lords Commissioners of the Admiralty," Old Jewry London, MS, 2 July 1783, repographic scan provided by the National Maritime Museum (NMM; REC/19), downloaded July 14, 2015, 100.

[8] The issue of the "Vouchers" is also confusing. Sharp repeats in the BL and the NMM documents that they accompany his missive to the Admiralty, and that only one copy of this expensive, large packet of documents exists; even today the only known transcription of the hearing in May is at the NMM, which suggests it could be Sharp's only copy. However, as I note above, the NMM document announces about itself that it is not the original sent to the Admiralty (it is marked "copy"), which suggests that the "Vouchers" included with it are not the originals, either, since they appear to be in the same handwriting—probably that of the shorthand writer whom Sharp hired to transcribe the hearing proceedings. To be clear: my research reveals that the letter and "Vouchers" at the NMM did not come from the Admiralty, and, yet, Sharp insists that there exists only one iteration of the "Vouchers," which he sent to the Admiralty; thus, it must be the case that, without Sharp's knowledge, someone made a copy of the (letter and) "Vouchers" and these are the documents now at the NMM.

[9] Sharp, NMM document, 96; Granville Sharp, [BL document, Copy of a Letter to Lords Commissioners of the Admiralty] "Paper by Glanville [sic] Sharp on the Case of 132 Murdered Negroes," in *Tracts 35* (Old Jewry London, MS: n.p., July 2, 1783), 3.

[10] Sharp, NMM document, 95, 100.

1966. That suggests it has always been in private hands."[11] Evidently, the NMM did not buy the manuscripts in REC/19 from a British government body, such as the Ministry of Defence, which has performed the functions of the Admiralty since 1964.[12] Thus, it appears that Sharp's original missive to the Admiralty is lost, as it is not at The National Archives (hereafter TNA), the only other place it is likely to be, given that the Kelsall affidavit is there. To quote George Hay, archivist at TNA, they "hold the Admiralty's correspondence for the [relevant] period ...—or ... what the Admiralty chose to preserve"; since TNA does not have a catalogued record of Sharp's missive, it would appear that the Admiralty "chose [not] to preserve" it.[13] According to the present records of the archives with holdings of Sharp's manuscripts on the *Zong* case—the NMM, the GA, TNA, and now the BL—there are only two extant manuscript copies of the two-part missive that Sharp sent to the Admiralty, the original having been destroyed or lost: besides the fair copy at the BL, the NMM holds a draft copy of the missive.

The BL's fair-copy manuscript of Sharp's missive to the Admiralty illustrates poignantly the writer's desire to present his case thoroughly and professionally. Walvin comments about the NMM holdings, "It had clearly taken Sharp a great deal of time and effort to draft and assemble his packet of documents."[14] This statement also applies to the two-part BL missive. The penmanship in the newly discovered BL document is perfectly legible and frankly beautiful; the lines of text are rigorously straight; and there are almost no deleted passages of text. None of these characteristics belong to the parallel NMM document, though. A comparison of the NMM and BL parallel manuscripts suggests that the former document is a draft of the latter, newly discovered missive. For example, in the parenthetical citations to the "Vouchers" in the missive

---

[11]Graham Thompson, emails to the author from the National Maritime Museum, June 22, 26, 2015.

[12]Portland would appear to be the most likely original owner of the Admiralty missive in the NMM, given that Sharp's letter addressed to Portland is part of the same holdings, but several unique features of the Admiralty missive in the NMM indicate strongly that it is Sharp's own copy of it, since these features are replicated in Hoare's *Memoirs*, which were "*Composed from His* [Sharp's] *Own Manuscripts*," as Hoare's long title attests.

[13]George Hay, email to the author from The National Archives, Kew, June 25, 2015. Please see note 10 on page 6 for the details of the Kelsall affidavit in TNA.

[14]James Walvin, *The Zong: A Massacre, the Law & the End of Slavery* (New Haven and London: Yale University Press, 2011), 168.

at the NMM, Sharp sometimes leaves space before the closing parentheses, presumably in order to insert the voucher and page numbers at a later time—and at one point in the BL document this space is filled with the relevant information. The copy of the detailed account in the NMM reads, "mistook Jamaica for Hispaniola. (V. 2. p 1   )," and the parallel section in the BL document appears thus: "mistook Jamaica for Hispaniola. (V. 2. p. 11. 17 & 18)," which suggests that Sharp filled in the missing numbers in the BL document once he had located them—after the NMM document was written.[15] This hypothesis also explains why several references to the "Vouchers" and other textual insertions in the NMM manuscript appear in a markedly lighter ink than in the rest of the same document: they were probably written at another time and with a different ink. Yet, the ink throughout the BL document is consistent in appearance, suggesting that it was copied out at one time, probably from the NMM document. Furthermore, at several points in the NMM document, Sharp inserts a carelessly omitted word or letters with a caret, but these passages are seamlessly written out in the BL document. For example, Sharp writes in the NMM document, "The Sickness & Mortality on Board the Zong, previous to the 29th Novr 1781 (the time when they began to throw the poor Negroes overboard alive) was ∧not occasioned by the want of Water."[16] The parallel passage in the BL document simply includes the word "not" as part of the original sentence, rather than as an insertion.[17] This circumstance is repeated six times, and each time Sharp amends the mistake in the BL document, contributing to the conclusion that the BL document was copied out from the NMM draft, and revealing the BL document as a more finished version of the Admiralty missive than the NMM copy.

Despite the conclusion that the two-part Admiralty letter in the NMM is a draft of the BL document, the NMM holdings of papers relating to the *Zong* remain hugely valuable as the most voluminous collection of contemporary manuscripts on the *Zong*. Baucom comments that the "packet of material" that Sharp sent to the Admiralty, which Baucom identifies as the contents of REC/19 at the NMM, consists

---

[15] Sharp, NMM document, 101; Sharp, BL document, 5. Here, Sharp omits his underlining of the place names in the BL document.

[16] Sharp, NMM document, 102.

[17] Sharp, BL document, 6; Sharp's double underlining.

of five documents: the first comprised a transcript of the appeals hearing on the case of the *Zong* held before Lord Mansfield at the court of King's Bench; the second was a letter Sharp addressed to the Lords Commissioners asking that they open a murder investigation; the third was his brief account of the massacre together with his arguments against the legal case for compensation advanced by the attorneys for the ship's owners; the fourth was a copy of another letter he had written, this to the Duke of Portland; the fifth was a copy of a petition the *Zong*'s insurance underwriters had sent to William Pitt in his capacity as chancellor of the Court of Exchequer requesting that the initial verdict reached in favor of the owners be set aside and a new trial ordered.[18]

The second and third items of this list comprise the two-part document that parallels the BL document. If the first item Baucom mentions is the original transcription of the hearing for an appeal that Sharp paid a shorthand writer to create and not a copy of it, then it is unique and what Sharp calls the "Vouchers" throughout the BL document: "a shorthand transcription of an appeal [of the March insurance trial decision] held on May 22 and 23, 1783, at the Court of King's Bench (Lord Mansfield, Chief Justice of King's bench presiding)," as Baucom notes.[19] Because Sharp only had one—very costly and long—transcription of the May hearing, these "Vouchers" were precious to him, as he maintains at the end of the cover letter of the BL document: "P. S To avoid delay I have sent my original Vouchers without preserving Copies of them; & as they are valuable, (the 2^d. alone having cost me £12.4.0) I must request—your Lordships to give orders that they may be returned to me as soon as the Business is concluded."[20] When one considers that Collingwood earned approximately five pounds a month as Captain of the *Zong*—"plus the value of the [two] 'privilege slaves'" for the entire journey to keep for himself or sell, as he wished, Shyllon notes—then Sharp's designation of the shorthand transcription as expensive appears in all its truth to a modern audience: at £12.4.0 for the second "Voucher" alone, the whole transcription was worth well more than two months' monetary wages for

---

[18] Baucom, "'*Signum*,'" 22–3. For more on REC/19 in the NMM, see also Rupprecht, "'Uncommon,'" 336; Walvin, *Zong*, 217; and Andrew Lewis, "Martin Dockray and the *Zong*: A Tribute in the Form of a Chronology," *Journal of Legal History* 28, no. 3 (2007): 357–70, 366, Taylor and Francis, accessed July 17, 2015.

[19] Baucom, *Specters*, 4.

[20] Sharp, BL document, 3.

a slave-ship captain.[21] Additionally, Sharp did not have a personal income in 1783: he had depended on his brothers for his maintenance since 1779, having quit the Ordnance Office on moral grounds.[22] Since the Admiralty apparently did not respond to his missive, we may assume that Sharp's request was unsatisfied and he never saw his "Vouchers" again.

Until recently, the only widely available transcription of the two-part Admiralty missive was Hoare's *Memoirs*, published in 1820.[23] Lyall's 2017 transcription of the NMM document (and the "Vouchers") is a vital new source for researchers interested in Sharp and the *Zong* case, but, prior to Lyall's book, the ease of accessing Hoare's text meant that many scholars of the *Zong* case consulted it.[24] And since the title

[21] Sharp, BL document, 3; Baucom, *Specters*, 10; Lewis, "Dockray," 358; Michael Lobban, "Slavery, Insurance and the Law," *The Journal of Legal History* 28, no. 3 (2007): 319–28, 323; F. O. Shyllon, *Black Slaves in Britain* (London and New York: Oxford University Press, 1974), ix, 525. Baucom states that Collingwood earned "the sale price of two slaves (for which he could expect something in the range of 30 pounds . . .)," but Lobban comments that "the slaves were valued in the policy at £30 a head. This [sum] reflected the expected sale price in Jamaica, rather than the African purchase price"; quoting Roger Anstey's, *The Atlantic Slave Trade and British Abolition, 1760–1810* (1975), Lobban later adds, "The average price in the 1780s of newly-landed slaves in the West Indies has been estimated at £36, which was indeed the price at which the *Zong*'s surviving slaves were sold" (323 n22). In other words, Collingwood could expect to make at least 60 pounds from the sale of his two "privilege slaves," should he choose to sell them, not 30 pounds. Since Collingwood died shortly after landing at Jamaica, he probably did not sell these Africans. Finally, Lewis notes that Collingwood's actual wage was 95 shillings a month, which was about five pounds (Lewis, "Dockray," 358).

[22] Anon., "Inhuman Traffic: Granville Sharp and the Sharp family," *Gloucestershire Archives Online Catalogue*, unpag., accessed July 3, 2015, http://www.gloucestershire.gov.uk/archives/learning-for-all/online-exhibitions/inhuman-traffic/, unpag.

[23] Hoare, *Memoirs*, 242–4, xvii–xxi.

[24] Leaving aside articles and other short works, the most notable books that cite Hoare's *Memoirs* have already been mentioned in the present study; these include those by Brown, Carey (*Sensibility*), and Carretta (*Self-Made*). Other books that use Hoare's *Memoirs* include: Paul Michael Kielstra, *The Politics of Slave Trade Suppression in Britain and France, 1814–1848: Diplomacy, Morality and Economics* (New York: Palgrave Macmillan, 2000); Peter Hogg, *The African Slave Trade and Its Suppression: A Classified and Annotated Bibliography of Books, Pamphlets and Periodical* (1973; Abingdon: Routledge, 2013); Frank N. Magill, *The 17th and 18th Centuries: Dictionary of World Biography* (Volume 4. Ipswich, MA: Salem Press, 1999. 10 vols); Dean Rapp, *Samuel Whitbread (1764–1815): A Social and Political Study* (New York: Garland Publishing, 1987); and Jeannine Marie DeLombard, *Slavery on Trial: Law, Abolitionism, and Print Culture* (Chapel Hill: University of North Carolina Press, 2009).

of Hoare's text announces that it was "*Composed from his* [Sharp's] *own Manuscripts, and other Authentic Documents in the Possession of his Family and of the African Institution*," it would seem to be a reliable version of the Admiralty missive on the *Zong*. However, Hoare's transcription does not meet today's scholarly standards and, more importantly, it omits several essential passages from Sharp's argument that are vital to our understanding of Sharp's approach to abolition. Since scholarship on Sharp and the *Zong* has relied so heavily upon Hoare's transcription to this point, it is worth exploring the differences between it and the NMM document—Hoare's source-text, I will argue—to see what we have been missing.

To this point, it has been unclear which copy of Sharp's two-part missive to the Admiralty Hoare used as his source-text when the Sharp family commissioned him to write the *Memoirs*.[25] Although it has been assumed that the manuscript Hoare consulted is at the GA, I have demonstrated that the GA does not have a copy of the Admiralty missive.[26] A comparison of the BL missive with the published Hoare transcription shows that Hoare did not use the BL document as his source-text, either. For instance, in *Memoirs*, Hoare follows the phrase "learned lawyer" with a footnote marker (a dagger: "†") that draws the reader's attention to the note, "I find the following note annexed to the original document of this letter, at this place:—'Memorandum. John Lee, Esq., a Yorkshire man, who spoke very broad in the provincial dialect of that county, which has seldom been so grossly profaned as by this lawyer?'"[27] The BL document contains the phrase "learned Lawyer" and the surrounding sentence, with slight variations (such as the capital "L" in "Lawyer"), but neither a footnote marker nor the relevant footnote is in it.[28] While it is not improbable that, during the transcription process, Hoare deleted several details of the manuscript he consulted, it is less likely that he would have inserted an entire footnote that did not exist in the original document and attribute it to Sharp. However, the NMM

[25] Christopher Leslie Brown, *Moral Capital: Foundations of British Abolitionism* (Chapel Hill: University of North Carolina Press, 2012), 171.

[26] See, for example, Walvin, *Zong*, 216; Parry, emails, 3, 8, 16, July 2015. I bought copies of the GA's holdings of all Sharp manuscripts relating to the *Zong* and confirm that they are not parallel to the BL or NMM documents.

[27] Hoare, *Memoirs*, 243.

[28] Sharp, BL document, 2.

manuscript does contain an asterisk footnote marker after the phrase "learned Lawyer" and a footnote that is parallel to the one about Lee in Hoare's *Memoirs*, suggesting that Hoare's source-text was the NMM document.

Other evidence indicating that the Hoare transcription is based on the NMM document concerns what is missing in the former and marked for deletion in the latter. With a pencil (unlike the ink of the main text), someone has marked up—essentially edited—the NMM document, suggesting deletions of words and whole passages that are reflected in the Hoare transcription, but not in the BL document. For instance, an entire section of text, beginning with "or rather, their meaning" and ending with a similar phrase ("their meaning") is marked for deletion in the NMM document.[29] The same passage is duly deleted from the Hoare transcription, but it nevertheless appears in the BL document.[30] A corresponding triad of evidence appears in the section that begins "So that the 6 Casks of Rain water" and ends with "never actually consumed."[31] Several other instances of this nature may be noted. Since the BL document appears to be in fair copy and does not account for these editorial suggestions, I conclude that they were not solicited by Sharp and may not even have been seen by him. These pencilled editorial suggestions in the NMM document were likely made by and for Hoare himself in preparation for transcribing and publishing the Admiralty missive in his *Memoirs*.

The copy of Sharp's two-part missive to the Admiralty in the NMM is very like the BL document in terms of formal features such as excessive underlining and multiple exclamation marks, but the Hoare transcription omits some of these details. For instance, in both documents Sharp comments, "the most obvious natural Right of Human Nature is at stake, viz.ᵗ the Right even to Life itself!!!"[32] Notably, these passages in both

[29] Sharp, NMM document, 103.

[30] Sharp, BL document, 7.

[31] Sharp, NMM document, 103; BL document, 8. Here and in subsequent references to both documents—in which I quote from only one manuscript (from either the NMM or BL, whichever appears first in the citation), but then also provide the page number for the parallel passage in the other manuscript—the reader should be aware that the formatting and exact wording is frequently different in the passage to which I refer with the second reference.

[32] Sharp, BL document, 13; NMM document, 108.

the BL and the NMM documents contain three exclamation marks, and the underlining is exactly the same between the two documents, even in the double underlining of the word "Life." If Hoare's source-text was the NMM document, as I argue it was, then these omissions exemplify how Hoare toned it down for his publication—and this change is significant because it misrepresents Sharp's attitude towards the *Zong* case as less than infuriated. Others have observed the passionate tone in Sharp's manuscripts. Rupprecht comments that "Sharp's rage becomes palpable as the account gathers rhetorical momentum, not least because much of the original text is furiously underscored."[33] Walvin, who consulted the Lloyd Baker holdings and the NMM documents, writes that Sharp's

> handwritten letters and annotations to what others wrote and published all fairly rattle with outrage: angry words are slashed across the page, and the text is speckled with passionate interjections. He dispatched angry missives left and right—long, furious letters—to any individual or organization he thought might help.[34]

I concur that the NMM document demonstrates Sharp's passion for his topic, and I would add that the BL document does, too. These manuscripts provide important insights into the intensity of Sharp's attitude that Hoare's text does not convey in its toned-down state. Indeed, Hoare's published transcription obscures much of Sharp's rage over his subject. It includes few of the dozens of exclamation marks and many other instances of underlining that appear in the BL and NMM documents (the former of which has 31 exclamation marks and the latter of which has 36). Notably, too, Sharp's other anti-slavery texts, such as those from 1776, reveal that excessive exclamation marks are a signature feature of his abolitionist writing. To temper such features is to misrepresent the letter to the Admiralty as being rather tame and unlike Sharp's published work from the previous decade.

Sharp's exclamation points are, indeed, remarkable for their excess. In two instances, he uses three exclamation points; at another, Sharp is so outraged that no fewer than four exclamation points will suffice to express his indignation. The most relevant section concerns the Solicitor

---

[33] Rupprecht, "Uncommon," 336.
[34] Walvin, *Zong*, 166.

General John Lee's defence. In the BL document, Sharp prefaces his quotation of Lee's words with this statement:

> I should not have taken notice of such an unreasonable argument & much less have troubled your Lordships with it, did not the Official Dignity of the Speaker, & his high Reputation as a Lawyer compel me to guard against the adoption of his avowed Doctrines in the present Case, lest precept, as well as impunity should encourage the Liverpool Traders to multiply their Murders to the disgrace of the English Name, & to the destruction of the human Species![35]

Sharp then quotes Lee:

> "If any Man of them" (said the learned Advocate for Liverpool Iniquity, speaking of the Murderers in the present Case "– if any Man of them" said he) "was allowed to be tried at the old Bailey for a murder I cannot help thinking" (said he) "if that charge of murder was attempted to be sustained & M.ʳ Stubbs adduced to prove the Evidence & the facts it would be folly & rashness to a degree of Madness, & so far from the Charge of Murder laying against these people there is not the least Imputation of Cruelty I will not say, but of impropriety not in the least"!!!![36]

Lest the Admiralty neglect these words, Sharp not only underlines the entire quotation by Lee and double-underlines the final phrase, but he also follows it with four exclamation marks in an apparent attempt to inspire sympathetic outrage in his readers. Uncharacteristically, Hoare himself seems unable to resist Sharp's energy at this point, as he includes three of the four exclamation marks that appear in his source-text, the NMM document.[37] But Hoare does not include any of the underlining in the NMM document, which is actually more excessive than in the BL document, since the phrase "least Imputation of Cruelty" is also double underlined in it. Intriguingly, too, the phrase "& Mʳ Stubbs adduced to prove the Evidence & the Facts" has been crossed through with pencil, as if for deletion, in the NMM document—and this phrase is in fact missing in the Hoare transcription. Here, then, is more proof both that

---

[35] Sharp, BL document, 11–12; NMM document, 107, wherein "Impunity," "Liverpool," "murders," and "English" are also underlined.

[36] Sharp, BL document, 12; NMM document, 107.

[37] Hoare, *Memoirs*, xix.

Hoare's source-text was the NMM document and that Hoare altered crucial features of Sharp's missive.

Sharp also uses underlining to stress the importance of his message. In some passages from the manuscripts, Sharp is so eager to emphasize a point that he underlines a word or phrase two or even three times, particularly in the detailed account (after the cover letter). Since Hoare replaces Sharp's underlining with italics, the energy of the multiple underlining is lost. Sharp underlines the names of the perpetrators he mentions, as if to burn them into the memories of his recipients, but he also underlines words that one can imagine he would shout if this letter were delivered orally. Crucially, too, Sharp tends to double-underline those words that lie at the conceptual centre of his argument, such as "Living Men," "Human Persons," and "cruelty & impropriety."[38] The following passage is a good example of how Sharp's method of underlining appears in the BL document:

> the said Luke Collingwood picked or caused to be picked out from the Cargo of the same Ship 133 Slaves, all, or most of whom were sick, or weak, and not likely to live, and ordered the Crew by turns to throw them into the Sea: which most inhuman Order was cruelly complied with.[39]

Sharp double-underlines the same words (beginning with "ordered" and ending with "Sea") in the NMM document, Hoare's source-text.[40] In addition to these formal changes, Hoare also removes most of Sharp's odd capitalizations, evident in both the NMM and the BL documents. These changes are significant. Sharp seems to anticipate that the recipients of the missive will only skim it, rather than read it over carefully, a situation that he attempts to remedy by using various methods of formatting and punctuation so that his most important points do not disappear among the many other statements he makes in this voluminous text. By removing many of these features of it, though, Hoare changes Sharp's message.

Why did the memoirist risk changing the tone of Sharp's manuscript so markedly by deleting these aspects of it? It may be that Hoare was required to regularize and formalize the manuscript copy by Sharp in

---

[38] Sharp, BL document, 12, 13; NMM document, 107, 108.

[39] Sharp, BL document, 7; NMM document, 102.

[40] Sharp, NMM document, 102.

accordance with the publisher's (Henry Colburn and Co.) demands; and perhaps Hoare himself wished to make the transcription appear more professional and consistent with formal publishing practices. This interpretation is strengthened upon consideration that Hoare corrects, or regularizes, Sharp's spelling at places, too, such as in Sharp's word "alledges," which Hoare spells "alleges."[41] Moreover, if the NMM document was indeed written down by the shorthand writer whom Sharp hired, as I have suggested—and not Sharp himself—then Hoare may have viewed his transcription of the NMM document as a helpful refinement of the shorthand writer's services and a scholarly improvement, rather than, as we view such changes today, unscholarly meddling with a source-text. While Hoare's methods may look like censorship, a more generous interpretation is that he wanted to present Sharp's words in the best light and reach the widest audience possible as a way of honouring Sharp's memory and hard work in the service of abolition. However, Hoare also sometimes eliminates the moving urgency that Sharp conveys in the manuscripts, which is more than half their power. Since Hoare's publication has been the most widely available to this point, these inaccuracies are important to acknowledge.

Even more crucially, several long passages appear in the BL missive and the NMM document that are not included in the widely used Hoare *Memoirs*. The first of these passages concerns how the murders were counted on the *Zong*—and, rather eccentrically, it reveals Sharp's interest in linguistics:

> their meaning, I apprehend, is that after the 2.^{d} time of throwing overboard (which seems to have been on the 30.th Novr See V. 2. P. 22) they counted the remaining Slaves (which Mr Stubbs acknowledges he did after each throwing over), & found by the decreased number of Slaves the next morning vizt on the 1.st December when they counted them, that 42 more Slaves had been thrown over; not that they were then (on the 1.st Dec.^{r}) thrown over; but only in the præter-pluperfect time,—had been vizt at the 2.^{d} time of throwing over, on the preceding day. This I take to be their meaning.[42]

[41] Sharp, BL document, 3; NMM document, 98; Hoare, *Memoirs*, 244.
[42] Sharp, BL document, 7; NMM document, 103.

In this summary of what Sharp calls "a Memorandum from the Deposition of Kelsall the Chief Mate" and what "M.ʳ Stubbs himself" told Sharp, Sharp avers that the crew members were not counting their victims carefully while they committed the murders, but that they only realized how many Africans they had killed by counting how many were left alive afterwards.[43] Sharp's eccentric use of the phrase "in the præter-pluperfect time" moreover reveals not only his interest in grammar (indeed, he combined this interest with his zeal for theology in *Remarks on the Uses of the Definitive Article in the Greek Text of the New Testament* (1798)), but, more importantly, the phrase highlights his effort to elucidate the dates and numbers of the murders on the *Zong*. As Sharp notes elsewhere in the detailed description, "there is some variation in the two Accounts, respecting the <u>number</u> of persons murdered."[44] He attempts to resolve this numerical confusion with the above statement. While Hoare's transcription does include a passage that provides the final number of victims, this unpublished segment from Sharp's missive reveals additional information concerning the timing of the murders, the murderers' heedlessness, and Sharp's determination to present the details of the event as clearly as possible in order to secure legal punishment for these crimes.

Also in the BL and NMM documents, but not Hoare's transcription of the Admiralty missive, are entire statements that expose Sharp's boldness in speaking truth to power—sometimes by stating religious truths. Sharp's assertiveness may seem surprising when one considers that this then-unemployed son of an Anglican cleric had a limited formal education. His former employment was of a somewhat lowly nature, too, as he had been "at a very early age withdrawn from the public grammar-school at Durham, before he had gained more than the first rudiments of the learned languages, and was sent to a smaller school," only to be apprenticed to a linen draper thereafter and, when the linen business failed, to become a clerk in the government Ordnance Office, which he eventually "quit in protest against the American war."[45] Davis comments that, despite these setbacks, as

---

[43] Ibid.

[44] Sharp, BL document, 2.

[45] G. M. Ditchfield, "Sharp, Granville (1735–1813)," *Oxford Dictionary of National Biography* (Oxford: Oxford University Press, 2004, 2012), unpag., accessed June 16, 2015, https://doi.org/10.1093/ref:odnb/25208; David Brion Davis, *The Problem of Slavery in the Age of Revolution, 1770–1823* (Oxford: Oxford University Press, 1999), 391.

the grandson of the Archbishop of York, and son of the Archdeacon of Northumberland, ... Granville had easy access to the bishops and peers of the realm. His wealthy older brothers were leading philanthropists, and the family, including Granville, won special esteem for their musical concerts, given from a summer barge, which delighted London's elite as well as the royal family itself.[46]

Additionally, two of Sharp's brothers were Anglican clergymen, while another was a respected physician.[47] The Sharp name was held in high regard, and Granville Sharp attempted to use it in the service of abolition. Nor was the *Zong* incident the first that inspired Sharp to request the Anglican nobility to help advance the anti-slavery cause. Shyllon reports that

> [A]s early as 15 May 1769, he had written to the Archbishop of Canterbury urging him to use his "exalted station both in church and state" towards the end of evils "which reflect not only dishonour, but the blackest guilt, on the British Government, so long as they are tolerated." He followed this up by soliciting the support of other bishops in this, the earliest campaign in England for the abolition of slavery and the slave trade.[48]

Armed with the confidence of hailing from an illustrious family of Anglican leaders, Sharp was eager to use his inherited clout to secure justice for the victims of the slave trade.

Accordingly, Sharp does not hesitate to berate England's Solicitor General, John Lee, in the BL copy of his cover letter to the powerful leaders of the British navy:

> Thus it was unhappily demonstrated that there is nothing, howsoever gross and absurd, which some professors of the Law accustomed to Sophistry, and hackneyed in the prostitution of their oratorical abilities for hire, will not undertake to justify, relying on their studied <u>powers of perversion</u>, like those "<u>double hearted Men</u> of old," <u>who said with our tongue we will prevail—our Lips are with us, who is Lord over us?</u>" But if we must one day "<u>render an Account of every idle word</u>." how much more awful will be the condemnation of that <u>perverse Oratory</u>, which patronizes and defends the

[46] Davis, *Problem*, 391.
[47] Ditchfield, "Sharp," unpag.
[48] Shyllon, *Black Slaves*, 136.

most violent of all <u>oppression</u>, even <u>wilful</u> <u>Murder</u>, the superlative degree
of unrighteousness![49]

Hoare's transcription does not include this passage, making it a pale
version of the more daring manuscripts in the BL and NMM. Not only
does Sharp insult one of the most eminent lawyers in Britain here, but he
also does so by appealing to a higher power than that of the law—God's
power—thereby undermining Lee's authority. In quoting from Matthew
12:36 and Psalm 12 in the Bible, Sharp reminds his recipients that, once
the legal sophistry and machinations of the slave traders has concluded,
they will all be judged by the Divine.[50] However, since Hoare's published version of the Admiralty missive does not contain the above passage about Lee and other defenders of slavery, the integrity of Sharp's
religious argument is undermined in it.

The source of Sharp's belief in his own ability to create positive
change appears to derive from his conviction that he was on the side
of right in the eyes of God, and that appealing to this realm of truth
would remind his worldly readers of their eternal, spiritual duty. Sharp
was, after all, a staunch Anglican from a family of clerics, a man who
had taught himself Greek and Hebrew in order to engage in theological
debate with ministers.[51] He firmly believed in and greatly feared Divine
justice, as is evident from "his commonplace books," which are filled
"with such headings as 'Retribution,' 'Demons and Devils,' 'Presages,'
'Right and Righteousness,' and 'Hell,' under the last of which he scrib-
bled 'the torments are everlasting,'" Brown reports.[52] Since the letter to
the Admiralty ends with the threat that England's tolerance of the slave
trade may "speedily involve the whole Nation in some such tremendous
Calamity as may unquestionably mark the avenging hand of God, who
has promised '<u>to destroy</u> the Destroyers of the Earth'!," it is therefore
clear that Sharp intends to revive his argumentative tactic from such texts

---

[49] Sharp, BL document, 2; NMM document, 96–7. As I note in the Appendix, opening
quotation marks should appear before the word "with."

[50] *The Holy Bible, Containing the Old and New Testaments Translated Out of the Original
Tongues and with the Former Translations Diligently Compared and Revised by His Majesty's
Special Command. Appointed to be Read in Churches. Authorized King James Version,* 1611
(Iowa Falls: World Bible Publishers, [n.d.]).

[51] Ditchfield, "Sharp," unpag.

[52] Brown, *Moral,* 174.

as *The Law of Retribution*, but here with a greater focus on a specific and recent event to impress upon his reader the immediacy of their danger.[53] Slavery may have seemed irrelevant and abstract to many eighteenth-century Britons, as the worst of it played out on distant ships on the Atlantic and plantations in the West Indies, but the reality of the trade in human flesh was revealed by the *Zong* trial: it involved British people, some of the pillars of their community, suing to be rewarded for mass murder, and it was heard in London in a courtroom with a jury of average Britons. Sharp encourages his readers to recognize that every Briton would pay eternally for allowing these crimes to go unpunished. If the horror of slavery was unknown before, it had arrived on British shores with the *Zong* trial, Walvin points out.[54] Similarly, God may be mostly unseen, but his justice would soon be felt on earth by every guilty individual, Sharp argues: Britain's time of reckoning for slavery had arrived with the *Zong* trial.

Another long passage that appears in the BL and NMM documents, but not the Hoare *Memoirs*, concerns the crew's excuse for the murders. Although the essential facts from this section are repeated elsewhere in the Hoare transcription, only this passage, excised by Hoare, includes Sharp's interpretation of such details. Writing of the rain that fell after the first two groups of Africans had been killed, Sharp suggests its divine significance in the following passage from the BL document:

> the 6 Casks of Rain water caught on the 1.st & 2.d Dec.r (only 7 days before this Opportunity of obtaining water from Jamaica) was not only a providential supply, but providentially demonstrated the iniquity of pretending a necessity to put innocent Men to a violent death, thro' the mere apprehension of a want, which (supposing it had taken place could not have afforded an admissible justification of the horrible deed – but which) did never really exist or take place at all in their case; because their Stock of Water was never actually consumed.[55]

The crux of the Gregson syndicate's argument in the initial insurance trial was what they called "necessity": because the *Zong* was dangerously low on water, the captain and crew killed the Africans in order

---

[53] Sharp, BL document, 15.

[54] Walvin, *Zong*, 178.

[55] Sharp, BL document, 8; NMM document, 103.

to save the lives of the remaining people on board, who, the Gregson syndicate claimed, surely would have died of thirst had their employees not reduced the number of people in need of water by 133 (the number of Africans they intended to drown). In this passage, Sharp rejects the *Zong* murderers' excuse completely, as he does in a similar passage that is reproduced in Hoare's *Memoirs*.[56] Sharp argues that they were never dangerously low on water, given that the rain had replenished their stock of it, and, never having moved to half-rations of water for anyone on the ship, the crew never even had "the mere apprehension of a want" of water. What is new in this passage—found in the manuscripts, but not the Hoare *Memoirs*—is Sharp's introduction of the notion of divine providence in the matter: the rain provided a "providential supply" of water that "providentially demonstrated" the evil in pretending that the murders were committed for want of water, Sharp claims. In other words, he contends that God supplied the rainfall specifically in order to preclude the possibility of excusing the murders through the plea of necessity. By using this reason as the basis for their insurance case, Sharp attests, the *Zong* crew and Gregson syndicate spurn two gifts from God—the rainwater and God's lesson regarding their evil intentions—and they thereby do infinitely worse than attempt to pervert the course of human justice through insurance fraud and attempting to get paid for mass murder.

To be sure, as a transcription of the NMM document (itself the draft of the BL document), Hoare's text is not reliable. Several additional examples of the above kind may be noted. For instance, Hoare does not include Sharp's postscript about the expensive "Vouchers" in the NMM document, a postscript that also appears in the BL document.[57] The memoirist gestures to the "Vouchers" in a footnote of his own ("This account was accompanied with various vouchers, to which all the passages marked with inverted commas are referred"), but he does not include Sharp's words from the NMM document: "P.S. To avoid delay I have sent my Original Vouchers without preserving Copies of them, & as they are valuable (the 2^d alone having cost me £12. .4 -) I must request your Lordships to give Orders that they may be returned to me as soon as

[56] Hoare, *Memoirs*, xix; Sharp, BL document, 9; NMM document, 105.
[57] Sharp, NMM document, 98; BL document, 3.

the Business is concluded.—."[58] Also with respect to this section, Hoare transcribes Sharp's valediction as "'With the greatest respect, my Lords,' &c. &c."; however, Sharp's actual valediction in the NMM document is: "I am with the greatest respect My Lords your Lordships most obedient & most humble Servant (Signed) Granville Sharp."[59] This difference is worth noting for a couple of reasons. To begin with, Sharp's longer greeting demonstrates his extreme respectfulness and desire to appear most humble before the Admiralty, probably so that he does not anger them by seeming too presumptuous, thereby undermining his purpose— specifically to convince the Admiralty to prosecute the *Zong* murderers. This rhetorical move may have been an attempt to undo some of the damage of the first hectic days after Sharp learned about the *Zong* massacre from Equiano, during which he notes in his diary that, on 22 March 1783, he "'Ordered Messrs. Heseltine and Lushington to commence a prosecution in the Admiralty Court, against all persons concerned in throwing into the sea one hundred and thirty Negro slaves, as stated on a trial at Guildhall on the 6th of this month.'"[60] Sharp wrote his letter to the Lords Commissioners of the Admiralty considerably later, on 2 July 1783; perhaps by that time Sharp realized that he did not follow protocol by "order[ing]" Sir Stephen Lushington and James Heseltine from the British High Court of Admiralty to pursue a murder case against the *Zong* crew, since such a criminal prosecution could only advance through the Admiralty's own exertions. In this case, Sharp would certainly have had to backtrack and attempt to convince the Admiralty that he respected their jurisdiction and autonomous right to prosecute "all Murders committed on board British Ships"—as Sharp puts it in the first sentence of his letter—on their own terms, rather than upon the orders

---

[58] Hoare, xvii; Sharp, NMM document, 98.

[59] Hoare, 244; Sharp, NMM document, 98.

[60] Qtd. in Hoare, *Memoirs*, 236; Jane Webster, "The *Zong* in the Context of the Eighteenth-Century Slave Trade," *Journal of Legal History* 28, no. 3 (2007): 285–98, 295. Incidentally, here Webster identifies Heseltine and Lushington as Sharp's lawyers, but, as I note in Chapter 2 (page 46), they are identified as partners connected to the "British High Court of Admiralty" in the official records of the Parliamentary debates from 1812 (Anon., *The Parliamentary Debates from the Year 1803 to the Present Time*, ed. T. C. Hansard (London: Longman, Hurst, Rees, Orme, and Brown, 1812), vol. 23, 777, *Google eBooks*, accessed 23 April 2018, https://books.google.ca/books?id=twlAAQAAMAAJ&printsec=frontcover&source=gbs_ge_summary_r&cad=0#v=onepage&q&f=false).

of a layman such as himself.[61] Because of Hoare's changes to Sharp's signature, however, his newly developed respectfulness to the Admiralty is not evident. Yet, the most egregious error in Hoare's transcription of the letter is that he spells the name of the ship "Zung" where Sharp calls it "Zurg" in the NMM document.[62] Since the name of the ship is already mired in confusion, Hoare's contribution to this linguistic chaos is unhelpful, to say the least.[63] Until very recently, Hoare's transcription has been the most accessible version of the letter, but I have demonstrated that Hoare changes many important passages and details that appear in both the BL document and the NMM document, rendering it an unreliable resource.

For all of these reasons, then, the BL document should be treated as the most reliable version of Sharp's missive to the Admiralty on the *Zong*. I have demonstrated the many ways in which Hoare's text is inaccurate. Additionally, as a fair copy of the missive to the Admiralty, the BL manuscript is more authoritative than the NMM draft and should be considered as closer to the original—presumably lost—version of the missive that Sharp actually sent to the Admiralty. Sharp intended to publish the BL document, and not the NMM document upon which the Hoare and Lyall transcriptions are based; Sharp perforce viewed the BL manuscript as a definitive version of his missive to the Admiralty. Serious scholarship on this episode in the history of slavery and abolition should be performed on the BL document, rather than on any version of the NMM document.

Sharp's missive to the Admiralty at the BL explicitly reveals Sharp's character, beliefs, intentions, and motivations in the cause of abolition. G. M. Ditchfield, author of the *ODNB* entry for Sharp, comments,

> Although Sharp was never a popular or even accessible writer, his work was of immense importance to the anti-slavery movement in Britain. It was partly through his efforts that it gained public attention and sympathy and that it transformed itself from a benign climate of opinion to a highly organized campaign. Thomas Clarkson regarded him as a founder of the

[61] Sharp, BL document, 1.
[62] Hoare, *Memoirs*, xvii, 242, 244; Sharp, NMM document, 95, 98, 99.
[63] Please see the discussion of the ship's name on page 14.

movement; according to the Whig Francis Horner, he was one of those who had started it.[64]

Given that Sharp was one of the first, great architects of the British abolition movement, his motivations are thus also those of the anti-slavery campaign itself. The BL document clarifies Sharp's interests and intentions with respect to the *Zong* case; by learning more about these efforts, we learn more about a major episode in the history of abolition. A devastating excoriation of British officials at the highest level, the BL document revises Ditchfield's assessment of Sharp's accessibility as a writer, too. It is an exciting, straightforward, and powerful missive. If it had been published in 1783, then it surely would have been read with fascination by many members of the public.

[64]Ditchfield, "Sharp," unpag.

CHAPTER 5

The Historical Significance
of the British Library Document

Abstract This chapter shows how Sharp's letter to the Admiralty came to be lost in the British Library by tracing its path through the libraries of two private collectors, the British Museum, and finally the British Library. It also advances several possible explanations for why the manuscript letter was inappropriately bound in a compiled volume of printed pamphlets and ends with a discussion of the other way in which the *Zong* case has remained hidden in text: historians have often misreported the facts of the case. The chapter then moves to consider the ramifications of the argument that Sharp's interest in publishing on slavery did not end in 1777, as scholars have assumed. It also explores an alternative history for the *Zong* case and abolition by considering what would have happened if Sharp had been successful in publishing the British Library letter, and it advances possible reasons for why Sharp never followed through with his plans to publish the letter to the Admiralty.

Keywords Archives · British Library · Revisionist history
Granville Sharp · Alternative history · Abolition · Quakers
Society for the Abolition of the Slave Trade

1   THE BURIAL OF THE BRITISH LIBRARY DOCUMENT AND THE TRUTH OF THE *ZONG*

Sharp's handwritten, fair-copy manuscript of his missive on the *Zong* to the Admiralty was doomed to archival burial in the British Library. Tuppen provides an informative explanation regarding how it became, in effect, lost in the Library's collections:

> The complete contents of the volume (including item 2, the Sharp item) were catalogued by the British Museum when the volume was acquired in the 19th century. We know this because there is a cataloguer's mark on the end page of item 2, and "Sharp" is underlined to show that a handwritten catalogue entry was made under his name. In the 19th century, cataloguing was done onto paper slips. At a later stage the slips were typed up to form the printed catalogue. However, the catalogue information for item 2 appears to have been overlooked when the British Museum printed books catalogue was created in the 19th century, as item 2 does not appear in the catalogue. It might be because the item is in manuscript, and the 19th-century cataloguer did not think it should be included in the books catalogue. For whatever reason, the Sharp document has never appeared in our printed catalogues and therefore has not been included in the online catalogue either. With many millions of items in the collection, no one had discovered that this particular item remained uncatalogued.[1]

After the cataloguer at the British Museum (the BL's predecessor body) noticed, but failed to record in print, the manuscript's odd presence in *Tracts 35*, the missive to the Admiralty became effectively lost in the BL.

Anyone looking for information on abolition, Sharp, or the *Zong* case would have no reason to search in *Tracts 35*, a volume comprised mostly of published medical pamphlets. So, why did the unknown compiler and binder of the volume neglect to separate Sharp's handwritten manuscript from the considerably less valuable printed pamphlets that surround it in *Tracts 35*? Several possible answers—including that the compiler was simply careless—present themselves. Working for Lettsom, he (and the compiler was almost certainly a man) must have created *Tracts 35* after Lettsom bought Baker's library in 1785, given that both Baker's and Lettsom's items are in the volume. Moreover, it is evident that the

---

[1] Sandra Tuppen, e-mails to the author from the British Library, June 18, 29, July 1, 2015.

volume was created before 1827, when the completed volume arrived at the British Museum. Other information about the sale of Lettsom's library indicates that *Tracts 35* was created earlier than 1815. Writing in *The Gentleman's Magazine* from 1815, Urban confirms not only Lettsom's purchase of Baker's library, but also the sale of Lettsom's own books some time before:

> In this library also was the collection of Classics formed by the learned and modest Mr. William Baker, printer, which Dr. Lettsom purchased on the death of the collector. The reader will partake of our regret, that the Doctor should have been compelled, by a train of adverse circumstances, at an advanced period of life, to dispose of so valuable a library.[2]

This information reveals that Lettsom sold his library before 1815. Probably, then, the British Museum acquired *Tracts 35* during the sale of Lettsom's library, in which case we know that *Tracts 35* was compiled before 1815, since it was already bound upon its arrival at the British Museum. The volume could not have been bound before 1787, the first date of publication for William Roscoe's *The Wrongs of Africa* (1787–1788), which also appears in it. However, if *Tracts 35* was bound in that year, when abolitionism first became a cultural force in England, then the compiler might not have recognized Sharp's early contributions to an abolitionist movement that was only beginning to materialize. It is conceivable that the compiler was plagued by ignorance regarding the missive's importance and did not think it valuable enough to separate it from the printed pamphlets in the volume.

However, if the volume was bound well after 1787 (but before 1815), an alternative explanation for this bibliographic mystery arises. It may be that the compiler was indeed aware of the manuscript's significance and did not wish to draw attention to it. He may have viewed it as an ugly reminder of British inhumanity, as did the Quakers and many other anti-slavery writers who mention the *Zong* case, as discussed in Chapter 2; after all, the missive contains Sharp's demands that the Admiralty bring numerous murder charges against the crew of the *Zong*, but these

---

[2] Sylvanus Urban, "Dr. John Coakley Lettsom, M.D.," *The Gentleman's Magazine, and Historical Chronicle*, vol. 85, pt. 2, issue 114 (London: Nichols, Son, and Bentley, 1815), 469–73, 471, *Google eBooks*, accessed July 17, 2015, https://books.google.ca/books/about/The_Gentleman_s_Magazine.html?id=oiM3AAAAYAAJ&redir_esc=y.

demands for justice went unanswered. In this case, the careless compilation of the BL document with printed matter of much less historical value may thus be regarded as a kind of active forgetting—a bibliographical suppression of national shame. It may also be that the compiler did not support abolishing slavery and therefore did not wish to highlight Sharp's powerful call for justice. Drescher argues that the lack of attention given to the *Zong* case demonstrates how reticent Britons were to engage with the abolitionist project at the time: "There is probably no better evidence of the difficulty of politicizing the abolitionist message after the silence of the war years than the muted public reaction to the *Zong* atrocity."[3] Perhaps, then, the compiler simply did not care about the plight of enslaved Africans and did not think the manuscript worthy of more selective handling.

Sharp's fair-copy missive at the BL was effectively buried between numerous other printed pamphlets in *Tracts 35*, while the volume itself became entombed among the other 56 million items in the Library.[4] In *Specters of the Atlantic*, Baucom calls for

> what is long past overdue: a return to the *Zong*, the sign it writes into the history of the modern, the state of history it reveals. And one way to begin to read that sign is to return, at last, to the decision that ... Granville Sharp made in identifying ... the *Zong* massacre as the age's decisive truth event, the decision he made in putting pen to paper and dispatching to the Lords Commissioners of the Admiralty his account of this event and the awful truth it demonstrated.[5]

This "awful truth" is none other than the official British acceptance—even sanction—of mass murder for financial gain. Shockingly, the failure of the Admiralty to punish the crew of the *Zong* for committing mass murder is the lesser outrage in this history. Much worse is that the slavers—the owners of the *Zong* and their employees—were to be *rewarded* with insurance money for the murder of 132 people. That the Gregson

[3] Seymour Drescher, "The Shocking Birth of British Abolitionism," *Slavery & Abolition* 33, no. 4 (2012): 571–93, 575.

[4] Anon., "Help for Researchers," *British Library*, accessed June 23, 2015, http://www.bl.uk/reshelp/findhelprestype/catblhold/all/major/majorcats.html.

[5] Ian Baucom, *Specters of the Atlantic: Finance Capital, Slavery, and the Philosophy of History* (Durham and London: Duke University Press, 2005), 123.

slave-owning syndicate was, evidently, never paid out after the underwriters' appeal is beside the point. What is significant is that, in a jury trial presided over by Lord Mansfield, the Lord Chief Justice of the country, the mass murder of enslaved people was officially declared remunerable.

So appalling is this truth that historians, British and otherwise, have refused to recognize it and have covered it with untruths that suggest a group shame extending beyond British borders. As early as 1836, Charles Stuart asserts in *A Memoir of Granville Sharp* that Mansfield "granted a new trial," and that "The result [of the new trial], was a verdict in favour of the underwriters."[6] However, the truth is that the insurers were in no way the victors in the insurance trial, the only trial on the *Zong* that ever happened and for which Mansfield granted only an appeal. Oldham comments, "No evidence has been discovered to show that a new trial was ever conducted."[7] In 1962, over a century after Stuart's text appeared, Daniel P. Mannix misleadingly claims that Mansfield "found for the underwriters" and asserts, "It was the first case in which an English court ruled that a cargo of slaves could not be treated simply as merchandise."[8] Since the *Zong* insurance trial was the earliest to deal with collecting insurance money for the mass jettisoning of human "cargo," it was, in fact, the first case in which an English court ruled that a cargo of enslaved people *could* be treated simply as merchandise, to turn Mannix's statement to its opposite and more accurate meaning.[9] Nor was the *Zong* massacre the last time enslaved Africans

---

[6]Charles Stuart, *A Memoir of Granville Sharp* (New York: American Anti-Slavery Society, 1836), 30–1, *Google eBooks*, accessed June 17, 2015, https://books.google.ca/books?id=eNxeks9xld4C.

[7]James Oldham, "Insurance Litigation Involving the *Zong* and Other British Slave Ships, 1780–1807," *Journal of Legal History* 28, no. 3 (2007): 299–318, 318n; see also Dave Gunning, *Race and Antiracism in Black British and British Asian Literature* (Liverpool: Liverpool University Press, 2010), 46.

[8]Daniel P. Mannix and Malcolm Cowley, *Black Cargoes: A History of the Atlantic Slave Trade 1518–1865* (New York: Penguin, 1962), 126–7. See Shyllon and Weisbord on Mannix's erroneous reportage of the *Zong* history (F. O. Shyllon, *Black Slaves in Britain* (London and New York: Oxford University Press, 1974), 192; Robert Weisbord, "The Case of the Slave-Ship *Zong*, 1783," *History Today* 19, no. 8 (1969): 561–7, 564). Notably, Mannix does not appear to have obtained his incorrect information on the *Zong* case from Stuart's early text, as he does not cite it in his work.

[9]Jane Webster, "The *Zong* in the Context of the Eighteenth-Century Slave Trade," *Journal of Legal History* 28, no. 3 (2007): 285–98, 298.

were treated as inanimate "cargo."[10] Finally, as recently as 2006, Lars Eckstein reports, "Sharp ... managed to bring the *Zong* case to court, where Collingwood and his crew, with enormous public interest, were put on trial before Judge Lord Mansfield."[11] Contrary to Eckstein's account, the slavers themselves—the Gregson syndicate who owned the *Zong*—were the ones to bring the case to court, not Sharp, and they did so in order to collect the insurance money for their lost "cargo" of 132 murdered Africans. Nor was Collingwood present in court at any time, having died in Jamaica shortly after the landing of the *Zong* in 1781. (Even Shyllon, an otherwise careful scholar, states, "On Collingwood's return to England, the owners of the *Zong* claimed from the insurers the full value of the murdered slaves.")[12] Weisbord calls Mannix's falsification of the *Zong*'s history "retrospective wishful thinking,"[13] but the repeated, conspicuous, and logically inexplicable nature of these historical fabrications, however inadvertently committed, suggests an attachment to an invented history of Britain—one that parallels the invented history of Mansfield as an abolitionist hero.[14]

The history of slavery and abolition has been shaped by, and suffered from, such resistance to the truth. Brown surmises that most Britons "resisted, for a time, thinking of the slave trade as a national crime. The very idea conflicted with what the British knew, or thought they knew, about the character of their overseas enterprise. In the public imagination, the British Empire was defined by its commitment to liberty."[15] Evidence of British belief in its devotion to liberty is everywhere in the nation's literary texts, such as in James Thomson's famous poem from 1740, "Rule, Britannia!," which announces,

---

[10] E.g. James Walvin, *The Zong: A Massacre, the Law & the End of Slavery* (New Haven and London: Yale University Press, 2011), 201–2. See page 22 for more on other slave-ship massacres.

[11] Lars Eckstein, *Re-membering the Black Atlantic: On the Poetics and Politics of Literary Memory* (Amsterdam: Editions Rodopi, 2006), 122.

[12] Shyllon, *Black Slaves*, 186.

[13] Weisbord, "Case," 564.

[14] Please see the discussion of Mansfield's abolitionist legacy beginning on page 32.

[15] Christopher Leslie Brown, *Moral Capital: Foundations of British Abolitionism* (Chapel Hill: University of North Carolina Press, 2012), 155.

The nations, not so blest as thee,
Must, in their turns, to tyrants fall;
While thou shalt flourish great and free,
The dread and envy of them all.
"Rule, ... [Britannia, rule the waves;
Britons never will be slaves."][16]

Thomson lauds Britain as immune to tyranny and slavery in its devotion to freedom—but it seems such characteristics only served native Britons since the mid-sixteenth century, when British involvement with the slave trade began. This truth hardly made a dint in the popular view of the national character, though, as is revealed in Henry Homes' (Lord Kames) encomium upon it from 1774, at the height of the slave trade:

The English are noted for love of liberty: they cannot bear oppression; and they know no bounds to resentment against oppressors. ... [N]o people are more noted for humanity: in no other nation do sympathetic affections prevail more: none are more ready in cases of distress to stretch out a relieving hand. Did not the English, in abolishing the horrid barbarity of torture, give an illustrious example of humanity to all other nations?[17]

Even more to the point are William Blackstone's remarks on how the British love of liberty is indivisible from Britishness itself. These comments are particularly notable here because they pertain to the status of enslaved people in England and were, in fact, quoted by Francis Hargrave, Somerset's lawyer, during the trial attended by Sharp and over which Mansfield presided: "this spirit of liberty is so deeply implanted in our constitution, and rooted even in our very soil, that a Slave or a Negro, the moment he lands in England, falls under the protection of

---

[16]James Thomson, "Rule, Brittania!" *The Poetical Works of James Thomson*, ed. W. M. Rossetti (London: Ward, Lock, & Co., 1880), 498–9, lines 7–11.

[17]Henry Home (Lord Kames), *Sketches of the History of Man Considerably Enlarged by the Last Additions and Corrections of the Author* (1774, 1778), 3 vols., ed. and intro. James A. Harris (Indianapolis: Liberty Fund, 2007), vol. 1, 344n, accessed August 30, 2017, http://oll.libertyfund.org/titles/kames-sketches-of-the-history-of-man-vol-1.

the laws, and with regard to all natural rights becomes *eo instanti* [at that moment] a freeman," to which is added, however, in the second edition of Blackstone's *Commentaries*, "though the Master's right to his service may possibly still continue."[18] Britons' belief in their own beneficence and commitment to liberty precluded their acceptance of their nation's considerable involvement in the slave trade. The British National Archives reports that Britain, "Together with Portugal, ... accounted for about 70% of all Africans transported to the Americas. Britain was the most dominant between 1640 and 1807 and it is estimated that Britain transported 3.1 million Africans (of whom 2.7 million arrived) to the British colonies in the Caribbean, North and South America and to other countries."[19] In the face of such overwhelming evidence, national self-deception about slavery continued.

We worry today about the political implications of information bubbles or "filter bubbles" in our access to news on the internet—that we only read the news that confirms our present beliefs, leaving us uninformed about the broader truth. Evidently, though, this problem is far from new. Slavery was allowed to proliferate so long in British history in part because Britons refused to recognize their considerable contribution to it. This culture of silence may have contributed to the burial of the BL document, too.

2   (RE)WRITING HISTORY

Abolitionists were aware of the danger that such ignorance presented to their cause. Clarkson writes in 1808,

> I attempted ... to show, that, though the sin of the Slave-trade had been hitherto a sin of ignorance, and might therefore have so far been winked at, yet as the crimes and miseries belonging to it became known, it would

[18] Quoted in James Oldham, *The Mansfield Manuscripts and the Growth of English Law in the Eighteenth Century* (Chapel Hill: University of North Carolina Press, 1992), vol. 2, 1233; Oldham quotes William Blackstone's *Commentaries on the Laws of England* (William Blackstone, *Commentaries on the Laws of England*, 4 vols. (Oxford: Clarendon, 1765–1769), vol. 1, 123). Oldham notes that it is uncertain who added the final phrase (1233).

[19] Anon., "British Transatlantic Slave Trade Records," *The National Archives*, accessed August 4, 2017, http://www.nationalarchives.gov.uk/help-with-your-research/researchguides/british-transatlantic-slave-trade-records/.

attach even to those who had no concern in it, if they suffered it to continue either without notice or reproach, or if they did not exert themselves in a reasonable manner for its suppression.[20]

The debate about the slave trade raged for far too long—sixteen years— in Parliament, while British slavery itself continued until 1833, but it must be noted that the popular spirit of abolitionism followed closely upon the broad dissemination of information about slavery. This causal pattern encourages questions about the potential course history might have taken if Sharp had succeeded in publishing his account of the *Zong* massacre, as I have argued was his intention when he sent the BL manuscript to Baker, his publisher. Webster's claim that Sharp's "transcript of the [trial] proceedings [in the NMM] is an invaluable document ... [and] nothing less than an artifact of the beginning of the end of the slave trade" is worth recalling here.[21] The same may also be said of the BL document, the rousing response of an influential anti-slavery campaigner to an iconic case in the history of slavery and abolition. Had Sharp's missive been widely accessible before Hoare's published transcription of it in the *Memoirs* of 1820, it might well have accelerated the historical course of abolition, which was shamefully slow. British Parliament rejected the first bill to abolish the trade in human flesh by an almost two-to-one vote in 1791; it was only in 1807 that both the Houses of Commons and Lords passed the Slave-Trade Act. The Slavery Abolition Act was finally passed in 1833, forty-two years after Parliament first considered abolishing the slave trade—and fifty years after Sharp wrote the BL missive to the Admiralty. We can never know if the publication of Sharp's letter would have hastened the abolition of slavery, but it surely would have attracted wide notice to the issue, given Sharp's spectacular claims: the missive categorizes the *Zong* incident as mass murder and holds British officials responsible for handling it appropriately, urging these authorities to deliver justice for the horrendous crimes. The publication of the missive would also have documented that Sharp's plea for justice was not answered, which would have imbued it with special urgency—and, presumably, its readers with a sense of outrage. Had Sharp's letter been published, the end of slavery might well have come sooner.

---

[20] Thomas Clarkson, *The History of the Rise, Progress, and Accomplishment of the Abolition of the African Slave-Trade, by the British Parliament*, 2 vols. (London: Longman, Hurst, Rees, and Orme, 1808), vol. 1, 423, *Online Library of Liberty*, accessed August 28, 2017, http://oll.libertyfund.org/titles/clarkson-the-history-of-the-abolition-of-the-african-slave-trade-vol-1.

[21] Webster, "Context," 295.

The *Zong* case became emblematic of the horrors of slavery once the abolitionism movement of the late 1780s was established, but, as Drescher notes, "The British public could read very little on the matter [of abolition or the *Zong*] before 1787. The *Zong* massacre became notorious after the mobilisation of abolitionism."[22] The amount of information about the *Zong* incident certainly was essential to its impact on the popular view of the slave trade, but the manner in which this information was conveyed is also worth considering. If Sharp's two-part missive to the Admiralty had been published, then it surely would have attracted much more attention to the *Zong* case than did any of the other publications about it, for Sharp's account is the most engaging and enraging of all. Of the monographs that mention the *Zong*, which I discuss in Chapter 2, not one provides the level of reliability and detail—not to mention irresistible passion—that Sharp includes in his missive to the Admiralty. None of these writers witnessed the *Zong* case being played out in a court of law as Sharp did when he attended the hearing for an appeal in May of 1783; based on transcriptions of this hearing, for which Sharp paid dearly, as well as personal discussions he held with witnesses to (and perhaps perpetrators of) the *Zong* massacre, Sharp's missive to the Admiralty stands as the longest, most trustworthy, and most accessible documentation of it. The BL document moreover establishes an undeniable fact about Britain in 1783: that the mass murder of enslaved Africans was not only accepted but rewarded on an official level.

Arguably, were it not for Sharp's involvement with the case, it might have gone unnoticed as merely another dispute over insurance, for the capital crime of murder was not mentioned until the hearing for an appeal. Webster remarks, "It is not unreasonable to argue that Sharp's presence in court—and [the] knowledge of his ongoing efforts to instigate criminal proceedings—had a significant bearing on the tone and language of the May 1783 hearing. Murder had been on no one's mind at the Guildhall sessions two months before, but that word was used nine times in the King's Bench."[23] Sharp's calculated use of the word "murder" in his missive to the Admiralty—27 times in 15 pages—changes the focus of the *Zong* case from the insurance of "cargo" to an atrocity, justice for which he demanded from the highest officials in the British navy. In his opening words to the Lords Commissioners of the Admiralty, Sharp leaves no room for an alternate interpretation of the significance of the *Zong* incident:

[22] Drescher, "Shocking," 576, 591.

[23] Webster, "Context," 295.

As the cognizance and right of enquiry concerning all Murders committed on board British Ships belongs properly to the Admiralty Department, I think it my Duty to lay before your Lordships two Manuscript Accounts wherein are stated from unquestionable authority the circumstances of a most inhuman and barbarous murder committed by Luke Collingwood the Master, Colonel James Kelsall, the Mate, and other persons, the Mariners or Crew of the Ship Zong or Zurg a Liverpool Trader freighted with Slaves &c. from the Coast of Africa.[24]

If Sharp had succeeded in publishing the BL document, then the language of ethics and human rights that permeates his missive to the Lords Commissioners of the Admiralty would have reached a wider audience and at a much earlier time than it did when Hoare published his transcription of it in 1820.

There is evidence that the British public was primed to respond positively to such an entreaty around the time that Sharp wrote his missive to the Admiralty. Only nine years later, many Britons responded with horrified fascination and outrage at the well-publicized trial of Captain John Kimber, who was tried for the murder of two African girls during the Middle Passage.[25] In "Reporting Atrocities: A Comparison of the Zong and the Trial of Captain John Kimber," Swaminathan compares the explosion of public interest in the 1792 Kimber trial with the lack of response to the Zong trial.[26] The Kimber trial probably captured the public imagination more than did the Zong case because Britons were by that time more aware of and responsive to abolitionist issues, which had been circulating widely since 1787. It is also notable that Kimber's crime—in one case whipping a girl to death while hanging her from her feet—garnered more interest from British readers because the victims were helpless young females, easy to imagine in their individuality and sympathize with in their femininity. Swaminathan comments about the reportage of the Kimber trial: "Each victim's age and physical condition

---

[24] Granville Sharp, [BL document, Copy of a Letter to Lords Commissioners of the Admiralty] "Paper by Glanville [sic] Sharp on the Case of 132 Murdered Negroes," in *Tracts 35* (Old Jewry, London, MS: n.p., July 2, 1783), 1.

[25] Srividhya Swaminathan, "Reporting Atrocities: A Comparison of the Zong and the Trial of Captain John Kimber," *Slavery & Abolition* 31, no. 4 (2010): 483–99, 484, 483.

[26] Swaminathan, "Atrocities," 483.

are marked, perhaps indicating that cruelty knows no boundaries, and Kimber disrespects each stage of womanhood. Age and gender are relevant in these descriptions insomuch as they may elicit greater sympathy in the reader."[27] I agree that the reading public was fascinated by the victims' femaleness, since Western culture—and particularly the popular eighteenth-century literature of sensibility—labels women as weak and in need of care, rendering Kimber's brutal treatment of these girls especially repugnant.

Brycchan Carey's excellent study *British Abolitionism and the Rhetoric of Sensibility: Writing, Sentiment and Slavery, 1760–1807* (2005) establishes convincingly the major role played by sentiment in the history of the anti-slavery movement in Britain, such as in Ramsay's *An Essay on the Treatment and Conversion of African Slaves in the British Sugar Colonies* from 1784, in which the author refers "to Granville Sharp and hold[s] him up as a sentimental hero, a model of active philanthropy, whose benevolence should be generally imitated," Carey comments.[28] Having been encouraged to exercise their powers of sensibility in response to anti-slavery texts for several years by the time of the Kimber trial in 1792, the British public was primed to respond with sympathy—a major aspect of literary sensibility—to the plight of the tortured and murdered African girls. Yet, in 1783, the year of the *Zong* trial and Sharp's letter to the Admiralty, the British public had not yet been taught by the popular abolition movement to identify the sufferings of kidnapped Africans in the slave trade as key targets for the exercise of their sympathy. Citing William Cowper's false claim that he was the first writer on abolition, Carey points out that the poet "had written lines clearly opposed to the slave trade as early as 1782"; since Cowper was one of the first to approach the topic in a sentimental style, though, readers were not yet accustomed to respond with vehement sympathy to such events as the *Zong* massacre.[29] This readership may also have found it more difficult to imagine the individual—and only partially feminine—tragedies that played out in the *Zong* massacre, given the great number of victims. Despite these important differences

[27] Swaminathan, "Atrocities," 491.

[28] Brycchan Carey, *British Abolitionism and the Rhetoric of Sensibility: Writing, Sentiment and Slavery, 1760–1807* (New York: Palgrave Macmillan, 2005), 112–13.

[29] Carey, *Sensibility*, 98.

between the cases, though, the fact that the Kimber trial attracted so much broad interest in 1792 suggests that Sharp's BL document might have attracted widespread sympathy for the abolitionist cause around this time, had he succeeded in publishing it. Focusing on the *Zong* massacre alone—a method replicated only in the newspaper article on the case in the *Morning Chronicle and London Advertiser* from 18 March 1783— Sharp's lengthy, outraged missive appeals to the reader in a way that no other period publication on the *Zong* does.

According to my research, Sharp published nothing devoted solely to the *Zong* case. Understandably, he did not want to publish his missive before the Admiralty had time to respond to it, but, when Baker died in 1785, the time would have been ripe for its publication. Even if the BL document was no longer accessible to him, Sharp could have composed another publishable copy of the missive from the document that Hoare transcribed for his *Memoirs*, now in the National Maritime Museum (NMM), but he did not do so. Why did he not advance his apparent plans to publish the BL missive to the Admiralty after 1785? Sharp might have felt disheartened after the failure of his remarkable efforts to obtain justice for the 132 murder victims of the *Zong*, not to mention the non-return of his valuable "Vouchers" from the Admiralty. It could be, too, that he eventually became too busy with his duties as the Chairman of the Society for the Abolition of the African Slave Trade and the Sierra Leone project to devote more time to publishing his letter to the Admiralty. Sharp may also have had misgivings about advancing this publication, as it implicated the powerful West India slavers, the Lords Commissioners of the Admiralty, and the top legal representatives in Britain in the acceptance of and reward for mass murder. I do not suggest that Sharp was personally afraid of his opponents, for he should be taken at his word when he claims in a letter that he considers it beneath him to hide his opinions when they could advance a worthy cause.[30] Certainly, publicizing the particulars of the *Zong* case could have advanced the cause of justice, but Sharp may have thought that this

[30] Prince Hoare, *Memoirs of Granville Sharp, Esq. Composed from His Own Manuscripts, and Other Authentic Documents in the Possession of His Family Authentic Documents in the Possession of His Family and of the African Institution* (London: Henry Colburn, 1820), 100, *Google eBooks*, accessed June 25, 2015–August 30, 2017, https://books.google.ca/books?id=PrUEAAAAIAAJ; also in Shyllon, *Black Slaves*, 120.

radical move could undermine the abolitionist cause and possibly even set the undecided against it. To be sure, Sharp's letter is bolder than most abolitionist publications of its time: unlike many accounts of the *Zong* case from the 1780s, Sharp's letter identifies by name each major player in the case, firmly laying responsibility for the crimes and injustices at the feet of the guilty individuals and groups, including the Admiralty itself, should it not prosecute the murders.

Sharp might well have helped to advance the anti-slavery cause by publishing his letter to the Admiralty shortly after he wrote it, at the height of abolitionist sentiment. Certainly, as Ramsay notes, Sharp was one of the few writers of his time who were willing to sacrifice their own comfort and safety to the "rage" of the "oppressor" and "relieve the sufferings of the wretched slave."[31] Again, then, we must ask: why did he not do so? It is not likely that Sharp was daunted by the prospect of publishing a text that he had composed some years before, as is evident from the 1805 publication of his work *Serious Reflections on the Slave Trade and Slavery, Wrote in March 1797*, which demonstrates that he was willing to publish work that was at least eight years old. Theoretically, then, he would have been willing to publish his letter to the Admiralty until at least 1791. However, those years presented their own obstacles to such a venture: opposition to anti-slavery activists had built to a dangerous pitch by that time. Indeed, later in the eighteenth century, pro-slavery advocates put increasing and even threatening pressure on abolitionists by linking Sharp, Benezet, and Clarkson with the French Revolutionaries through their contacts with the *Amis des Noirs*, such as Jacques-Pierre Brissot de Warville (1754–1793), abolitionists in France. Significantly, so-called "Jacobin" sympathy was an offence punishable by jail or worse in Britain at that time.[32] Even more alarmingly, after the Haitian slave revolution in 1791, slavers—who euphemistically called themselves "West Indian planters" in the newspapers—accused

---

[31] James Ramsay, *An Essay on the Treatment and Conversion of African Slaves in the British Sugar Colonies* (London: James Phillips, 1784), 105.

[32] "Scrutator," *Morning Chronicle and London Advertiser*, London, December 11, 1788 [links to letter from 6 March 1792], issue 6113, unpag., *17th–18th Century Burney Collection Newspapers*, accessed July 11, 2017. Brissot (the "de Warville" is commonly dropped) would become a leader of the Girondins in Revolutionary France and was guillotined.

abolitionists of counselling enslaved Africans in the Caribbean to murder them.[33] While Sharp may have thought it was beneath him to withhold his abolitionist sentiments with respect to his personal safety, he may have reasoned that—should his publication of the letter to the Admiralty result in his incarceration or worse, thereby hindering his fight for abolition—he would not be advancing the cause of justice.[34]

Nevertheless, the years following 1783 should have been a fortuitous time for Sharp to have published his letter to the Admiralty on the *Zong*. The Quakers began to organize their powerful public opposition to slavery in the same year as the letter's composition:

> In June 1783, just months after the conclusion of the American War of Independence, the Religious Society of Friends, then ending its annual summer gathering in London, presented a petition to the House of Commons. Signed by 273 Quakers, this petition called for abolition of the British traffic in African men, women, and children.[35]

W. O. Blake, an American writer, provides a short account of the long history of anti-slavery sentiment among the Quakers in his text from 1861, noting that "George Fox, the venerable founder of the society of the Quakers, took strong and decided ground against the slave-trade. ... When he was in the island of Barbadoes, in the year 1671, he delivered himself to those who attended his religious meetings" to reject slavery, and in 1727 the Quakers in London took the "resolution" to reject the slave trade altogether, which was followed with the pronouncement in 1761 that any Quaker who was a slave-owner would be expelled from Quaker society.[36] The Quaker method of abolition was successful in part because they published their abolitionist sentiments widely in newspapers and with presses owned and operated by Quakers, with the result that "Every major antislavery tract printed in England from 1783

[33] Anon., *Diary or Woodfall's Register*, London, August 13, 1789, issue 118, unpag., Gale: *17th–18th Century Burney Collection Newspapers*, accessed June 16, 2017; Anon., *Morning Chronicle*, unpag.

[34] Hoare, *Memoirs*, 100; also in Shyllon, *Black Slaves*, 120.

[35] Brown, *Moral*, 1.

[36] W. O. Blake, *The History of Slavery and the Slave Trade, Ancient and Modern* (Columbus, OH: H. Miller, 1861), 169, 170.

through 1787 came off the presses of Quaker printer James Phillips,"
Brown notes.[37] Through their shared interest in advancing abolition,
Sharp was in close contact with the Quakers, having corresponded
since the early 1770s with Benezet, through whom he began a correspondence with Benjamin Rush, and then as a founding member of the
Society for the Abolition of the African Slave Trade in 1787, of which
most of the founding members were Quakers.[38] After Sharp's plans to
publish the BL document with Baker were derailed—perhaps by the latter's death in 1785—he, presumably, might have approached Phillips,
the Quakers' main publisher, with the work. After all, Phillips published
abolitionist works by other non-Quakers, such as Ramsay's *Essay* from
1784.[39] However, the Quaker approach to the cause was considerably
less aggressive than was Sharp's. If he had offered his missive to the
Admiralty to a Quaker press, then the editor might have rejected it out-
right as too antagonistic—although Sharp's uncharacteristic call in the
Admiralty missive to put "an entire stop to the Slave Trade," rather than
slavery as a whole, suggests that he was trying to ameliorate his position somewhat, perhaps in order to garner Quaker support for his effort
to obtain justice for the *Zong* murders.[40] (He received it from at least
one Quaker: Dillwyn, an American, reportedly "hoped in 1783 that the
Zong case would go some way toward exposing the inhumanities of the
traffic" in humans.)[41] If the BL missive had gone to press in the 1780s,
then the publication would have been unparalleled in its boldness and
the truths it reveals about the British slave trade, as well as the unique

[37] Brown, *Moral*, 426.

[38] Hoare, *Memoirs*, 118.

[39] J. Watt, "Ramsay, James (1733–1789)," *Oxford Dictionary of National Biography* (Oxford: Oxford University Press, 2004), unpag., accessed August 28, 2017, https://doi.org/10.1093/ref:odnb/23086.

[40] Sharp, BL document, 15.

[41] Brown, *Moral*, 426.

evidence it provides regarding the villainy of British officials at the highest levels, both in the military and the law. Its potential effects on the history of abolition are impossible to ascertain, though. Perhaps the missive would have met with the same paucity of response that Sharp's other abolitionist texts did, in contrast with the less combative publications of the Quakers.

Nevertheless, the argument that Sharp makes in the letter to the Admiralty and the evidence it provides are so striking that its burial in the archives seems equivalent to the loss of an early chance to advance the abolition of slavery. Surely its publication would have caused soul-searching at all levels of British society. Brown comments,

> several in Britain would propose that the nation, not merely individuals, bore responsibility for colonial slavery and the Atlantic slave trade. No one espoused this view during the American war with more vigor than Granville Sharp. His personal campaign for government action against slavery and the slave trade between 1772 and 1781 represented, in a proper sense, the beginnings of British abolitionism.[42]

Sharp's key positions are repeated with great power and rhetorical flourish in the missive to the Admiralty from 1783. The shocking nature of the case might have attracted supporters to Sharp's cause and helped to establish his "take no prisoners" brand of abolitionism had he succeeded in publishing it.

---

[42] Brown, *Moral*, 160.

CHAPTER 6

Conclusion: Revisiting the History of Abolition

Abstract The conclusion confirms the historical significance of the newly discovered Sharp manuscript at the British Library, arguing that it reminds us of Sharp's importance for the abolition movement and provides vital primary textual evidence of the *Zong* episode.

Keywords Abolition · Granville Sharp · Primary textual evidence Archives

With the discovery of the BL document, we are reminded of Sharp's immense energy for and dedication to the abolition of slavery—not to mention that he was one of the first to fight for the cause. This lengthy, handwritten, and meticulously crafted missive contributes greatly to our impression of the man revealed in Hoare's *Memoirs*, one who appears nearly obsessed with achieving justice for the victims of the *Zong* massacre immediately after hearing about it. Addressing the reader, Hoare writes:

> Let us first see his [Sharp's] own Manuscript notes of the transaction.

> MS. "March 19.—Gustavus Vasa [Equiano], a Negro, called on me, with an account of one hundred and thirty Negroes being thrown alive into the sea, from on board an English slave ship.

© The Author(s) 2018
M. Faubert, *Granville Sharp's Uncovered Letter and the* Zong *Massacre*,
https://doi.org/10.1007/978-3-319-92786-2_6

"20th.—Called on Dr. Bever this evening, to consult about prosecuting the murderers of the Negroes.

"21st.—Called on the Bishops of Chester [Porteus] and Peterborough, and General Oglethorpe, and Dr. Jebb.

"22d.—Ordered Messrs. Heseltine and Lushington to commence a prosecution in the Admiralty Court, against all persons concerned in throwing into the sea one hundred and thirty Negro slaves, as stated on a trial at Guildhall on the 6th of this month.[1]

Sharp clearly viewed the *Zong* incident as a watershed moment, and perhaps as one that could activate an anti-slavery movement in Britain. For three successive days after Equiano's visit, he approached many of his most illustrious contacts, as well as some influential new acquaintances, to tell them about the case, probably in the hope that simply hearing about the horrors of the massacre would inspire them, once and for all, to help end slavery. He had tried to enlist several of these people— Porteus, Hinchcliffe, Oglethorpe, and Jebb—in the cause during his involvement with legal cases concerning slavery in the 1770s, but he did not succeed in convincing his illustrious Anglican contacts to do their Christian duty and fight for the victims of Britain's nefarious slave trade. The shocking nature of the *Zong* case would finally inspire them to agitate for abolition, Sharp seems to have reasoned.

The *Zong* case certainly moved Sharp to throw himself into the fray again, some years after the disappointments of the 1770s, when Mansfield refused to decide clearly against slavery in the cases of Strong, Lewis, and Somerset. Sharp could only have been frustrated and disillusioned after the failures of the previous decade: despite Sharp's many passionate, indignant, and learned publications on the matter, he did not move Mansfield to recognize in a court of law that slavery was already illegal under British law. In *Appendix* from 1772, Sharp demands,

---

[1] Prince Hoare, *Memoirs of Granville Sharp, Esq. Composed from His Own Manuscripts, and Other Authentic Documents in the Possession of His Family Authentic Documents in the Possession of His Family and of the African Institution* (London: Henry Colburn, 1820), 236, *Google eBooks*, accessed June 25, 2015–August 30, 2017, https://books.google.ca/books?id=PrUEAAAAIAAJ. The source text lacks closing quotation marks.

when the Laws of the Land, and especially the Habeas Corpus Act, are expressly and clearly on one Side of the Question [of whether a human can be property under British law] … and when the only plea on the other side of the Question is absolutely without Foundation either in Natural Equity or the established Law and Customs of this Country, what room can there be for doubt? and how would a Judge be able to justify an Arrest of Judgment in such a case?[2]

However reasonable Sharp's question is, the "Judge" in question—none other than Mansfield—did "Arrest" his "Judgment in such a case," and with little justification. He merely sidestepped the question. It must have seemed to Sharp that he had learned the fine points of British law to no avail, a reasonable conclusion that would explain the six-year lacuna in Sharp's writing after 1777. And, yet, judging by his productivity after he learned of the *Zong* case in 1783, it seems that Sharp's personal devotion to abolition had not wavered, after all.

On the second day of his whirlwind tour of visits to influential leaders in March of 1783, Sharp appealed again to Bishop Beilby Porteus, as he had in the 1770s. In a text from 1807, the year that the Houses of Commons and Lords passed the Slave-Trade Act, Porteus could therefore write knowledgeably of Sharp's contributions to the anti-slavery movement. Here, Porteus appears anxious to remind his reader of Sharp's pioneering spirit and indomitable devotion to the cause:

"It ought to be remembered … in justice to a most worthy man, no less remarkable for his modesty and humility, than for his learning and piety, I mean Mr. Granville Sharp, that the first publication which drew the attention of this country to the horrors of the African trade, came from his pen; and that at his own expense, and by his own personal exertions, he liberated several Negroes from a state of slavery."[3]

---

[2] Granville Sharp, *An Appendix to the Representation: (Printed in the Year 1769) of the Injustice and Dangerous Tendency of Tolerating Slavery, or of Admitting the Least Claim of Private Property in the Persons of Men in England* (London: Benjamin White, and Robert Horsefield [sic], 1772), 19–20.

[3] Quoted in Robert Hodgson, *Works of the Right Reverend Beilby Porteus, Late Bishop of London: With His Life* (London: T. Cadell, 1823), 218, *Google eBooks*, accessed July 14, 2015, https://books.google.ca/books?id=1L4OAAAAIAAJ.

In this passage, Porteus appears concerned that history had already forgotten Sharp's efforts in the cause of anti-slavery. Meanwhile, lying dormant in the blandly titled *Tracts 35* was the seed of Sharp's greater fame, a potential publication that could have secured Sharp's reputation in the history of abolition: the fair-copy manuscript of his powerful missive to the Admiralty on the *Zong*.

Although historians dispute the direct influence of the *Zong* case on the course of abolition, it is nevertheless recognized widely as a symbol of the horrors of slavery. 2007 was the bicentenary anniversary of the abolition of the slave trade, and suddenly the *Zong* was everywhere, an unquiet ghost demanding justice. James Walvin reports that

> a replica *Zong* sailed into the port of London [in 2007]. A church ministry, the Centre for Contemporary Ministry, keen to promote awareness about the history of slavery and the slave trade, raised £300,000 for the lease of an old square rigger, the *Madagascar*—and temporarily renamed it the *Zong*. For a few weeks it was moored alongside the *HMS Belfast* in London and hosted a series of commemorations of the *Zong* killings and the slave trade.[4]

Scholars, too, recognized the occasion by invoking the *Zong* case: the *Journal of Legal History* devoted an entire volume to the exploration of it.[5] Even if the public reaction to it was muted in the eighteenth century, the *Zong*'s ongoing legacy demonstrates that Sharp correctly identified the massacre as exemplary of the horrors of slavery, both with respect to its events and its ideological assumptions. I have demonstrated that the only media account of the *Zong* massacre in the 1780s was the article that Equiano brought to Sharp when he apprised him of it. Sharp's efforts to have the crew prosecuted for murder helped to publicize the case, though; he was unsuccessful on a legal level, but Sharp nevertheless drew attention to it, such that several influential abolitionists wrote of the massacre thereafter and, according to Jane Webster, Clarkson's very career as an abolitionist writer was "surely inspired by the *Zong* tragedy."[6]

---

[4] James Walvin, *The Zong: A Massacre, the Law & the End of Slavery* (New Haven and London: Yale University Press, 2011), 207.

[5] *Journal of Legal History* 28, no. 3 (2007).

[6] Jane Webster, "The *Zong* in the Context of the Eighteenth-Century Slave Trade," *Journal of Legal History* 28, no. 3 (2007): 285–98, 296.

The shocking details of the incident would seem to ensure its salvation from historical obscurity, but the legal outcome of the case and dearth of reportage about it suggest, rather, that it would have been forgotten had Sharp not attempted to use the details of the case as evidence for the prosecution of 132 murders.

Little archival evidence exists on this iconic case in the history of abolition. Collingwood's logbook from the *Zong*'s voyage from the Cape Coast of Africa to Black River, Jamaica, is missing, as is the final missive that Sharp actually sent to the Lords Commissioners of the Admiralty. Meanwhile, the copy at the National Maritime Museum (NMM) is merely a working draft of the BL document, as I have shown. Since the BL document is the only fair copy of Sharp's two-part missive—which includes the detailed description and letter requesting that the crew of the *Zong* be prosecuted for murder—it should be consulted first by scholars of the *Zong* episode. The BL document is substantially different from the draft in the NMM, and in ways that reveal its more advanced editorial state; very likely, it is the cognate of the missive that Sharp actually mailed to the Lords Commissioners of the Admiralty. The unearthing of the BL document provides historians of abolition with a valuable and genuine artefact of the *Zong* episode.

Sharp's reputation as an abolitionist is not as eminent as it should be. Davis summarizes the common view of Sharp's anti-slavery activity in 1780s when he writes,

> Granville Sharp published seven separate tracts on parliamentary reform and another seven on the virtues of replacing a standing army with a free militia between 1777 and 1786. He wrote one on slavery [*The Law of Liberty, or, Royal Law* (1777)]. … Sharp's declining attention to the anti-slavery cause during the 1780s hints that even ardent abolitionists might need the pressure of events to sustain their commitment.[7]

However, Sharp's fervent efforts on behalf of the *Zong* victims in 1783 shows that his commitment to the anti-slavery cause remained strong into the 1780s. After attending the hearing for an appeal, he wrote letters to several important people in order to achieve justice for the victims

---

[7] David Brion Davis, *The Problem of Slavery in the Age of Revolution, 1770–1823* (Oxford: Oxford University Press, 1999), 200.

of the *Zong* and, I have shown, even planned to publish on the case. His failure to accomplish the former goal says more about the debased state of the British establishment of the time than it does about Sharp's devotion to this important cause. The BL document transforms even our most generous understanding of how far Sharp was willing to go in his campaign for the *Zong* victims, not to mention our view of the historiography of slavery in general and the *Zong* in particular.

I have established that Sharp intended to publish his letter to the Admiralty on the *Zong*. If he had accomplished his goal, then this publication would have been his only text on slavery in the 1780s and the boldest, most accessible of all of Sharp's anti-slavery publications. In it, Sharp foregoes his usual abstractions and references to the Bible to describe, in visceral terms, a contemporary event that reveals the true horrors of slavery—and he does so while naming the perpetrators of these atrocities and revealing, through the missive's very addressees, the governmental body responsible for allowing 132 murders to go unpunished. Had the BL document been published, it might well have caused an uproar on both sides of the slavery debate and perhaps even a public scandal—thereby securing Sharp's place as a great abolitionist, rather than, as he appears now, an early and unfairly overlooked figure.

Correction to: Equiano, Sharp, Mansfield, and the *Zong* Massacre: History and Significance

Correction to:
Chapter 2 in: M. Faubert, *Granville Sharp's Uncovered Letter and the* Zong *Massacre,*
https://doi.org/10.1007/978-3-319-92786-2_2

In the original version of the book, the following correction should be incorporated:

In page 57 of Chapter 2, the text "As for Sharp's significance... (And that the Society...his primacy in the Society.)" should be replaced with the newly added text "Prince Hoare... was formed in 1787", and the text "Anon., Morning Chronicle and London Advertiser, unpag." in footnote 146 should be replaced with the newly added text "Prince Hoare, Memoirs of Granville Sharp... accessed June 25, 2015–August 30, 2017, https://books.google.ca/books?id=PrUEAAAAIAAJ, 383".

The correction chapter and the book have been updated with the change.

The updated online version of this chapter can be found at
https://doi.org/10.1007/978-3-319-92786-2_2

© The Author(s) 2018
M. Faubert, *Granville Sharp's Uncovered Letter and the* Zong *Massacre,*
https://doi.org/10.1007/978-3-319-92786-2_7

APPENDIX: TRANSCRIPTION AND IMAGES OF SHARP'S MISSIVE TO THE ADMIRALTY ON THE *ZONG* AT THE BRITISH LIBRARY

© The Editor(s) (if applicable) and The Author(s) 2018

M. Faubert, *Granville Sharp's Uncovered Letter and the* Zong *Massacre*,
https://doi.org/10.1007/978-3-319-92786-2

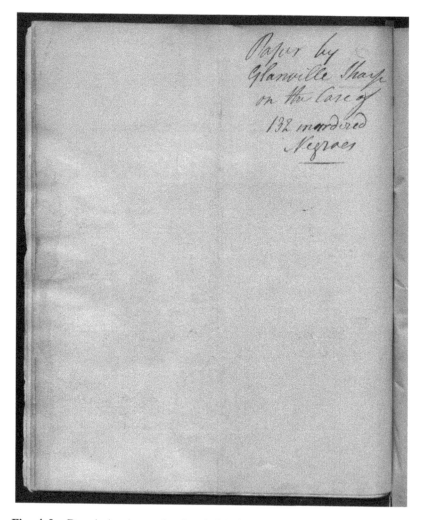

Fig. A.1 Description in another hand, BL document, © British Library Board General Reference Collection T.35.(2), folios 1–15

Paper by Glanville [sic] Sharp on the Case of 132 murdered <u>Negroes</u>[1]

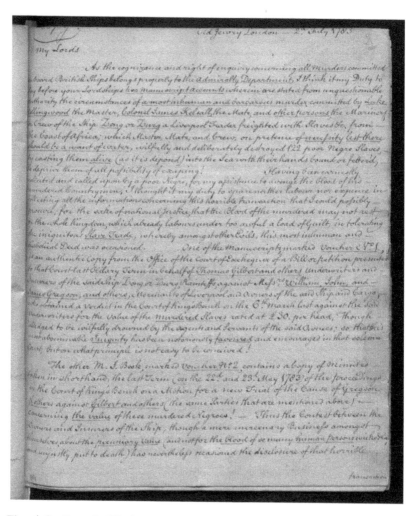

Fig. A.2 Page 1, BL document, © British Library Board General Reference Collection T.35.(2), folios 1–15

Copy.[2]   Old Jewry London – 2.[d] July 1783
My Lords

 As the cognizance and right of enquiry concerning all Murders committed on board British Ships belongs properly to the Admiralty Department,
I think it my Duty to lay before your Lordships two Manuscript Accounts
wherein are stated from unquestionable authority the circumstances of a most
inhuman and barbarous murder committed by Luke Collingwood the Master,
Colonel James Kelsall, the Mate, and other persons, the Mariners or Crew
of the Ship Zong or Zurg a Liverpool Trader freighted with Slaves &c. from
the Coast of Africa; which Master, Mate, and Crew, on pretence of necessity
lest there should be a want of water, wilfully and deliberately destroyed
122 poor Negro Slaves, by casting them alive (as it is deposed) into the
Sea with their hands bound or fetter'd, to deprive them of all possibility of escaping!   Having been earnestly solicited and called upon
by a poor Negro, for my assistance to avenge the blood of his murdered Countrymen, I thought it my duty to spare neither labour nor
expence in collecting all the information concerning this horrible transaction that I could possibly procure; for the sake of national Justice, that
the Blood of the murdered may not rest on the whole Kingdom, which
already labours under too awful a load of Guilt, in tolerating the iniquitous
Slave Trade, whereby amongst other Evils, this most inhuman and diabolical
Deed was occasioned.   One of the Manuscripts, marked Voucher N.[o] 1.,
is an authentic Copy from the Office of the Court of Exchequer of a Bill or petition presented to that Court last Hilary Term in behalf of Thomas Gilbert and
others Underwriters and Insurers of the said Ship Zong or Zurg, Plaintiffs, against
Mess.[rs] William, John, and James Gregson, and others, Merchants of Liverpool
and Owners of the said Ship and Cargo, who obtained a verdict in the Court of
King's Bench on the 6.th March last against the said Underwriters for the value
of the Murdered Slaves rated at £30. per head, Though alledged to be wilfully
drowned by the agents and Servants of the said Owners; so that this most abom-
inable Iniquity has been notoriously favoured and encouraged in that solemn
Court; but on what principle is not easy to be conceived!
 The other M.S. Book, marked Voucher N.[o] 2, contains, a Copy of
Minutes taken in shorthand, the last Term (on the 22.[d] and 23.[d] May
1783) of the proceedings in the Court of King's Bench on a Motion for
a new Trial of the Cause of Gregson & others against Gilbert and others
(the same Parties that are mentioned above) concerning the value of
these murdered Negroes! – Thus the Contest between the Owners and
Insurers of the Ship, though a mere mercenary Business amongst themselves, about the pecuniary value (and not for the blood of so many
human Persons wickedly and unjustly put to death) has nevertheless occasioned
the disclosure of that horrible

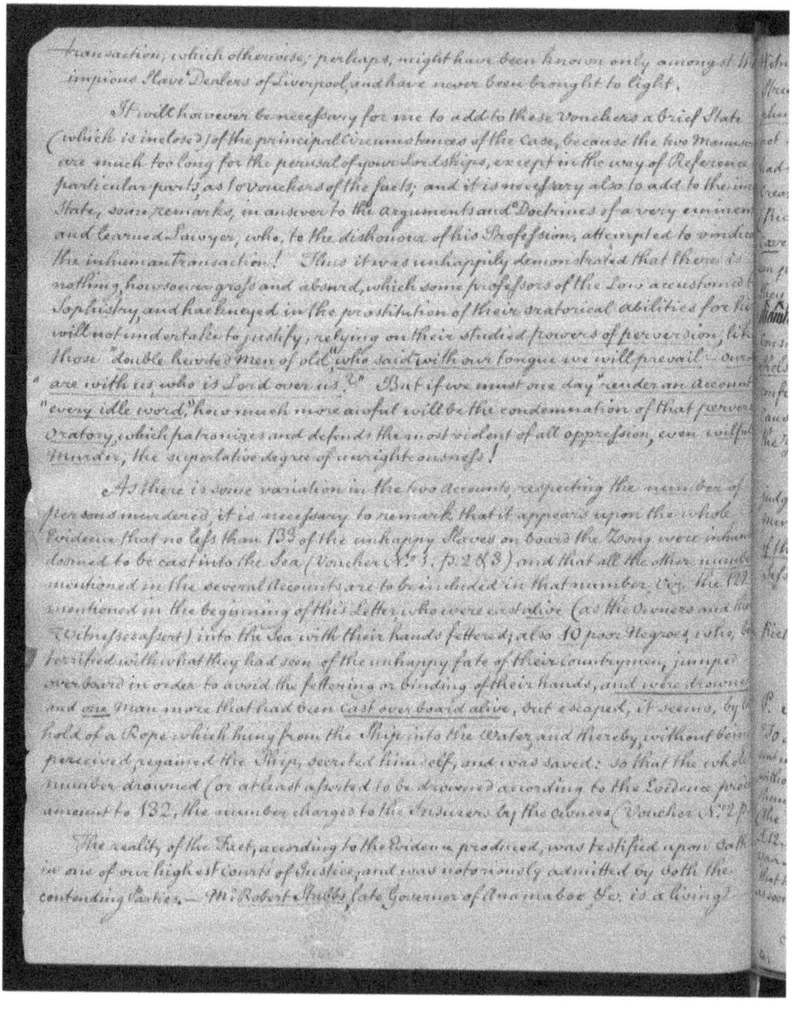

Fig. A.3 Page 2, BL document, © British Library Board General Reference Collection T.35.(2), folios 1–15

[/ 2] transaction, which otherwise; perhaps, might have been known only amongst the impious Slave Dealers of Liverpool, and have never been brought to light.

It will however be necessary for me to add to these Vouchers a brief State[ment] (which is inclosed) of the principal Circumstances of the Case, because the two Manuscripts are much too long for the perusal of your Lordships, except in the way of Reference to particular parts, as to Vouchers of the facts; and it is necessary also to add to the inclosed State[ment], some remarks, in answer to the arguments and Doctrines of a very eminent and learned Lawyer, who, to the dishonour of his Profession, attempted to vindicate the inhuman transaction! Thus it was unhappily demonstrated that there is nothing, howsoever gross and absurd, which some professors of the Law accustomed to Sophistry, and hackneyed in the prostitution of their oratorical abilities for hire, will not undertake to justify, relying on their studied <u>powers of perversion</u>, like those "<u>double hearted Men</u> of old," <u>who said ³with our tongue we will prevail – our Lips are with us, who is Lord over us</u>?" But if we must one day "<u>render an Account of</u> <u>every idle word</u>," how much more awful will be the condemnation of that <u>perverse Oratory</u>, which patronizes and defends the most violent of all <u>oppression</u>, even <u>wilful Murder</u>, the superlative degree of unrighteousness!

As there is some variation in the two Accounts, respecting the <u>number</u> of persons murdered, it is necessary to remark that it appears upon the whole Evidence that no less than 133 of the unhappy Slaves on board the Zong were inhumanly doomed to be cast into the Sea (Voucher N.º 1. P. 2 & 3) and that all the other <u>numbers</u> mentioned in the several Accounts, are to be included in that number, Viz. the 122 mentioned in the beginning of this Letter, who were cast <u>alive</u> (as the Owners and their Witnesses assert) into the Sea with their hands fettered; also <u>10</u> poor Negroes, who, being terrified with what they had seen of the unhappy fate of their Countrymen, jumped overboard in order to avoid the fettering or binding of their hands, <u>and were drowned</u>; and <u>one</u> Man more that had been <u>cast overboard alive</u>, but escaped, it seems, by laying hold of a Rope which hung from the Ship into the Water, and thereby, without being perceived, regained the Ship, secreted himself, and was saved: so that the whole number drowned (or at least asserted to be drowned according to the Evidence produced) amount to 132, the number charged to the Insurers by the Owners (Voucher N.º 2 P. 49).

The reality of the Fact, according to the Evidence produced, was testified upon Oath in one of our highest Courts of Justice; and was notoriously admitted by both the contending Parties. – M.ʳ <u>Robert Stubbs</u>, late Governor of Anamaboe, &c. is a living

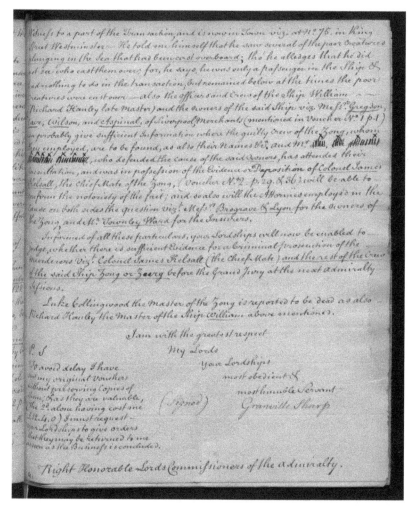

Fig. A.4 Page 3, BL document, © British Library Board General Reference Collection T.35.(2), folios 1–15

[/ 3] Witness to a part of the Transaction, and is now in Town viz. at N.º 75. in King Street Westminster – He told me himself that he saw several of the poor Creatures plunging in the Sea that had been cast overboard; tho' he alledges that he did not see who cast them over; for, he says, he was only a passenger in the Ship & had nothing to do in the transaction; but remained below at the times the poor Creatures were cast over – Also the officers and Crew of the Ship William (Richard Hanley late Master) and the Owners of the said Ship viz. Mess.ʳˢ Gregson, Cave, Wilson, and Aspinal, of Liverpool, Merchants (mentioned in Voucher N.º 1 p. 1) can probably give sufficient Information where the guilty Crew of the Zong, whom they employed, are to be found, as also their Names &cᵃ. and M.ʳ X X XX XXXX XXX⁴, who defended the cause of the said Owners, has attended their Consultation, and was in possession of the Evidence or Deposition of Colonel James Kelsall, the Chief Mate of the Zong, (Voucher N.º 2. p. 29. & 36) will be able to confirm the notoriety of the fact; and so also will the Attornies employed in the Cause on both sides the question viz.ᵗ Mess.ʳˢ Brograve & Lyon for the Owners of the Zong, and M.ʳ Townley Ward for the Insurers.

Informed of all these particulars, your Lordships will now be enabled to judge, whether there is sufficient Evidence for a Criminal prosecution of the Murderers Viz.ᵗ Colonel James Kelsall (the Chief Mate) and the rest of the Crew of the said Ship Zong or Zurg before the Grand Jury at the next Admiralty Sessions.

Luke Collingwood the Master of the Zong is reported to be dead as also Richard Hanley the Master of the Ship William above mentioned.

I am with the greatest respect

P. S   My Lords
To avoid delay I have   Your Lordships
sent my original Vouchers   most obedient &
without preserving Copies of   most humble Servant
them; & as they are valuable, (Signed)   Granville Sharp
(the 2ᵈ. alone having cost me
£12.4.0) I must request –
your Lordships to give orders
that they may be returned to me
as soon as the Business is concluded.

Right Honorable Lords Commissioners of the Admiralty.

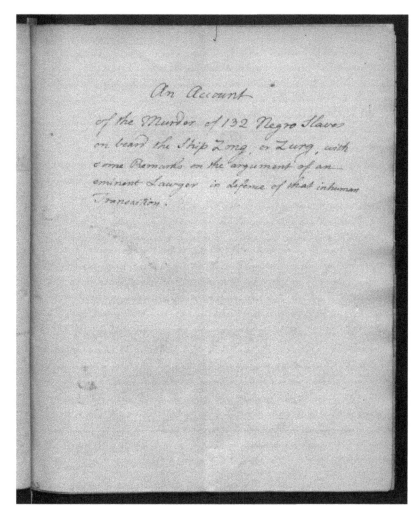

Fig. A.5 Page 4, BL document, © British Library Board General Reference Collection T.35.(2), folios 1–15

[5][/ **4**] An Account
of the Murder of 132 Negro Slaves
on board the Ship Zong, or Zurg, with
some Remarks on the argument of an
eminent Lawyer in defence of that inhuman
Transaction.

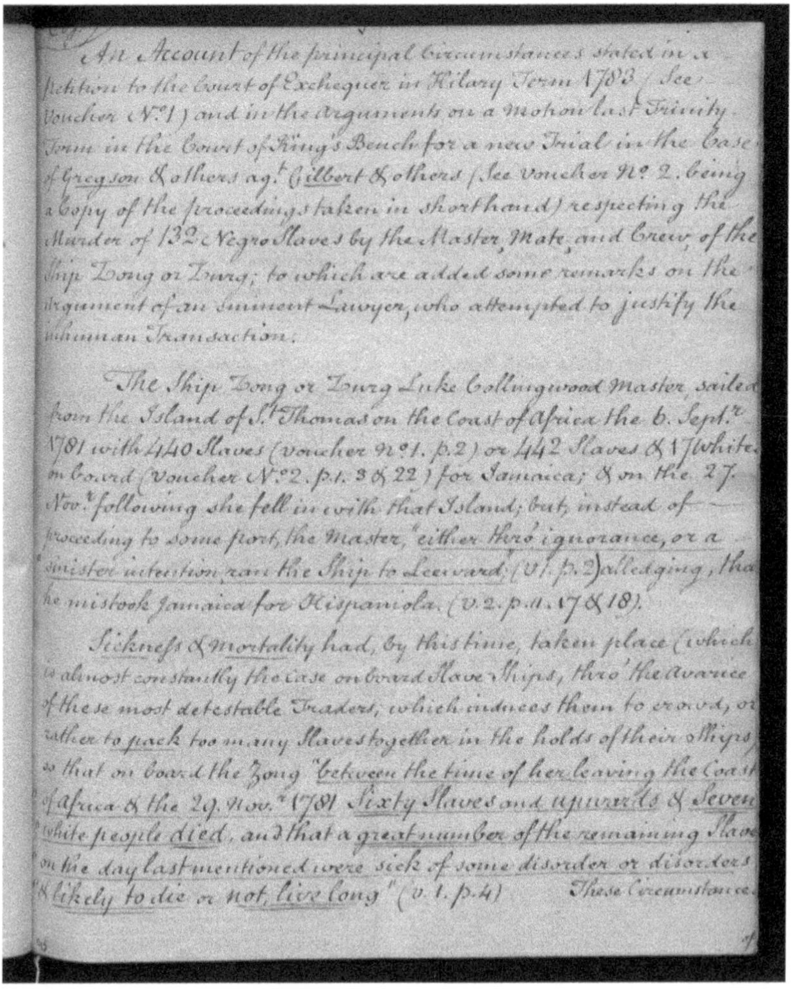

An Account of the principal Circumstances stated in a
petition to the Court of Exchequer in Hilary Term 1783 (See
Voucher N.º 1) and in the arguments on a motion last Trinity
Term in the Court of King's Bench for a new Trial in the Case
of Gregson & others ag.ᵗ Gilbert & others (See voucher N.º 2. being
a Copy of the proceedings taken in shorthand) respecting the
Murder of 132 Negro Slaves by the Master, Mate, and Crew of the
Ship Zong or Zurg; to which are added some remarks on the
argument of an Eminent Lawyer, who attempted to justify the
inhuman Transaction.

   The Ship Zong or Zurg Luke Collingwood Master, sailed
from the Island of S.ᵗ Thomas on the Coast of Africa the 6. Sept.ʳ
1781 with 440 Slaves (voucher N.º 1. p.2) or 442 Slaves & 1 White
on board (Voucher N.º 2. p.1. 3 & 22) for Jamaica; & on the 27.
Nov.ʳ following she fell in with that Island; but, instead of
proceeding to some port, the Master, either thro' ignorance, or a
sinister intention ran the Ship to Leeward (V.1. p.2) alledging, that
he mistook Jamaica for Hispaniola. (v.2. p.1. 17 & 18).

   Sickness & Mortality had, by this time, taken place (which
is almost constantly the case onboard Slave Ships, thro' the avarice
of these most detestable Traders; which induces them to crowd, or
rather to pack too many Slaves together in the holds of their Ships)
so that on board the Zong "between the time of her leaving the Coast
of Africa & the 29. Nov.ʳ 1781 Sixty Slaves and upwards & Seven
white people died, and that a great number of the remaining Slaves
on the day last mentioned were sick of some disorder or disorders
& likely to die or not live long" (v.1. p.4)   These Circumstances

Fig. A.6 Page 5, BL document, © British Library Board General Reference
Collection T.35.(2), folios 1–15

[/ 5] copy[6]

An Account of the principal Circumstances stated in a petition to the Court of Exchequer in Hilary Term 1783 (See Voucher N.º 1) and in the Arguments on a Motion last Trinity Term in the Court of King's Bench for a new Trial in the Case of <u>Gregson</u> & others ag.ᵗ <u>Gilbert</u> & others (See Voucher N.º 2. being a Copy of the proceedings taken in shorthand) respecting the Murder of 132 Negro Slaves by the Master, Mate, and Crew, of the Ship Zong or Zurg; to which are added some remarks on the Argument of an eminent Lawyer, who attempted to justify the inhuman Transaction.

The Ship Zong or Zurg Luke Collingwood Master, sailed from the Island of S.ᵗ Thomas on the Coast of Africa the 6. Sept.ʳ 1781 with 440 Slaves (voucher N.º 1. P. 2) or 442 Slaves & 17 White[s][7] on board (voucher N.º 2. P. 1. 3 & 22) for Jamaica; & on the 27. Nov.ʳ following she fell in with that Island; but, instead of proceeding to some port, the Master, "<u>either thro' ignorance, or a sinister intention, ran the Ship to Leeward</u>"; (V 1. P. 2) alledging, tha[t] he mistook Jamaica for Hispaniola. (V. 2. p. 11. 17 & 18).

<u>Sickness</u> & <u>Mortality</u> had, by this time, taken place (which is almost constantly the Case on board Slave-Ships, thro' the Avarice of these most detestable Traders; which induces them to crowd, or rather <u>to pack</u> too many Slaves together in the holds of their Ships, so that on board the Zong "<u>between the time of her leaving the Coast</u> of Africa & <u>the 29. Nov.ʳ 1781 Sixty Slaves and upwards</u> & <u>Seven white people died</u>, and that a <u>great number of the remaining Slave[s] on the day last mentioned were sick of some disorder or disorders</u> & <u>likely to die</u> or <u>not, live long</u>" (v. 1. P. 4)   These Circumstances

of Sickness & Mortality are necessary to be remarked; and also
the consequence of them viz.ᵗ that the Dead & dying Slaves
would have been a dead loss to the owners (and, in some
proportion, a loss also to the persons employed by the owners)
Some pretence or expedient had been found to throw the loss upon
the Insurers (V. N.º 1. p. 4. V. N.º 2. p. 8. 14) as in the case of Jetson
or Jetson viz: a plea of necessity to cast overboard some part of a
Cargo to save the rest.   These Circumstances, I say, are neces.
to be remarked; because they point out the most probable …
inducement to this enormous wickedness.

The Sickness & Mortality on board the Zong previous to the
29. Nov.ʳ 1781 (the time when they began to throw the poor Negroes
overboard alive) was not occasioned by the want of Water; for it
was proved that they did not discover, till that very day the 29
Nov.ʳ (or the preceding day) that the Stock of fresh Water was
reduced to 200 Gallons (as M.ʳ Stubbs has inform'd me) yet the
same day or in the Evening of it, before any Soul had been put to
short allowance (V. 2. p. 5. 6. 18 & 52) and before there was any
present or real want of Water, "the master of the Ship called
together a few of the officers & told them to the following effect,
that "if the Slaves died a natural death it would be the loss of the
"Owners of the Ship; but if they were thrown alive into the Sea, it
"would be the loss of the Underwriters &c. (V. 1. p. 4) and "to palliate
"the inhuman proposal he the said Collingwood pretended that it
"would not be so cruel to throw the poor sick wretches (meaning
"such Slaves) into the Sea as to suffer them to linger out a few
"days under the disorders with which they were afflicted or …
"expressed himself to the like effect" (ibid) To which proposal
the Mate (whose Name is Colonel James Kelsall. V. 1 p. 3) objec.

[/ 6] of Sickness & Mortality are necessary to be remarked; and also the consequence of them viz.ᵗ that the Dead & dying Slaves would have been a dead loss to the Owners (and, in some proportion, a loss also to the persons employed by the Owners) unless some pretence or expedient had been found to throw the loss upon the Insurers (V. N.º 1. P. 4. V. N.º 2. p. 8. 14) as in the case of Jetsam or Jetson⁸ i:e: a plea of Necessity to cast overboard some part of a Cargo to save the rest.   These Circumstances, I say, are necessary to be remarked; because they point out the most probable inducement to this enormous wickedness.

   The Sickness & Mortality on board the Zong previous to the 29. Nov.ʳ 1781 (the time when they began to throw the poor Negroes overboard alive) was not occasioned by the want of water; for it was proved that they did not discover, 'till that very day the 29.ᵗʰ Nov.ʳ (or the preceding day) that the Stock of fresh water was reduced to 200 Gallons (as M.ʳ Stubbs has inform'd me) yet the same day or in the Evening of it, before any Soul had been put to short allowance (V. 2. P. 5. 6. 18 & 52) and before there was any present or real want of water, "the Master of the Ship called together a few of the Officers & told them to the following effect; that "if the Slaves died a natural death it would be the loss of the Owners of the Ship; but if they were thrown alive into the Sea, it would be the loss of the Underwriters" &c. (V. 1. P. 4) and "to palliate the inhuman proposal he the said Collingwood pretended that it would not be so cruel to throw the poor sick Wretches (meaning such Slaves) into the Sea as to suffer them to linger out a few days under the disorders with which they were afflicted or expressed himself to the like effect" (ibid) To which proposal the Mate (whose Name is Colonel James Kelsall; V. 1. P. 3) objected

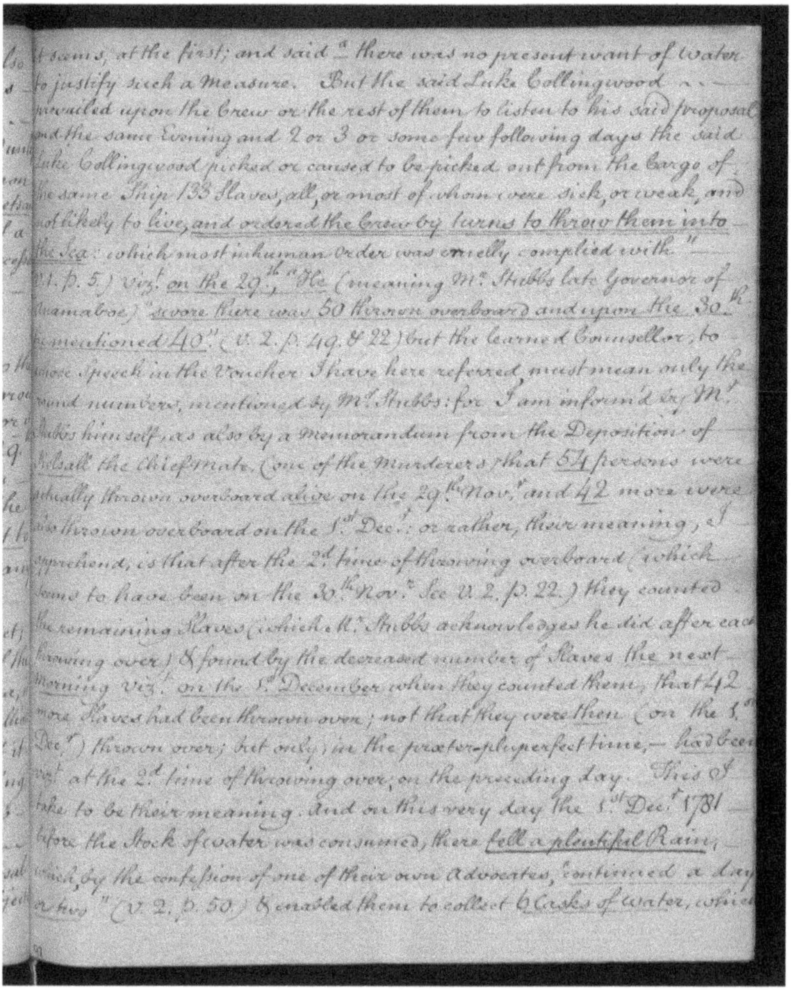

…seems, at the first; and said there was no present want of water to justify such a measure. But the said Luke Collingwood prevailed upon the crew or the rest of them to listen to his said proposal and the same evening and 2 or 3 or some few following days the said Luke Collingwood picked or caused to be picked out from the cargo of the same Ship 133 Slaves, all, or most of whom were sick, or weak, and not likely to live, and ordered the crew by turns to throw them into the Sea: which most inhuman order was cruelly complied with" (1. p. 5) viz. on the 29th, "He (meaning Mr. Stubbs late Governor of Anamaboe) swore there was 50 thrown overboard and upon the 30th mentioned 40". (v. 2. p. 49. & 22) but the learned Counsellor, to whose speech in the Voucher I have here referred, must mean only the round numbers, mentioned by Mr. Stubbs: for I am inform'd by Mr. Stubbs himself, as also by a Memorandum from the Deposition of Kelsall the Chief mate (one of the Murderers) that 54 persons were actually thrown overboard alive on the 29th Nov. and 42 more were thrown overboard on the 1st Dec.: or rather, their meaning, I apprehend, is that after the 2d time of throwing overboard (which seems to have been on the 30th Nov. See v. 2. p. 22.) they counted the remaining Slaves (which Mr. Stubbs acknowledges he did after each throwing over) & found by the decreased number of Slaves the next morning viz. on the 1st December when they counted them, that 42 more Slaves had been thrown over; not that they were then (on the 1st Dec.) thrown over; but only, in the preter-pluperfect time,— had been cast at the 2d time of throwing over, on the preceding day. This I take to be their meaning. And on this very day the 1st Dec. 1781 before the Stock of water was consumed, there fell a plentiful Rain; which by the confession of one of their own Advocates, "continued a day or two" (v. 2. p. 50.) & enabled them to collect 6 Casks of water, which…

Fig. A.8 Page 7, BL document, © British Library Board General Reference Collection T.35.(2), folios 1–15

[/ 7] it seems, at the first; and said – "there was no present want of water to justify such a Measure. But the said Luke Collingwood prevailed upon the Crew or the rest of them to listen to his said proposal and the same Evening and 2 or 3 or some few following days the said Luke Collingwood picked or caused to be picked out from the Cargo of the same Ship 133 Slaves, all, or most of whom were sick, or weak, and not likely to <u>live, and ordered the Crew by turns to throw them into the Sea</u>: which most inhuman Order was cruelly complied with" (V. 1. P. 5.) vizt <u>on the 29.th, "He</u> (meaning Mr Stubbs late Governor of Anamaboe) "<u>swore there was 50 thrown overboard and upon the 30.th he mentioned 40.</u>" (V. 2. P. 49. & 22) but the learned Counsellor, to whose Speech in the Voucher I have here referred, must mean only the round numbers, mentioned by Mr Stubbs: for I am inform'd by Mr Stubbs himself, as also by a Memorandum from the Deposition of <u>Kelsall</u> the Chief Mate. (one of the Murderers) that <u>54</u> persons were actually thrown overboard <u>alive</u> on the 29.th Novr and <u>42</u> more were also thrown overboard on the 1.st Dec.^{r}: or rather, their meaning, I apprehend, is that after the 2.^{d} time of throwing overboard (which seems to have been on the 30.th Novr See V. 2. P. 22) they counted the remaining Slaves (which Mr Stubbs acknowledges he did after each throwing over), & found by the decreased number of Slaves <u>the next</u> <u>morning</u> vizt <u>on the 1.st December</u> when they counted them, that 42 more Slaves had been thrown over; not that they were <u>then</u> (on the 1.st Dec.^{r}) thrown over; but only in the præter-pluperfect time, – <u>had been</u> vizt at the 2.^{d} time of throwing over, on the preceding day. This I take to be their meaning. And on this very day the 1.st Decr 1781 before the Stock of water was consumed, there <u>fell a plentiful Rain</u>, which, by the confession of one of their own Advocates, "<u>continued a day or two</u>" (V. 2. P. 50.) & enabled them to collect <u>6 Casks of Water</u>, which

was full allowance for 11 days; (v.2.p.24) or for 23 days at half
allowance; whereas the Ship actually arrived at Jamaica on 21 days
afterwards viz: on the 22d Decr 1781 (v.1.p.2). They seem also to
have had an opportunity of sending their Boat for water no less
than 13 days sooner viz: on the 9th Dec: when they "made the west
End of Jamaica distant 2 or 3 Leagues only" as I am informed by a
person who was on board: So that the (6 Casks of Rum Water caught
on the 1st & 2d Dec: only 7 days before this opportunity of obtaining
water from Jamaica) was not only a providential supply, but
providentially demonstrated the iniquity of pretending a necessity
to put innocent Men to a violent death, thro' the mere apprehension
of a want, which (supposing it had taken place could not have afforded
an admissable justification of the horrible deed but which) did not
really exist or take place at all in their case; because their Stock of
water was never actually consumed. And yet notwithstanding
this proof of a possibility, that they might perhaps obtain further
Supplies by Rain; or that they might be able to hold out with
their now increased Stock of Water, till they might chance to meet
with some Ship or be able to send to some Island for a further
Supply; they, nevertheless, cast 26 more human persons alive into
the Sea even after the Rain! (v. no 2. p.23.24.25.48.49. & 50)
whose hands were also fettered, or bound; & which was done, it seems
in the sight of many other unhappy Sufferers, that were being
up upon the Deck for the same detestable purpose whereby 10 of
these poor miserable human Creatures were driven to the Lamentable
Necessity of jumping overboard (v.2.p.24.48 & 49) to avoid the
fettering or binding of their hands, & were likewise drowned!

Fig. A.9 Page 8, BL document, © British Library Board General Reference Collection T.35.(2), folios 1–15

[/ 8] was full allowance for 11 days; (V. 2. P. 24) or for 23 days at half Allowance; whereas the Ship actually arrived at Jamaica in 21 days afterwards viz.ᵗ on the 22.ᵈ Dec.ʳ 1781 (V. 1. P. 2). They seem also to have had an opportunity of sending their Boat for Water no less than 13 days sooner viz: on the 9.ᵗʰ Dec.ʳ when they "made the West End of Jamaica distant 2 or 3 Leagues only" as I am inform'd by a person who was on board: So that the 6 Casks of Rain water caught on the 1.ˢᵗ & 2.ᵈ Dec.ʳ (only 7 days before this Opportunity of obtaining water from Jamaica) was not only a providential supply, but providentially demonstrated the iniquity of pretending a necessity to put innocent Men to a violent death, thro' the mere apprehension of a want, which (supposing it had taken place could not have afforded an admissable justification of the horrible deed – but which) did never really exist or take place at all in their case; because their Stock of Water was never actually consumed. And yet notwithstanding this proof of a possibility, that they might perhaps obtain further supplies by Rain; or that they might be able to hold out with their now increased Stock of Water, till they might chance to meet with some Ship or be able to send to some Island for a further supply; they, nevertheless, cast 26 more human persons alive into the Sea even after the Rain! (V. N.º 2. P. 23. 24. 25. 48. 49. & 50) whose hands were also fettered, or bound; & which was done, it seems, in the sight of many other unhappy Sufferers, that were brought up upon the Deck for the same detestable purpose, whereby 10 of these poor miserable human Creatures were driven to the lamentable Necessity of jumping overboard (V. 2. P. 24. 48. & 49) to avoid the fettering or binding of their hands, & were likewise drowned!

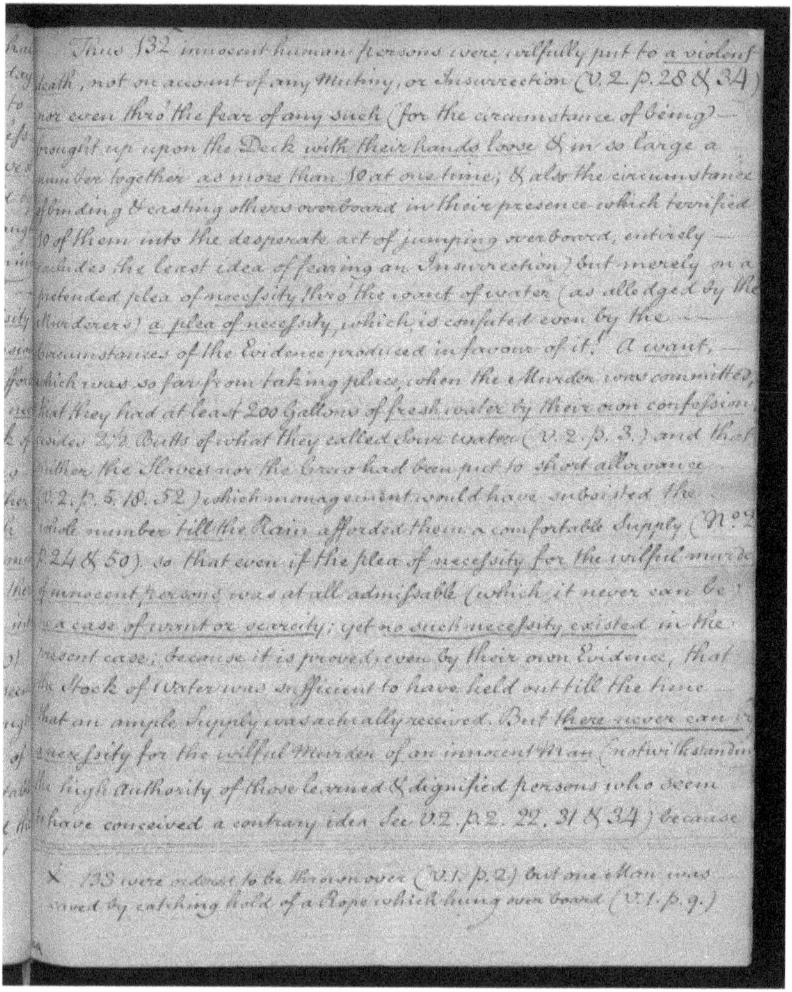

Thus 132 innocent human persons were wilfully put to a violent death, not on account of any Mutiny, or Insurrection (V.2. p. 28 & 34) nor even thro' the fear of any such (for the circumstance of being brought up upon the Deck with their hands loose & in so large a number together as more than 10 at one time; & also the circumstance of binding & casting others overboard in their presence which terrified 10 of them into the desperate act of jumping overboard, entirely excludes the least idea of fearing an Insurrection) but merely on a pretended plea of necessity thro' the want of water (as alledged by the Murderers) a plea of necessity, which is confuted even by the circumstances of the Evidence produced in favour of it. A want, which was so far from taking place, when the Murder was committed, that they had at least 200 Gallons of fresh water by their own confession besides 2½ Butts of what they called Sour water (V. 2. p. 3.) and that neither the Slaves nor the Crew had been put to short allowance (V. 2. p. 5. 18. 52) which management would have subsisted the whole number till the Rain afforded them a comfortable Supply (N° 2 p. 24 & 50) so that even if the plea of necessity for the wilful murder of innocent persons was at all admissable (which it never can be) in a case of want or scarcity; yet no such necessity existed in the present case; because it is proved, even by their own Evidence, that the Stock of Water was sufficient to have held out till the time that an ample Supply was actually received. But there never can be a necessity for the wilful Murder of an innocent Man (notwithstanding the high authority of those learned & dignified persons who seem to have conceived a contrary idea See V. 2. p. 2. 22. 31 & 34) because

X   133 were ordered to be thrown over (V. 1. p. 2) but one Man was saved by catching hold of a Rope which hung overboard (V. 1. p. 9.)

Fig. A.10 Page 9, BL document, © British Library Board General Reference Collection T.35.(2), folios 1–15

[/ 9] Thus 132^{X9} innocent human persons were wilfully put to <u>a violent death</u>, not on account of any Mutiny, or Insurrection (V.2. P. 28 & 34) <u>nor even thro'</u> <u>the fear of any such</u> (for the circumstance of being brought up upon the Deck <u>with their hands loose</u> & in so large a number together <u>as more than 10 at one</u> <u>time</u>; & also the circumstance of binding & casting others overboard in their presence which terrified 10 of them into the desperate act of jumping overboard, entirely excludes the least idea of fearing an Insurrection) but merely on a pre-tended plea of <u>necessity thro' the want of water</u> (as alledged by the Murderers) <u>a</u> <u>plea of necessity,</u> which, is confuted even by the Circumstances of the Evidence produced in favour of it! A <u>want</u>, which was so far from taking place, when the Murder was committed, that they had at least 200 Gallons of <u>fresh water by their</u> <u>own confession</u>, besides 2/2 Butts of what they called Sour water (V. 2. P. 3.) and that neither the Slaves nor the Crew had been put to <u>short allowance</u> – (V. 2. P. 5. 18. 52) which management would have subsisted the whole number <u>till the Rain</u> afforded them a comfortable Supply (N.° 2 P. 24 & 50). so that even if the plea of <u>necessity for the wilful murde[r]</u>^{10} <u>of innocent persons</u> was at all admissable (which it never can be) <u>in a case of want or scarcity</u>; yet <u>no</u> <u>such necessity existed</u> in the present case; because it is proved, even by their own Evidence, that the Stock of Water was sufficient to have held out till the time that an ample Supply was actually received. But <u>there never can be a</u> <u>necessity</u> for the <u>wilful Murder of an innocent Man</u> (notwithstanding the high Authority of those learned & dignified persons who seem to have conceived a contrary idea See V. 2. P. 2. 22. 31 & 34) because

---

^{11}X   133 were ordered to be thrown over (V. 1. P. 2) but one Man was saved by catching hold of a Rope which hung over board (V. 1. P. 9.)

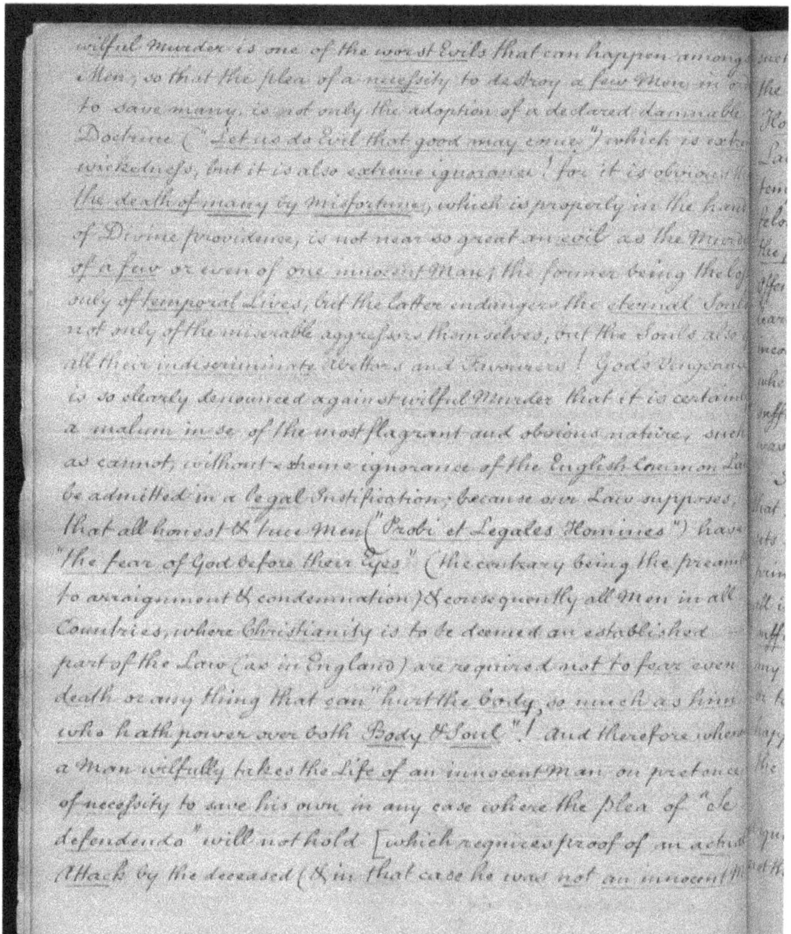

Fig. A.11 Page 10, BL document, © British Library Board General Reference Collection T.35.(2), folios 1–15

[/ 10] <u>wilful Murder</u> is one of the <u>worst Evils</u> that can happen amongst Men, so that the plea of a <u>necessity</u> to destroy <u>a few Men</u> in order to save <u>many</u>, is not only the adoption of a declared <u>damnable</u> Doctrine ("<u>Let us do Evil that good may come</u>")[12] which is <u>extreme wickedness</u>, but it is also <u>extreme ignorance</u>! for it is <u>obvious</u> that <u>the death of many by Misfortune</u>, which is properly in the hand of Divine providence, is not near so great an <u>evil</u> as the <u>Murder of a few</u> or even of <u>one innocent Man</u>; the former being the loss only of <u>temporal Lives</u>, but the latter endangers the <u>eternal Souls</u>, not only of the miserable aggressors themselves, but the Souls also of all their <u>indiscriminate</u> Abettors and Favourers! God's Vengeance is so clearly denounced against <u>wilful Murder</u> that is certainly a <u>malum in se</u>[13] of the most flagrant and obvious nature, such as cannot, without extreme ignorance of the <u>English Common Law</u> be admitted in a <u>legal</u> Justification; because our Law supposes, that all <u>honest & true Men</u> ("<u>Probi et Legales Homines</u>") have "<u>the fear of God before their Eyes</u>" (the contrary being the preamble to arraignment & condemnation) & consequently all Men in all Countries, where <u>Christianity</u> is to be deemed an established part of the Law (as in England) are required <u>not to fear</u> even <u>death</u> or any thing that <u>can "hurt the body, so much as him who hath power over both Body & Soul</u>"! And therefore whenever a Man <u>wilfully takes the Life of an innocent Man</u> on pretence of <u>necessity to save his own</u> in any case where the plea of "<u>Se defendendo</u>" will not hold [[14]<u>which requires proof of an actual Attack</u> by the deceased (& in that case he was <u>not</u> an innocent Man) such an attack as must be inevitable by any other means than the death wound] such a man I say is guilty of a felonious Homicide and also of (what is equally cognizable by our common Law) a gross contempt of God, in being more afraid of death & of temporal Sufferings than of God's eternal Judgment; so that the felonious disposition which our Law condemns viz! the "not having the fear of God before his Eyes' is clearly marked upon such an offender, & upon all his abettors & Defenders! And therefore a learned & dignified Lawyer did certainly place himself, very inconsiderately, under the same felonious description of Mind, when he asserted in behalf of these Murderers — "I could not suffer another man to live" (said he) when the single question was whether I should prefer my Life to his "&c (v. 2. p. 33).

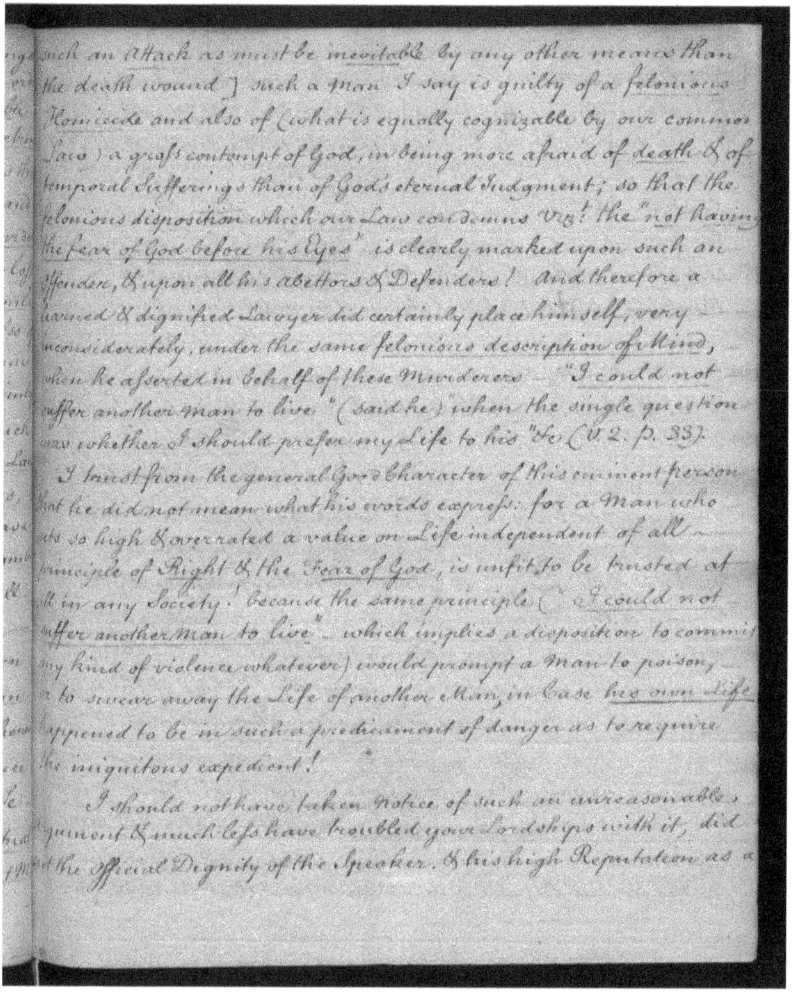

    I trust from the general Good Character of this eminent person that he did not mean what his words express. for a Man who sets so high & overrated a value on Life independent of all principle of Right & the Fear of God, is unfit to be trusted at all in any Society! because the same principle ("I could not suffer another Man to live" which implies a disposition to commit any kind of violence whatever) would prompt a Man to poison, or to swear away the Life of another Man, in Case his own Life happened to be in such a predicament of danger as to require the iniquitous expedient!

    I should not have taken notice of such an unreasonable argument & much less have troubled your Lordships with it, did not the official Dignity of the Speaker, & his high Reputation as a

Fig. A.12   Page 11, BL document, © British Library Board General Reference Collection T.35.(2), folios 1–15

[/ 11] such an <u>Attack</u> as must be <u>inevitable</u> by any other means than the death wound] such a Man I say is guilty of a <u>felonious</u> <u>Homicide</u> and also of (what is equally cognizable by our common Law) a gross contempt of God, in being more afraid of <u>death</u> & of temporal Sufferings than of God's eternal Judgment; so that the felonious disposition which our Law condemns vizt: the "<u>not hav-ing the fear of God before his Eyes</u>". is clearly marked upon such an Offender, & upon all his Abettors & Defenders! And therefore a learned & dignified Lawyer did certainly place himself, very inconsiderately, under the same <u>felonious description of Mind</u>, when he asserted in behalf of these Murderers – "<u>I could not</u> suffer another man to live" (said he) "when the single question was whether I should prefer my Life to his" &c. (V. 2. P. 33).

I trust from the general Good Character of this eminent person that he did not mean what his words express: for a Man who sets so high & overrated a value on Life independent of all principle of <u>Right</u> & the <u>Fear of God</u>, is unfit to be trusted at all in any Society! because the same principle ("<u>I could not suffer another Man to live</u>" – which implies a disposition to commit any kind of vio-lence whatever) would prompt a Man to poison, – or to swear away the Life of another Man, in Case <u>his own Life</u> happened to be in such a predicament of dan-ger as to require the iniquitous expedient!

I should not have taken notice of such an unreasonable argument & much less have troubled your Lordships with it, did not the Official Dignity of the Speaker, & his high Reputation as a

Lawyer compel me to guard against the adoption of his immor[al]
Doctrines in the present Case, lest precept, as well as impun[ity]
should encourage the Liverpool Traders to multiply their mo[st]
to the disgrace of the English Name & to the destruction of th[e]
human Species! "If any man of them" (said the learne[d]
Advocate for Liverpool Iniquity, speaking of the Murderers [in]
the present Case "if any man of them" said he) "was allowed
" to be tried at the old Bailey for a murder I cannot help —
" thinking (said he) "if that charge of murder was attempted to [be]
" sustained & Mr. Stubbs adduced to prove the Evidence & the fa[cts]
" it would be folly & rashness to a degree of madness, & so far
" from the Charge of Murder laying against these people there [is]
" not the least Imputation of Cruelty I will not say, but of —
" impropriety not in the least"!!!! (V.2.p.33)   This destru[ction]
of Living Men he considered, it seems, as if it were merely "th[e]
" Case of Chattels of Goods:— "it is really so" (says he) V.2.p.31.) "[it]
" the Case of throwing over Goods, for to this purpose, & the —
" purpose of this Insurance, they are Goods & property, and whet[her]
" right or wrong we have nothing to do with &c".   But at the
same time, he ought not to have forgot the Nature of these Goo[ds]
or property; for that is the most material circumstance of the c[ase]
& yet he, either indiscriminately overlooked, or criminally supp[ressed]
this most indispensable point of Consideration viz! that it is als[o]
the case of throwing over Living Men! and that, notwithstan[ding]
they are, in one sense, unhappily considered as Goods or Chattel[s]
(to the eternal disgrace of this Nation) yet that, still, they are [men]

Fig. A.13 Page 12, BL document, © British Library Board General Reference Collection T.35.(2), folios 1–15

[/ 12] Lawyer compel me to guard against the adoption of his avowed Doctrines in the present Case, lest precept, as well as impunity should encourage the Liverpool Traders to multiply their Murders to the disgrace of the English Name, & to the destruction of the human Species!   "If any Man of them" (said the learned Advocate for Liverpool Iniquity, speaking of the Murderers in the present Case "– if any Man of them" said he) "was allowed to be tried at the old Bailey for a murder I cannot help thinking" (said he) "if that charge of murder was attempted to be sustained & M.ʳ Stubbs adduced to prove the Evidence & the facts it would be folly & rashness to a degree of Madness, & so far from the Charge of Murder laying against these people there is not the least Imputation of Cruelty I will not say, but of impropriety not in the least" !!!! (V. 2. P. 33)   This destruction of Living Men he considered, it seems, as if it were merely "the case of Chattels of Goods: – "it is really so" – (says he) V.2. P. 31.) "it is the Case of throwing over Goods; for to this purpose, & the purpose of this Insurance, they are Goods & property and whether right or wrong we have nothing to do with &c".   But, at the same time, he ought not to have forgot the Nature of these Goods or property; for that is the most material Circumstance of the case & yet he, either indiscriminally[15] overlooked, or criminally suppressed this most indispensable point of Consideration viz.ᵗ – that it is also the case of throwing over Living Men! and that, notwithstanding they are, in one sense, unhappily considered as Goods or Chattels (to the eternal disgrace of this Nation) yet that, still, they are Men;

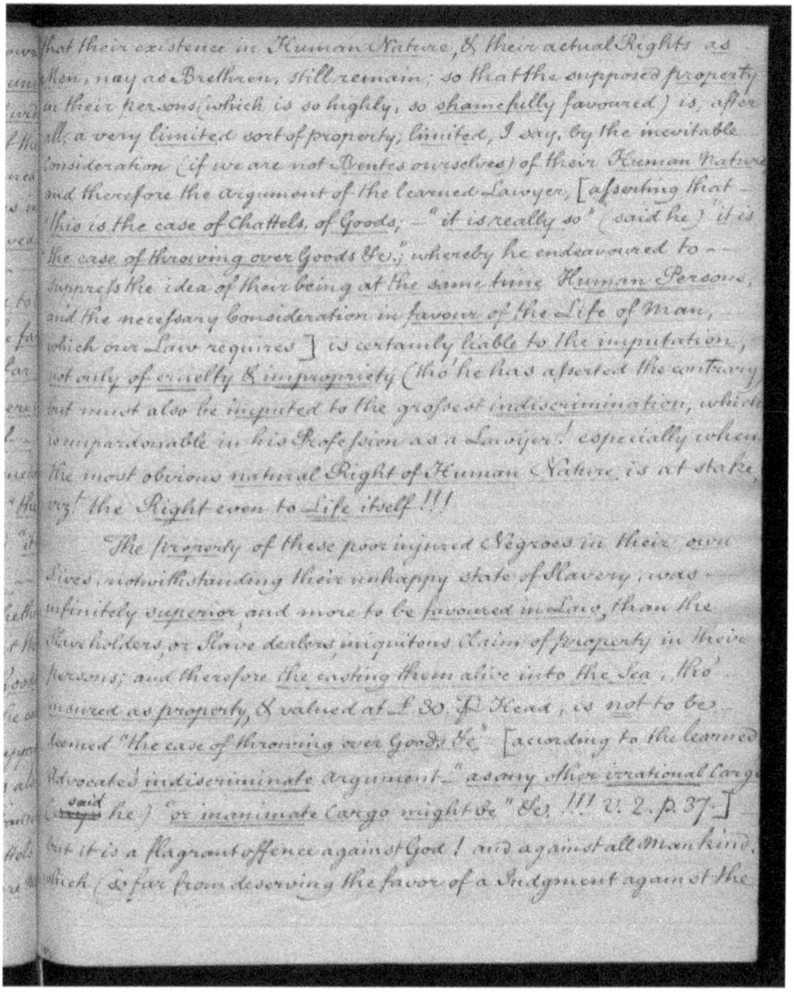

that their existence in Human Nature, & their actual Rights as Men, nay as Brethren, still remain; so that the supposed property in their persons (which is so highly, so shamefully favoured) is, after all, a very limited sort of property; limited, I say, by the inevitable consideration (if we are not Brutes ourselves) of their Human Nature and therefore the argument of the learned Lawyer, [asserting that this is the case of Chattels, of Goods; — "it is really so" (said he) it is the case of throwing over Goods &c.; whereby he endeavoured to — suppress the idea of their being at the same time Human Persons, and the necessary consideration in favour of the Life of Man, which our Law requires] is certainly liable to the imputation, not only of cruelty & impropriety (tho' he has asserted the contrary) but must also be imputed to the grossest indiscrimination, which is unpardonable in his Profession as a Lawyer! especially when the most obvious natural Right of Human Nature is at stake, viz! the Right even to Life itself!!!

The property of these poor injured Negroes in their own Lives, notwithstanding their unhappy state of Slavery, was infinitely superior and more to be favoured in Law, than the Slaveholders, or Slave dealers iniquitous claim of property in their persons; and therefore the casting them alive into the Sea, tho' insured as property, & valued at £30 P. Head, is not to be deemed "the case of throwing over Goods &c" [according to the learned Advocate's indiscriminate argument - "as any other irrational Cargo (said he) or inanimate Cargo might &c." &c !!! v. 2. p 37.] but it is a flagrant offence against God! and against all Mankind, which (so far from deserving the favor of a Judgment against the

Fig. A.14 Page 13, BL document, © British Library Board General Reference Collection T.35.(2), folios 1–15

[/ 13] that their existence in <u>Human Nature</u>, & their actual Rights <u>as Men</u>, nay as Brethren, still remain; so that the supposed <u>property</u> in their persons (which is so highly, so <u>shamefully</u> favoured) is, after all, a very <u>limited</u> sort of property; <u>limited</u>, I say, by the inevitable Consideration (if we are not <u>Brutes</u> ourselves) of their <u>Human Nature</u>, and therefore the Argument of the learned Lawyer, [[16]asserting that – "<u>this is the case of Chattels, of Goods</u>; – "<u>it is really so</u>" (said he) "<u>it is the case of throwing over Goods &c.</u>"; whereby he endeavoured to suppress the idea of their being <u>at the same time</u> <u>Human Persons</u>, and the necessary Consideration <u>in favour of the Life of Man</u>, which our Law requires] is certainly <u>liable to the imputation, not only of cruelty & impropriety</u> (tho' he has asserted the contrary) but must also be <u>imputed</u> to the grossest <u>indiscrimination</u>, which is unpardonable in his Profession as a Lawyer! especially when the most obvious <u>natural Right of Human Nature</u> is at stake, viz.[t] the <u>Right</u> even to <u>Life itself</u>!!!

The <u>property</u> of these poor injured Negroes in their <u>own</u> <u>Lives</u>, notwithstanding their unhappy state of Slavery, was infinitely <u>superior</u>, and more to be <u>favoured in Law</u>, than the Slaveholders, or Slave dealers, iniquitous claim of <u>property</u> in their persons; and therefore <u>the casting them alive into the Sea</u>, tho' <u>insured as property</u>, & valued at £30. P̶ Head, is <u>not</u> to be deemed "<u>the case of throwing over Goods &c</u>" [[17]according to the learned Advocate's <u>indiscriminate</u> Argument" – "<u>as any other irrational Cargo</u> (s̶a̶y̶s̶ said he) "<u>or inanimate Cargo might be</u>" &c. !!! V. 2. P. 37.] but it is a flagrant offence against God! and against all Mankind. which (so far from deserving the favor of a Judgment against the

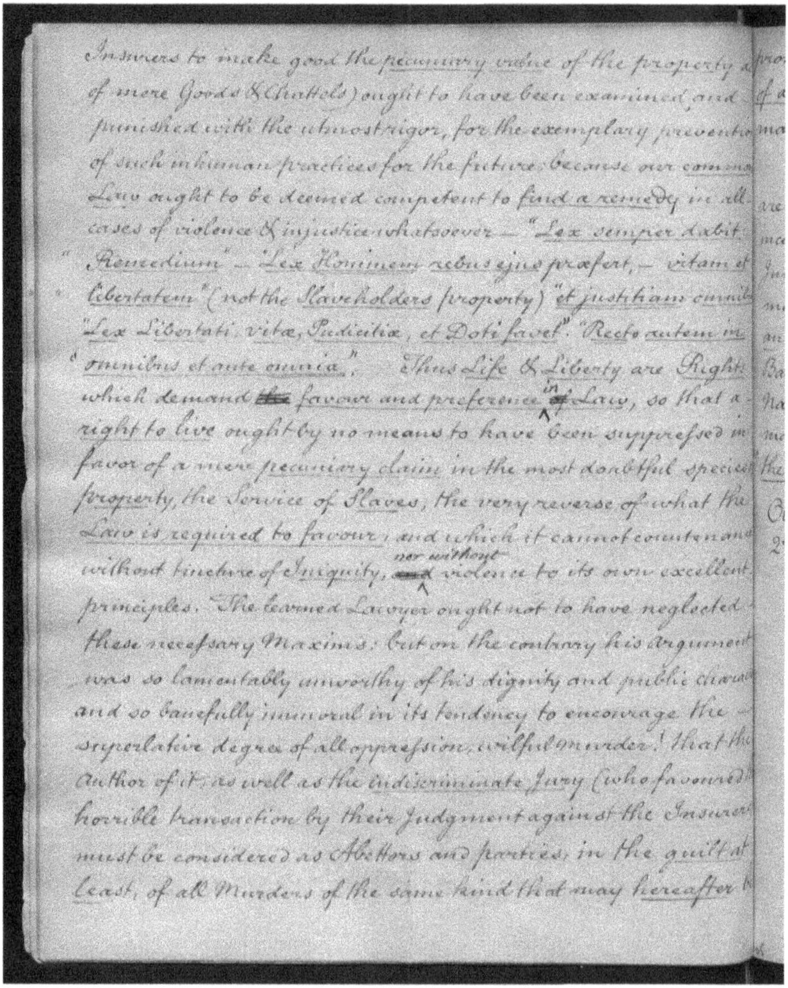

Fig. A.15 Page 14, BL document, © British Library Board General Reference Collection T.35.(2), folios 1–15

[/ 14] Insurers to make good the pecuniary value of the property as of mere Goods & Chattels) ought to have been examined, and punished with the utmost rigor, for the exemplary prevention of such inhuman practices for the future; because our common Law ought to be deemed competent to find a remedy in all cases of violence & injustice whatsoever – "Lex semper dabit Remedium" – "Lex Hominem rebus ejus præfert, – vitam et libertatem" (not the Slaveholders property) "et justitiam omnibus Lex Libertati, Vitæ, Pudicitiæ, et Doti favet". "Recto autem in omnibus et aute omnia".[18] Thus Life & Liberty are Rights which demand the favour and preference^in of Law, so that a right to live ought by no means to have been suppressed in favor of a mere pecuniary claim in the most doubtful species of property, the Service of Slaves, the very reverse of what the Law is required to favour, and which it cannot countenance without tincture of Iniquity, and ^nor without violence to its own excellent principles. The learned Lawyer ought not to have neglected these necessary Maxims: but on the contrary his Argument was so lamentably unworthy of his dignity and public character and so banefully immoral in its tendency to encourage the superlative degree of all oppression, wilful Murder! that the Author of it, as well as the indiscriminate Jury (who favoured the horrible transaction by their Judgment against the Insurers) must be considered as Abettors and parties, in the guilt at least, of all Murders of the same kind that may hereafter be promoted by this failure of Justice, & by the lamentable want of distinction between good & evil which has been so notoriously manifested in this inhuman Business!

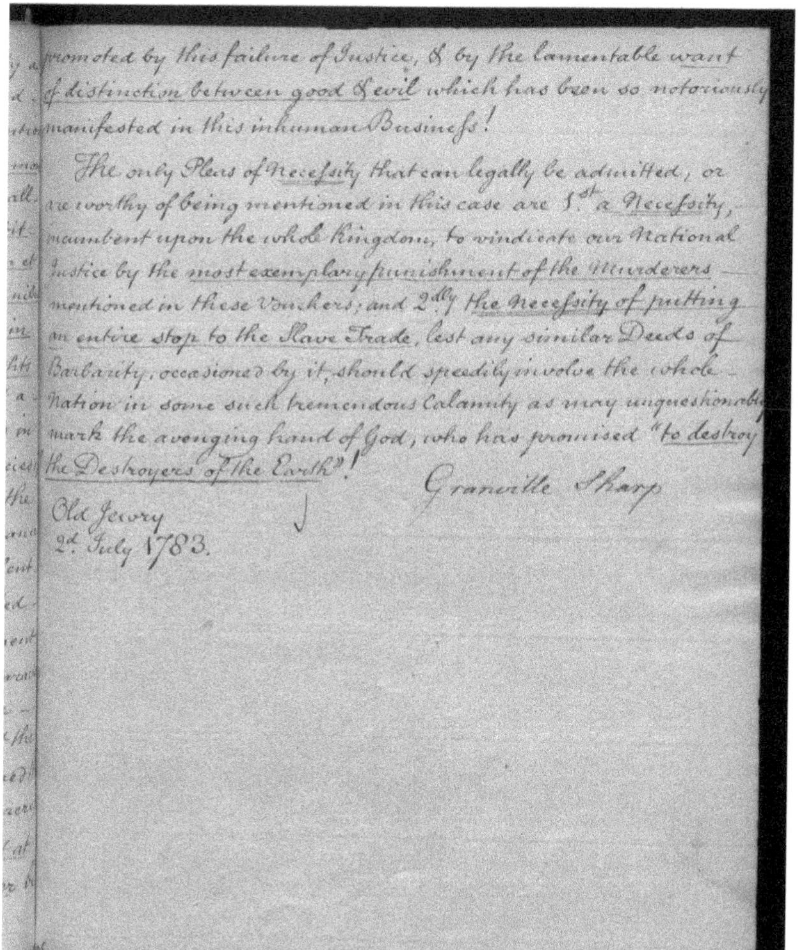

The only Pleas of Necessity that can legally be admitted, or are worthy of being mentioned in this case are 1st a Necessity, incumbent upon the whole Kingdom, to vindicate our National Justice by the most exemplary punishment of the Murderers mentioned in these Vouchers; and 2dly the Necessity of putting an entire stop to the Slave Trade, lest any similar Deeds of Barbarity, occasioned by it, should speedily involve the whole Nation in some such tremendous Calamity as may unquestionably mark the avenging hand of God, who has promised "to destroy the Destroyers of the Earth"!

Granville Sharp

Old Jewry
2d. July 1783.

Fig. A.16 Page 15, BL document, © British Library Board General Reference Collection T.35.(2), folios 1–15

[/ **15**] promoted by this failure of Justice, & by the lamentable <u>want</u> <u>of distinc-</u> <u>tion between good & evil</u> which has been so notoriously manifested in this inhu- man Business!

The only Pleas of <u>Necessity</u> that can legally be admitted, or are worthy of being mentioned in this case are 1.st <u>a Necessity</u>, incumbent upon the whole Kingdom, to vindicate our National Justice by the <u>most exemplary punishment</u> <u>of the Murderers</u> mentioned in these Vouchers; and 2.dly <u>the Necessity of put-</u> <u>ting an entire stop to the Slave Trade</u>, lest any similar Deeds of Barbarity, occa- sioned by it, should speedily involve the whole Nation in some such tremendous Calamity as may unquestionably mark the avenging hand of God, who has prom- ised "<u>to destroy the Destroyers of the Earth</u>"![19]

Granville Sharp

Old Jewry
2.^d July 1783.

NOTES

1. This transcription is of the first title page, not in Sharp's hand, of the two-part BL document. Another title page appears after the three-page cover letter, which follows. The table of contents lists the document as "Sharp on the Murder of 132 Negroes".

2. The word "Copy" is circled and most of it is cut off at the top of the page. With regard to the images of the BL document that appear opposite, please note that some words were cut off in the scanning process at the BL, but I created my transcription from the original letter.

3. A small horizontal mark appears before "with" in this quotation. Since opening quotation marks should appear in this place, Sharp may have meant this mark to be opening quotation marks, but it does not look like them. The complete section of Psalm 12 to which Sharp refers is as follows: "Help, LORD; for the godly man ceaseth; for the faithful fail from among the children of men./ They speak vanity every one with his neighbour: *with* flattering lips *and* with a double heart do they speak./ The LORD shall cut off all flattering lips, *and* the tongue that speaketh proud things:/ Who have said, With our tongue will we prevail; our lips *are* our own: who *is* lord over us?" (*The Holy Bible, Containing the Old and New Testaments Translated Out of the Original Tongues and with the Former Translations Diligently Compared and Revised by his Majesty's Special Command. Appointed to be Read in Churches. Authorized King James Version*, 1611 (Iowa Falls: World Bible Publishers, [n.d.]), Psalm 12: 1-4). The phrase "render an Account of every idle word" refers to Matthew 12:36: "But I say unto you, That every idle word that men shall speak, they shall give account thereof in the day of judgment."

4. Five words are crossed out with Xs. Most of the words under the Xs are thus rendered illegible, but I can discern the name "Lee" as the first word. John Lee, Solicitor General, represented the Gregson syndicate in court.

5. The phrase "Right Honorable Lords Commissioners of the Admiralty" is at the bottom of the final page of what I call the "cover letter" of Sharp's missive; the page following it on the same sheet of paper is blank. Facing that blank page, and on a new sheet of paper, is the second title page: with text on one side of the sheet of paper, it contains a single phrase describing the detailed account in the pages thereafter.

6. As at the start of the cover letter, the top of this page has what appears to be the encircled word "copy," but it is almost entirely cut off.

7. The page is cut off here, but a small mark appears at the end of the word "White" that appears to have pluralized it, as proper grammar would

dictate. The same occurrence happens at the end of this paragraph, where the final t of the word "that" is cut off.

8. Sharp ms to mean "jettison" here.
9. The footnote marker "X" is half cut off at the top of the page.
10. The second r in "murder" has been cut off at the right-hand edge of the page.
11. Sharp's X at the bottom of this page is a footnote marker to match the X at the top of the page ("Thus 132^X"). To divide his main discussion from this footnote, Sharp draws three closely spaced lines across the bottom of the page and above the footnote, given above.
12. Romans 3:8.
13. Latin phrase meaning "wrong [evil or criminal] in itself." The subsequent Latin phrase means "good and lawful men," while "*se defendendo*" means "self-defense."
14. Unusually, these square brackets are Sharp's.
15. Sharp seems to have meant "indiscriminately," as Hoare transcribes it (Prince Hoare, *Memoirs of Granville Sharp, Esq. Composed from His Own Manuscripts, and Other Authentic Documents in the Possession of His Family Authentic Documents in the Possession of His Family and of the African Institution* (London: Henry Colburn, 1820), xx, *Google eBooks*, accessed June 25, 2015–August 30, 2017, https://books.google.ca/books?id=PrUEAAAAIAAJ). This word is spelled "indiscriminatly" in the NMM document (Granville Sharp, [NMM document] "Copy of a Letter to Lords Commissioners of the Admiralty," Old Jewry London, MS, 2 July 1783, repographic scan provided by the National Maritime Museum (NMM; REC/19), downloaded July 14, 2015, 107).
16. Again, these opening and closing brackets are Sharp's.
17. These brackets are also Sharp's.
18. I am hugely thankful to Liesl Smith for providing me with the following Latin translations (e-mail to the author, July 2, 2015):
    "*Lex semper dabit remedium.*" The law will always give a remedy.
    "*Lex hominem rebus ejus præfert, vitam et libertatem et justitiam omnibus.*" The law places a man before his possessions, life and liberty and justice before all.
    "*Lex libertati, vitæ, pudicitiæ, et doti favet; recto autem in omnibus et ante omnia.*" The law protects/favors liberty, life, chastity and dower; however, it favors the right in all things and before all things.
19. From Revelations 11:18: "The nations raged, but your wrath came, and the time for the dead to be judged, and for rewarding your servants, the prophets and saints, and those who fear your name, both small and great, and for destroying the destroyers of the earth."

INDEX

A

Abolition movement, 3, 7, 9, 28, 32, 42, 44, 56, 97, 110

Abolition of slavery, 2–11, 23–30, 32, 33, 36–40, 42–44, 47–50, 52, 54, 56, 57, 60, 62, 72–74, 84, 86, 89, 91, 96, 97, 100, 101, 104, 107–110, 112–115, 117–122

Admiralty, 3, 5, 6, 9–11, 15, 16, 23, 39, 46, 48, 49, 51, 52, 57, 60, 61, 63–65, 67, 72–81, 83–87, 90, 92, 95, 96, 100–102, 107–115, 120, 122, 131, 156, 157

Admiralty Court, 95, 118

African Institution, 4

Africanus, 50–52

   Leigh, William, 50

   Remarks on the Slave Trade, and the Slavery of the Negroes. In a Series of Letters (1788), 50, 51

America, 33, 36, 65, 106

American Revolution, 38

American Revolutionary War (1775–1783), 90, 113, 115

American war. *See* American Revolutionary War (1775–1783)

Amis des Noirs, 112

Anamaboe, or Anomabu, 16, 129, 139

Anglicans, 28, 90–92, 118

Annis, John, 23

Anti-slavery. *See* Abolition of slavery

Archbishop of Canterbury. *See* Cornwallis, Frederick, Archbishop of Canterbury (1713–1783)

Archbishop of York. *See* Sharp, John, Archbishop of York (1645–1714)

Archdeacon of Northumberland. *See* Sharp, Thomas, Archdeacon of Northumberland (1693–1758)

Austen, Jane, 8

B

Baker, William, 68–72, 77, 101

Baker, William Lloyd, 67–69, 77

Barbados, 29, 113

Basker, James, 29

Baucom, Ian, 9, 10, 56, 78, 81–83, 102

Belle, Dido Elizabeth, 32

Belle (2014), 32

Benezet, Anthony, 57, 72, 112, 114

© The Editor(s) (if applicable) and The Author(s) 2018
M. Faubert, *Granville Sharp's Uncovered Letter and the Zong Massacre*,
https://doi.org/10.1007/978-3-319-92786-2

A Short Account of That Part of Africa, Inhabited by the Negroes (1762), 72
Bever, Thomas, 118
Bible, 30, 92, 122, 131
  Scripture, 38
Bicknell, John, 29
Bishop Hinchcliffe, 59–60
Bishop of Chester. *See* Porteus, Beilby
Bishop of Peterborough. *See* Hinchcliffe, John
Bishop Porteus, 59
Black River, 15, 20, 49, 121
Blackstone, William, 105, 106
  Commentaries on the Laws of England (1765), 15, 46, 106
Blake, W.O., 45, 113
BL. *See* British Library (BL)
Britain, 6, 8–10, 22, 23, 27, 30–37, 56, 65, 66, 92, 93, 96, 104–106, 108, 110–112, 115, 118
British Empire, 9, 35, 39, 104
British Library (BL), 2–5, 8–10, 16, 19, 39, 62, 64, 66, 67, 70, 123
British Library (BL) document, 3–6, 9–11, 14, 15, 17, 20, 26, 32, 47, 60–97, 100–115, 117, 121, 122
British Museum, 63, 100, 101
British Parliament, 107
Brograve and Lyon, Mrs., 131
Brown, Christopher Leslie, 27–29, 42, 43, 46, 47, 56, 83, 84, 92, 95, 104, 113–115
Burroughs, R., 5

C
Cape Coast, 14, 16, 121
Carey, Brycchan, 4, 28, 29, 43, 54, 110
Caribbean, 106, 113

Carretta, Vincent, 25, 26, 83
Chater, Kathleen, 30
Clarkson, Thomas, 4, 7, 27–29, 43–45, 47, 56, 57, 96, 106, 107, 112, 120
  An Essay on the Slavery and Commerce of the Human Species, Particularly the African (1786), 47
  The History of the Rise, Progress, and Accomplishment of the Abolition of the African Slave-Trade, by the British Parliament (1808), 28, 45, 56, 107
Coleridge, S.T., vii
Colley, Linda, 45
Collingwood, Luke, 2, 6, 10, 15–17, 42, 48–52, 73, 82, 83, 88, 104, 109, 121, 127, 131, 135, 137, 139
The Committee for the Relief of the Black Poor, 64
Cooper, Thomas, 15, 45, 48
  Letters on the Slave Trade (1787), 15, 45, 48
Cornwall Chronicle, 15
Cornwallis, Frederick, Archbishop of Canterbury (1713–1783), 91
Cotter, William R., 36
Court of Exchequer, 65, 82, 127, 141
Court of King's Bench, 22, 34, 35, 50, 76, 82, 127, 135
Cowley, Malcolm, 103
Cowper, William, 28, 110
Cugoano, Ottobah, 24, 53, 54
  Thoughts and Sentiments on the Evil and Wicked Traffic of the Slavery and Commerce of the Human Species, Humbly Submitted to the Inhabitants of Great-Britain (1787), 53

D

Davis, David Brion, 4, 29, 30, 33, 44, 90, 91, 121
Day, Thomas, 29
DeLombard, Jeannine Marie, 83
de Warville, Jacques-Pierre Brissot, 112
Digges, Thomas, 26
Dillwyn, William, 56, 65, 114
Ditchfield, G.M., 3, 27, 29, 30, 38, 90–92, 96, 97
Dockray, Martin, 6
Douglas, Starr, 64
Drescher, Seymour, 24, 44, 102, 108
Duke of Portland, 60, 73, 76, 77, 82

E

Earl of Liverpool, 62
Eckstein, Lars, 104
Edwards, Bryan, 72, 73
 The History, Civil and Commercial, of the British West Indies (1818-1819), 72, 73
Equiano, Olaudah, 4, 6–8, 22–27, 39, 46, 53–55, 58, 65, 66, 95, 117, 118, 120
Exchequer, 6, 16
 affidavit in the, 17, 51

F

Faubert, Michelle, viii
Fisher, Ruth Anna, 4
Fothergill, John, 65
Fox, George, 113

G

GA. *See* Gloucestershire Archives (GA)
Galabin, John William, 71, 72

The Gentleman's Magazine, 46, 47, 101
Ghana, 14
Gilbert, Thomas, 127
 underwriters, 20, 22, 47, 51, 54, 55, 73, 82, 103, 127, 137
Gloucestershire Archives (GA), 67–70, 80, 84
Greene, Jack P., 50
Gregory, George, 15, 47, 48
 Essays Historical and Moral (1785), 15, 47
Gregson, Cave, Wilson, and Aspinal, 131
Gregson, James, 127
Gregson slave-trading syndicate, 14, 17, 20, 21, 32, 50, 93, 94, 104, 135
Gregson *vs.* Gilbert insurance trial (1783), 18
Guildhall, 48, 50, 95, 108, 118
Gunning, Dave, 18, 103

H

Habeus Corpus, 31, 119
Haitian slave revolution, 112
Hanley, Richard, 14, 16, 131
Hargrave, Francis, 105
Hay, George, 80
Heseltine, James, 46, 95, 118
Hinchcliffe, John, 27, 65, 76, 118
Hispaniola, 20, 81, 135
Hoare, Prince, 4, 10, 11, 15, 23, 24, 26, 27, 35, 38, 42–46, 57, 60, 64–66, 68, 69, 74, 76, 77, 80, 83–90, 92–96, 107, 109, 111, 113, 114, 117, 118, 157
 Memoirs of Granville Sharp, Esq. Composed from his [Sharp's] *own Manuscripts, and other Authentic*

Documents in the Possession of his Family and of the African Institution (1820), 4, 10, 11, 23–27, 35, 38, 42, 44–46, 57, 60, 63–66, 69, 74, 77, 80, 83–85, 87, 89, 93–96, 107, 111, 113, 114, 117, 118, 157
Hodgson, Robert, 119
Hogg, Peter, 83
The Holy Bible, 92, 156
Home, Henry (Lord Kames), 105
Horner, Francis, 97
House of Commons, 27, 107, 113, 119

I
Inoculation, 5, 61
Insurers
  underwriters, 20, 22, 47, 51, 54, 55, 73, 82, 103, 127, 137
Island of St. Thomas, 135

J
Jamaica, 10, 15–17, 20, 30, 31, 33, 48, 49, 52, 73, 81, 83, 93, 104, 121, 135, 141
Jebb, Sir Richard, 27, 66, 118
Jenner, Edward, 61

K
Kelsall, James, 2, 6, 16–20, 49, 51, 52, 80, 90, 109, 127, 131, 137, 139
Kerr, James, 29
Kielstra, Paul Michael, 83
Kimber, John, 40, 109
King George III, 66
King's Bench, 19, 51, 82, 108
Kippax, 71
Krikler, Jeremy, 21, 22

L
Lascelles, Edward Charles Ponsonby, 4
Law, British, 8, 21, 22, 24, 30–34, 36–38, 41, 43, 52, 72, 91, 106, 108, 115, 118
  British legal system, 49, 58
  court, 7, 17, 21, 22, 133
  trial, 7, 10, 17, 19, 21, 22, 33–36, 41, 42, 45, 48, 50, 51, 55, 65, 73, 74, 82, 95, 103–105, 107, 109–111, 118
Lee, Solicitor-General John, 42, 87
Leigh, William. *See* Africanus
Letter of Marque, 14
Lettsom, John Coakley, 61–66, 68–71, 100, 101
  History of Coffee, by the late Dr. John Fothergill (1809), 65
  A Letter to Sir Robert Barker, Knt., F. R. S. and George Stacpoole, Esq.; Upon General Inoculation (1778), 61–62
Lewis, Andrew, 6, 14, 15, 82
Lewis, Thomas, 3, 29, 31, 32, 39, 51, 52, 118
  Rex *vs.* Stapylton case of 1771, 31, 41
Lisbon earthquake, 38
Lisle, David, 29
Liverpool, 2, 18, 21, 42, 62, 70, 73, 87, 109, 127, 131, 149
Liverpool syndicate, Gregson and partners, 14
Lloyd Baker, Thomas J., 70
Lobban, Michael, 83
London Medical Society, 63
Lords Commissioners of the Admiralty, 4, 5, 10, 46, 64, 78, 95, 102, 108, 109, 111, 121, 131
Lushington, Stephen, 46, 95, 118
Lyall, Andrew, 10, 14–16, 18–20, 40, 52, 58, 76, 83, 96

"James Kelsall's Answer" from the Documents in the Exchequer (1783), 18

M

Magill, Frank N., 83
Mannix, Daniel P., 103, 104
Mansfield, Lord, 6, 8, 10, 22, 27–44, 62, 82, 103–105, 118, 119
May, Stephen J., 4
McBride, Dwight A., 46, 53
Meeting for Suffering Committee on the Slave Trade, 65
Methodism, 25
Middle Passage, 21, 24, 109
Moore, Norman, 66
Moore, Sean, viii
Morning Chronicle and London Advertiser, 21, 23, 46, 50, 52, 55, 111, 112

N

The National Archives (TNA), 6, 19, 80, 106
National Maritime Museum (NMM), 3, 6, 9–11, 15, 47, 68, 72, 74–81, 83–90, 92–96, 107, 111, 121
Newton, John, 53, 54, 56
    Thoughts upon the African Slave Trade (1788), 53, 54
NMM. *See* National Maritime Museum (NMM)
North, Lord, 27
North and South America, 106

O

Oglethorpe, General, 27, 65, 118
Oldham, James, 6, 17–19, 31, 32, 35, 41, 51, 54, 55, 74, 103, 106

Old Jewry, 2, 15, 16, 57, 79, 127, 155
Ordnance Office, 34, 83, 90

P

Paley, Ruth, 33, 35, 36
Park, James Allan, 54
Parliament, 7, 22, 33, 56, 57, 73, 107
Parliamentary acts against slavery in the colonies (1833), 29
Parliamentary acts against the slave trade (1807), 29
Parry, Andrew, 67, 69, 84
Payne, J.F., 61, 62
Perceval, Spencer, 62
Pettigrew, Thomas Joseph, 62–64, 66, 69
Philip, M. NourbSe, 14, 15, 18
Phillips, James, 48, 114
Pitt, William, 82
Pollard, Albert Frederick, 4
Porteus, Beilby, 27, 55, 65, 76, 77, 118–120
Prime Minister of Britain, 76
Prince of Wales, 66

Q

Quakers, 7, 15, 28, 43, 48, 50, 56, 57, 62, 64, 72, 101, 113–115. *See also* The Society of Friends
Queen Charlotte, 25, 57

R

Ramsay, James, 42, 43, 48–50, 56, 110, 112, 114
    An Essay on the Treatment and Conversion of African Slaves in the British Sugar Colonies (1784), 43, 48, 110, 112, 114
Rapp, Dean, 83
Richard [ship], 16

Richard of Jamaica [ship], 15
Robertson, James, 22
Roscoe, William, 62, 101
    The Wrongs of Africa (1787), 62,
    101
Rupprecht, Anita, 15, 22, 46, 56, 60,
    77, 82, 86
Rush, Benjamin, 64, 114

S
Sally and Rachell [ship], 14
Sears, Christine A., 50
*17th- and 18th-Century Burney
    Newspapers Collection*, 46
Sharp, Granville, 2–5, 15, 16, 23,
    27–29, 33, 34, 36, 37, 39, 42,
    43, 50, 60, 63–65, 67–72, 76,
    79, 83, 90, 91, 95, 102, 109,
    110, 115, 119, 121, 125, 157
    *An Account of the Ancient Division
        of the English Nation into
        Hundreds and Tithings* (1784),
        71
    *An Appendix to the Representation
        of the Injustice and Dangerous
        Tendency of Tolerating Slavery*
        (1772), 30
    *An Essay on Slavery: Proving from
        Scripture its Inconsistency
        with Humanity and Religion*
        (1773), 37
    *The Just Limitation of Slavery: In
        the Laws of God, Compared
        with the Unbounded Claims of
        the African Traders and British
        American Slaveholders* (1776),
        36
    *The Law of Liberty: Or, Royal Law,
        by which All Mankind Will
        Certainly be Judged! Earnestly
        Recommended to the Serious
        Consideration of all Slaveholders*

    and Slavedealers (1777), 37,
    38, 121
    *The Law of Passive Obedience, Or
        Christian Submission to Personal
        Injuries* (1776), 37
    *The Law of Retribution: A Serious
        Warning to Great Britain
        and Her Colonies, Founded
        on Unquestionable Examples
        of God's Temporal Vengeance
        Against Tyrants, Slave-holders,
        and Oppressors* (1776), 37
    *Remarks on the Uses of the Definitive
        Article in the Greek Text of the
        New Testament* (1798), 90
    *A Representation of the Injustice
        and Dangerous Tendency of
        Tolerating Slavery* (1769), 29,
        30, 33, 72
    *Serious Reflections on the Slave Trade
        and Slavery, Wrote in March
        1797* (1805), 112
    Sharp's letter to the Admiralty, 4,
        11, 39, 47, 52, 60, 76, 78–80,
        82, 83, 94, 111, 131, 161
Sharp, James, 30
Sharp, John (brother), 26
Sharp, John, Archbishop of York
    (1645–1714), 91
Sharp, Mary, 70
Sharp, Thomas, Archdeacon of
    Northumberland (1693–1758),
    91
Sharp, William, 29, 70
Shepherd, Verene A., 16
Sheridan, Richard B., 73
Shyllon, F.O., 3, 4, 22, 25, 27, 28,
    30–35, 45, 46, 48, 53, 55, 82,
    83, 91, 103, 104, 111
Sierra Leone, 4, 26, 28, 60, 64, 72,
    111
Slavery, 3, 4, 6–8, 23, 24, 26, 27,
    29–39, 41–44, 53, 54, 56, 58,

62, 72, 92, 93, 96, 104–108, 113–115, 118–122, 157
Slaves, 2, 5, 17–20, 22, 25, 31, 32, 35, 39–41, 43, 49, 51, 54, 70, 73, 76, 82, 88, 89, 95, 103–105, 118, 127, 133, 139, 141, 143, 145, 149
Slave Trade, 1–3, 6, 8, 9, 20, 21, 24–26, 37, 43, 54–57, 60, 91, 92, 104–108, 110, 113–115, 118, 120, 127, 161
Smeathman, Henry, 64
Smith, Gregory, 41
Smith, Liesl, 159
Society for the Abolition of the African Slave Trade, 3, 7, 28, 43, 56, 57, 111, 114
The Society of Friends, 56, 113. See also Quakers
Somerset, James, 3, 29, 31–36, 39, 41, 47, 52, 72, 105, 118
Sons of Africa, 24, 53
St. James's Chronicle or the British Evening Post, 35, 38
Stapylton, Robert, 31
Stewart, Charles, 31, 33
Strong, Jonathan, 3, 29, 30, 32, 39, 113, 118
Stuart, Charles, 4, 103
A Memoir of Granville Sharp (1836), 103
Stuart, John. See Cugoano, Ottobah
Stubbs, Robert, 16, 17, 19, 51, 52, 87, 89, 90, 133, 143, 145, 155
Swaminathan, Srividhya, 39, 40, 44, 45, 54, 56, 109, 110
Sylvanus Urban, 70, 101

T
Tedder, H.R., 68, 71
Thompson, Graham, 79, 80
Thomson, James, 104, 105
"Rule, Britannia!" (1740), 104

TNA. See The National Archives (TNA)
Tuppen, Sandra, 5, 62, 63, 100

U
Urban, Sylvanus, 101

V
Vaccination, 61
Vassa, Gustavus. See Equiano, Olaudah
Vice-Admiralty Courts, 14

W
Walvin, James, 4, 14–17, 19, 21, 22, 29, 46, 50, 51, 67, 80, 84, 86, 93, 104, 120
The Zong [book], 67
Ward, Townley, 135
Webster, Jane, 6, 14, 22, 95, 103, 107, 108, 120
Wedgwood abolitionist medal, 7
Weisbord, Robert, 3, 4, 6, 45, 46, 103, 104
West, Benjamin, 57
West Indies, 31, 33, 62, 93
Wilberforce, William, 4, 73
William [ship], 14, 16, 135
William, John, 127
Williams, Gomer, 27
Wollstonecraft, Mary, 25

Y
Yorke and Talbot decision, 1729, 30

Z
Zong case, 3, 4, 6–10, 14, 15, 21, 24, 27, 28, 32, 35, 36, 39, 41, 44–58, 60, 65, 74, 76, 77, 80, 83, 86, 95, 97, 100–102,

104, 108, 109, 111, 112, 114,
118–120

Zong trial, 10, 23, 40, 45, 48, 53,
71, 73, 93, 103, 109, 110

Zong massacre, 3, 6, 7, 14–22, 17, 44,
46, 47, 53, 54, 56, 65, 75, 95,
102, 103, 107, 108, 110, 111,
117, 120

Zong, ship, 2–11, 14–22, 26, 27, 32,
39, 41, 42, 45–51, 53–55, 57,
58, 60, 65–70, 72–74, 76, 77,
79, 81–84, 89–91, 93–96, 100,
102–104, 107–109, 111, 113,
114, 118, 120–123, 127, 133,
135, 139, 141, 143

Zorgue/De Zorg. See Zong, ship

Zung. See Zong, ship

Zurg. See Zong, ship

Printed in the USA
CPSIA information can be obtained
at www.ICGtesting.com
LVHW010903271023
762000LV00045B/93